The Death of Dylan Thomas

THE DEATH
OF
DYLAN THOMAS

JAMES NASHOLD MD
AND GEORGE TREMLETT

MAINSTREAM
PUBLISHING

EDINBURGH AND LONDON

First published in Great Britain in 1997 by
MAINSTREAM PUBLISHING COMPANY (EDINBURGH) LTD
7 Albany Street
Edinburgh EH1 3UG

ISBN 1 85158 977 5

A catalogue record for this book is available from the British Library

The photograph on the back of the jacket is incorrectly credited to George Tremlett; the credit should in fact read © Norah Summers

Typeset in Centaur
Printed and bound in Great Britain by Butler and Tanner Ltd, Frome

For Elizabeth and Jane

'Though lovers be lost love shall not'

— from *And death shall have no dominion*
by Dylan Thomas

Contents

Preface

What does it matter how a man dies? Is not the fact of death enough in itself? The answers may be clear enough for most of us, but not to the poets or those heroic figures of war and legend who give their lives for a nobler cause. For them, a 'good death' is a matter of lifelong importance. They hope to die with a sword in their hands, love in their hearts and the last unfulfilled dream of victory in their eyes.

This was especially true of Dylan Thomas, who scarcely looked like a romantic hero. He was less than 5 feet 4 inches tall, asthmatic, plagued by gout and grossly overweight, but he was a wonderfully funny man, wrote beguilingly beautiful love letters to Caitlin, his wife, and continually compared himself with Keats, Byron and Shelley, saying he, too, would be dead before he was 40. He had his reasons for saying that and kept to his forecast, dying, so the legend has it, after drinking '18 straight whiskies' in less than an hour and a half. These were not the tiny tots of whisky served in British pubs either, but the larger, American tumbler size. It was enough to kill anyone, and Thomas is said to have remarked cheerily 'I think that's the record', before slipping into a coma at the Chelsea Hotel in Greenwich Village. He was rushed to St Vincent's Hospital, New York, where he died nearly five days later without regaining consciousness.

Caitlin's desperate flight across the Atlantic to be at his bedside gave the story a romantic edge, and this was subsequently magnified by the claims of John Malcolm Brinnin in *Dylan Thomas in America* that Dylan was a hopeless drunkard who was really in love with someone else.

Upon this imagery of drink, death and the eternal triangle an intriguing legend was born, and no one seriously questioned it for nearly 40 years – until one of the co-authors of this book, George Tremlett, suggested in *Dylan Thomas: In the Mercy of His Means* (1991) that much of Brinnin's narrative was secondhand, based on just one unreliable source, and that the medical facts did not add up.

In the winter of 1994, the other co-author, American doctor James Nashold, ordinarily based at the Duke University Medical Center in Durham, North Carolina, was staying in Cambridge, studying morbid anatomy at King's College as part of his postgraduate training in neurosurgery. Shortly before they were due to return home to the United States, Nashold and his wife Elizabeth planned a short holiday, he to visit Laugharne, Dylan Thomas's home town, and she to go to Rhyl, North Wales, where her family came from. Their itinerary included an overnight stay in Hay-on-Wye, where Nashold bought a copy of Tremlett's book. He read it in one sitting and the same evening tried to track Tremlett down. Not finding him in the telephone book, he phoned Brown's Hotel, which features prominently in the legend, and asked, 'Does anyone there know George Tremlett?' As it happened, Tremlett was standing three or four feet away from the phone, having his evening pint.

'There's some American on the phone. Says he's a brain surgeon and has got to see you at once,' said the landlord, Tommy Watts, relaying the message with more than a twinkle in his eye.

(Stranger things than this have happened in the bar of the Brown's. Dylan Thomas used to jump on a table and recite poetry. Male voice choirs have been known to drop in unexpectedly and sing for hours, and one day former US President Jimmy Carter walked in through the door with his wife Roslyn, their daughter Amy and six Secret Servicemen who seized control of the lavatories in case foreign agents slipped in through the back door. Richard Burton and Elizabeth Taylor used to call occasionally, and Charles Bronson was once spotted sitting in a corner, drinking a beer and not saying a word. Four or five film crews turn up every summer, making documentaries on Dylan Thomas for TV stations around the world, and the wily locals have managed to sell 'Dylan's very own dartboard' at least 20 times.)

Nashold and Tremlett met the next day. Nashold was still excited. With his lifelong interest in neurosurgery, which was also his father's profession, he had spotted several clues in Tremlett's narrative that indicated to him that the whole foundation of 'The Thomas Legend' was faulty. In particular, the story of the '18 straight whiskies' could not be true, the drugs used were inappropriate and overprescribed, and there were evidently several pieces missing from the narrative.

With his knowledge of the chemistry and neurology of the human brain, Nashold could see that Thomas's death was not as straightforward as the legend suggested. Why was everyone so quick at the time to blame alcohol? Why did they make no allowance for the body's ability to metabolise alcohol? If the 18 straight whiskies story could be refuted, as Tremlett had done with the help of the New York lawyer Eric Corbett Williams, how could Thomas have died of alcoholic poisoning five days later? Why were no laboratory tests taken when Thomas's problems first manifested themselves? Why was the truth concealed from his widow? Whose reputation was being protected by this cover-up? The doctors', the hospital's, Brinnin's or the mysterious mistress's?

☆   ☆   ☆

That first time they met, Nashold and Tremlett ran briefly through the anecdotal evidence concerning Thomas's health, with Tremlett saying that when collaborating with Mrs Thomas on her memoir *Caitlin* (1986), she told him she had never been able to establish a satisfactory explanation of Dylan's death. 'It always seemed strange to me,' she said, 'but no one would ever tell me what happened. When I last saw him before he went to New York, Dylan seemed tired, but no worse than that . . . He was always complaining about his health, gout, asthma or other chest infections, but was a much stronger man than anyone ever suspected. Much of what he said about his health was exaggerated. That was how he used to get his mother's attention as a child and he was just the same with me. When I used to tell him that if he was that bad he ought to see a doctor, he just wouldn't go, unless he had broken one of his bones. That was his main problem, breaking bones. His mother used to say they were just like chicken bones. Apart from that his health wasn't too bad at all.'

Tremlett also said he had long been mystified by the fact that several of Thomas's closer friends, including Dr Daniel Jones, Mervyn Levy, Fred Janes, Colin Williams, Douglas Williams, Reggie Smith and Glyn Jones, insisted that Dylan was not a particularly heavy drinker when he was in Laugharne, London or Swansea, and was never seen with anything but a glass of beer.

'Have you spoken to his doctor?' asked Nashold.

'Too late,' said Tremlett, explaining that the Thomases' family doctor in St Clears, Dr Hughes, was now dead, although he had once met Dr Elwyn James, who had treated Thomas in Swansea before the war and expressed surprise at the medical details given in the biographies by Constantine Fitzgibbon and Paul Ferris.

'What – you mean none of the doctors have been interviewed?' exclaimed Nashold, and it was that comment which led directly to this book. The methodology has been unusual. Nashold returned to North Carolina early in the summer of 1994 to complete a programme of medical work while Tremlett was busily writing his biography *David Bowie* (1996), but they corresponded by letter and fax and kept in touch by phone, gradually putting their different perspectives of Dylan and Caitlin together and comparing notes.

In September 1995, Nashold and his wife spent a week in Laugharne going through all the background material, and Nashold then decided to take a sabbatical through most of 1996, during which he traced and interviewed friends of Dylan and Caitlin in New York; the doctors and nurses who attended Dylan in his final days; Brinnin, who is now in his eighties and living in Florida; Rollie McKenna, who photographed Dylan and Caitlin in Laugharne and New York; Dave Slivka, who prepared Thomas's death mask, and his former wife Rose Slivka who looked after Caitlin when Dylan died; Peter and Florence Grippe, who were friends in New York, and several more who requested anonymity. In all, Nashold conducted 29 separate interviews. Tremlett then married this manuscript with his, working in totally new material relating to Caitlin's life after Dylan died and her long-running dispute with the trustees of the Dylan Thomas Estate. The finishing touches were added when Nashold returned to Laugharne at the end of February 1997.

✳   ✳   ✳

Something is always missing in every biography of Dylan and Caitlin Thomas: the humour that bound them together and the jollity of the man. What so many people loved in him was a special social gift that came directly from the days of music hall. He was a richly inventive comedian, and a master of an almost forgotten skill: the shaggy-dog story. This was what made him such lively company in public bars. The gift is not easily described, because Thomas's skill lay in building up a story layer by layer, pausing for laughter with each new twist before delivering a punchline. His timing was superb.

In one typical story, once heard by Lawrence Durrell, he said he had lost his shoes in a pub and spent all day looking for them, returning to all 13 pubs where he had drunk that day, with old men crawling under tables to help him and getting stuck, and being nearly tattooed by an elderly Indian . . . 'until finally, I got back home and found the shoes standing beside my bed. I had simply forgotten to put them on . . .'

His death was a tragedy because he was, like so many actors, artists and musicians, a deeply emotional, whimsical, gentle man, dependent wholly on the people around him for support. In New York, he did not receive it. As both Dame Edith Sitwell and Pamela Hansford Johnson observed, he attracted appalling friends.

✳   ✳   ✳

This is an extraordinary story, setting what happened against his career and life with Caitlin. Parts of it make uncomfortable reading, but without discussing the physical facts of his death and autopsy one cannot establish how Dylan Thomas died and why the truth was kept from his widow and children for more than 40 years. Had the whole story been made available at the time to the New York State authorities, we believe there would have been a public inquest followed by a civil claim for damages and, possibly, a charge of malpractice. But the truth remained well hidden.

Does it really matter after all these years? We think so. Several lives were ruined by what happened in New York in November 1953. Falsehood denied Dylan Thomas the respect his work deserved. He was no alcoholic. He was a man with easily treatable illnesses, who needed a good doctor and true friends. With proper treatment he would have lived another 30 or 40 years. Caitlin was plunged into a desperate misery from which she never recovered – and yet, despite all that was written about the man she loved, Caitlin kept her faith in him. Theirs remained a true love story right to the end.

James Nashold MD
Durham, North Carolina

George Tremlett
Laugharne, Wales

May 1997

1

Leaving for the Last Time

Three times he came back to the front door of Pelican to kiss his mother goodbye. Three times as the frail, white-haired lady stood in the hallway of her home, supporting herself on two sticks.

Caitlin waited impatiently on the bus. In less than a year his father and sister had died, and now Dylan Thomas was holding the family together, but Caitlin was always more brittle, decisive, with less time for niceties. 'Hurry up,' she called, knowing they had barely enough money for the fares from Laugharne to Carmarthen, and the train to Swansea where Thomas planned to cash post-dated cheques with friends because his bank manager would not allow him to borrow any more money to fund his fourth trip to the United States.

This was a familiar financial situation for them both – improvidence cursed their lives – but Caitlin was also angry. She did not want him to go back to New York less than five months after his last visit, was suspicious of his motives, and sensed something was happening between them over which she had no control.

'Come on,' she said, as Thomas, a lumpy figure in a tweed jacket and rumpled trousers, stepped back across the pavement to give Mrs Florence Thomas one final kiss as she stood on the doorstep, waiting to wave as the bus disappeared down the street. No one else minded the brief delay because this was a happy-go-lucky rural bus service that barely kept to its timetable, with passengers dropped off or picked up wherever they wished, the drivers often calling at pubs along the route for a drink, and sometimes even ferrying pigs and chickens to market.

The date was Friday, 9 October 1953, and the Thomases were on their way to London to spend a week with friends, the music-hall comedian and tenor Harry Locke and his wife Cordelia, before Dylan caught the plane to New York. And what could be more natural than him wanting to reassure his mother he would soon be back? But Caitlin thought it odd. Dylan had never gone back before like that. No one knew he was leaving Laugharne for the last time and would never see Brown's Hotel, his writing shed, The Boat House, the herons on the estuary, his mother or his children again.

There was a tension between the Thomases throughout that fateful journey and the week that followed. Dylan was torn between family loyalties and West Wales, where he had always written his best work, and his new life in the United States, where success beckoned at every turn. To stay in Laugharne meant being subjected to constant fights with Caitlin over money, work and women, and he was no longer finding peace in his workshed on The Cliff. A military testing station had opened nearby and the boom of exploding bombs and missiles shook every building in the town. New York and America seemed to answer all his problems, with their constant offer of reading tours, public performances and writing commissions, but Caitlin was against all this and did not know that he also had a mistress there, Liz Reitell.

Apart from these uncertainties and hidden stresses, Dylan Thomas was coping with the new demands success in America imposed upon his life. Subsequent biographers were to claim that his writing powers were diminished, but this can be refuted. What had happened was that his new acclaim as a public performer, reading his works to packed university audiences across North America, broadened his appeal until he found himself working in several different genres.

In that summer of 1953, between returning from his third American tour at the end of May and leaving Laugharne in the October, Thomas revised *Under Milk Wood*, which he first presented on stage in New York with a cast of American actors, preparing it as a radio script for the BBC producer Douglas Cleverdon; wrote and recorded six programmes for the BBC, including the now-famous short story *The Outing*; continued work on his novel, *Adventures in the Skin Trade*; worked on two major poems, including the unfinished *Elegy* in memory of his father; made plans for a London stage play, *Two Streets*, with Philip Burton, who was due to be its director; worked upon an idea for a cinema film with the renowned director Michael Powell, based upon Homer's *Odyssey*; wrote at least 36 letters of varying length to his literary agent, publishers and friends, and made detailed plans for the most exciting project of all, the libretto he was planning to work on with Stravinsky during that fourth tour. He proposed to stay at Stravinsky's home in California while they created a new opera set in some futuristic Garden of Eden, where the world begins all over again after a nuclear holocaust.

This was hardly the schedule of an unreliable man, or one whose life was destroyed by alcohol, but Caitlin continued to taunt him for neglecting what she called his 'real work': the poetry upon which his reputation largely rested.

These nightly barbs, fuelled by whisky when she joined him at the bar in Brown's, turned nastier once they began walking home to The Boat House, often unsteady on their feet, urinating against trees or in doorways and sometimes crawling on their hands and knees down the cockleshell-strewn path to their front door for fear of toppling over the low garden wall onto the mudbanks below or, if the tide was in, straight into the River Taf. Although they had once been the happiest of couples, their relationship had been under stress since Caitlin learned of Dylan's sexual affair with the mysterious 'Pearl' during his first American tour, and thereafter Caitlin clung to the wreckage, pleading poverty, threatening to go home to her mother, desperately reminding Dylan of his responsibilities to his mother, her and their children and stealing money from his pockets when he was drunk to fund the family budget, all the while insisting he was neglecting the only thing that really mattered in life: his poetry.

Her complaints became a mantra, repeated to friends and family and picked up by biographers when they came to assess Dylan's life in later years, but they were less than half a convincing truth. She overlooked something else in the sad scenario. The man was ill. He needed help.

✻　✻　✻

Dylan Thomas returned home from his third visit to the United States with his arm in a sling. After a dinner party in New York, he fell downstairs while on his way with Liz Reitell to see Arthur Miller's new play, *The Crucible*. The arm was broken, and he probably knew this straightaway – for Thomas was forever breaking bones – but with him in considerable pain they continued with their plans for the evening until they were eventually asked to leave the theatre because his groans were upsetting other members of the audience.

When they returned to his room at the Chelsea Hotel, Thomas still refused to go to hospital, so Reitell called in her own doctor, Milton Feltenstein, who had already treated him on several occasions for fatigue, gout, asthma and gastritis. Feltenstein set the arm in a cast, and a few days later (28 May) made a second cast, shortly before Thomas caught the plane back to London.

For such a secretive man, this incident posed several dilemmas. Thomas

17

dared not say the fall happened after a dinner party, for then Caitlin would want to know what dinner party, where, who else was there and who he was with. Likewise, had he said he was on his way to the theatre, she would have asked with whom, knowing it was unlikely that he would have gone on his own. She knew enough of his friends in New York for Thomas to worry whether she might make enquiries, especially bearing in mind the presently fragile state of their marriage.

Reitell, Brinnin and the photographer Rollie McKenna have confirmed what really happened that night, but Thomas invented a totally different story that avoided him having to answer those awkward questions. To his eldest son, Llewelyn, he wrote that he had broken his arm tripping over a suitcase in his hotel room.[1] Other friends were told his arm was broken in an altercation with a group of sailors. Either explanation served its purpose, but once he returned to Britain the suitcase-in-the-dark story was the one he told and the one which became accepted by his biographers. It was generally assumed Dylan was drunk.

Superficially, this may seem a minor incident, nothing more than a little white lie designed to hide the truth from his wife, but its significance lies in the fact that this enabled Thomas to conceal the existence of his mistress and all mention of his visits to her doctor. Until the day she died, Caitlin had no way of knowing how Feltenstein used his 'winking needle' during that third visit to inject Thomas with shots of cortisone and ACTH, another form of cortisone, to sober him up before performances, including the rehearsals for his first reading of *Under Milk Wood*, or that her husband was prescribed other drugs to counteract bouts of fatigue, gout, asthma and gastritis.

At that time, cortisone was a new 'wonder drug' whose side effects were largely unknown, and Caitlin had no means of knowing what was the matter with Dylan when she met him on his return to London. Despite his ragged appearance, they spent two days at Margaret Taylor's home enduring what was in effect a non-stop party that began with the Queen's coronation, before going back home to Laugharne. 'I was too determined to enjoy myself to care very much what happened to him,' she admitted to Tremlett, adding that 'the poor bugger looked totally shagged out'. In their book *Caitlin*, she said:

> I didn't know how shattered he was; I thought it was just immense fatigue due to bad living, so I wasn't feeling very amiable or sympathetic. I was now nursing such an enormous resentment that, in a way, I wanted to torment him by dancing around and being gay . . . When we eventually got back to Laugharne, Dylan was almost too shattered to work. He looked miserable, and though he soon slipped back into his old routine, he didn't seem happy

to be at home with me and the children. He went around to see his mother in the mornings, and to see Ivy at the Brown's, but he didn't really become his old self again, though he still didn't think of going to see a doctor, of course.[2]

Caitlin's description was a devastatingly honest and detailed portrait of a man clinically depressed and sick. In New York, only a day before his departure for England, he had made several recordings for Caedmon Records. His face was bloated and there was vomit on his suit. 'He was morose, and I was horrified by his condition,' remembers Barbara Holdridge at Caedmon,[3] who edited the slurred edges of his voice out of the recording. 'A few days before I had seen him reading, dressed in a smart tweed suit, white shirt and bow tie – and now he looked a wreck. I wondered who was looking after him.'

This radical change in Dylan's appearance was captured by Rollie McKenna, whose photographs were later published in *Portrait of Dylan* (1986). Gone were the sparkling eyes, pug nose, round cheeks and full mouth that made his face so memorable, replaced by fat which stretched and distorted his face. His neck was fuller, too, and the rolls of fat seen in the open collar of his shirt made him look like a hideous distortion of his former self. Most of Dylan's friends mistook his bloated face and ruddy complexion as signs of too much drinking. Even Igor Stravinsky, who met Dylan in Boston during his third tour, commented: 'He was nervous, however, chain-smoking the whole time, and he complained of severe gout pains . . . "but I prefer the gout to the cure; I'm not letting a doctor shove a bayonet into me twice a week". His face and skin had the colour and swelling of too much drinking.'[4] The 'bayonet' referred to the fact that Feltenstein was already giving him twice-weekly shots of cortisone for gout and gastritis. Thomas was also using an inhaler for asthma and was drinking much less alcohol under Reitell's strict supervision.

Swollen or bloated facial features have since become recognised side effects of cortisone and ACTH use. They usually occur in patients where chronic doses are prescribed for a number of illnesses. Dylan shared this side effect with another famous personality who was equally secretive about his true state of health, for political rather than personal reasons: President John F. Kennedy. In his biography *President Kennedy, Profile of Power*, Richard Reeves describes how long-term use of cortisone, which Kennedy took because he was suffering from Addison's disease, left him complaining that his face felt 'puffed up' after injections. 'This isn't my face; that's not me,' Kennedy said one morning as he looked in a White House mirror.[5] For Kennedy and Thomas, the benefits far outweighed the side effects – or so they thought. Both men suffered bouts of low energy, especially Kennedy, who had a genetic shortage of cortisone. The injections lifted them up, giving them the energy to continue functioning at a boosted pace.

Without the injections, Kennedy would have died long before he became President. Addison's disease left him with a serious shortage of cortisol in the adrenal gland, and the cortisone was so vital to him that his father, Joseph Kennedy Snr, secreted doses in bank safety deposit boxes all over the world in case of emergency. Dylan, on the other hand, was taking cortisone for three medical reasons: painful gout, gastritis and hangovers which threatened to interfere with his reading performances.

✳   ✳   ✳

Cortisone, with its related form ACTH, was discovered in 1948. When doctors first began using it regularly in the early '50s, little was known about its long-term side effects and its interaction with other diseases such as diabetes. It was then an expensive drug, and that tended to limit its use and the quantities prescribed. Originally it was used to treat patients with rheumatic fever and rheumatism, but a wide range of allergic and inflammatory diseases were dramatically improved with cortisone, including asthma and skin, eye and gastrointestinal complaints. In Dylan's case, gout and gastritis − chronic conditions due to too much alcohol and not enough food − were both ameliorated by cortisone, and Feltenstein thus became the first physician to make Dylan feel better through his treatment of those nagging, but non-fatal, disorders. Nevertheless, using cortisone for sobering up patients was a controversial practice in 1953 according to psychiatrists familiar with the treatment of alcoholism in New York at the time.

Two schools of thought existed over the use of cortisone for chronic alcoholism in the early '50s. Academics opposed prescribing cortisone to sober up patients because it made treatment of their underlying problems more difficult and delayed the analysis necessary for psychiatric treatment. Physicians in private practice complained they did not have the luxuries of the university psychiatrists with large staffs of doctors and nurses. They treated patients in the real world where alcoholics tried to maintain normal lives and jobs. After a binge of drinking, patients had to sober up fast to be able to return to work and function properly. Cortisone injections boosted the patient's sense of well-being instantly and, so it seemed, could be repeated indefinitely, depending only on the chronicity of the bouts of sobering up. Some physicians even claimed cortisone reduced dependency on alcohol, though this is no longer believed.

In addition to their chronic use of cortisone, Dylan Thomas and President

Kennedy also shared another interesting but significant medical habit: the use of 'uppers'. In Kennedy's case, this was metamphetamine, and in Thomas's, benzedrine. With both men, their complaint of low energy levels was the main reason for these medicines being used at all. Kennedy maintained the glow, energy and appeal of a vibrant national leader by using amphetamines, while Thomas was able to sustain himself through long nights of drinking and carousing that his fragile constitution would never otherwise have allowed.

Although this was not known at the time, Dylan Thomas was also diabetic and prescribing cortisone to him was a fatal error. This was because the increase in his body's metabolism caused by cortisone also increased the levels of his blood sugar, or glucose. In most people, this would be balanced by an increased liberation of insulin, which maintains a steady state of sugar in the body. In an adult diabetic who does not take insulin, chronic use of cortisone has the disastrous effect of not only increasing blood sugar levels, creating a state of hyperglycaemia, but also decreasing the effectiveness of what little insulin is available. Thus, the net effect of cortisone on a diabetic is to cause hyperglycaemia in the bloodstream *and also* hypoglycaemia in tissues and cells, because so little of the glucose in the bloodstream can be utilised. Some of the symptoms of decreased availability of glucose include low blood pressure, blackouts, low energy, chronic debility, headaches, mood swings, infections, abdominal pain and vomiting which might mimic gastritis. From the many descriptions of his behaviour, it is clear Dylan Thomas suffered all these symptoms during and after his third visit to the United States.

We have also confirmed that Feltenstein was prescribing this treatment at that time. He became so distressed when he realised the consequences that he went to see a fellow doctor, Dr Joseph Lehrman (a pseudonym), and admitted making the mistakes that led to Thomas's death.[6] However, it also has to be said that Dylan Thomas was a far from ideal patient. He failed to tell Feltenstein that he was diagnosed as possibly diabetic as early as 1933 and had done nothing whatsoever about it. Feltenstein, for his part, did not press Thomas for details of his medical history and neither did he carry out the basic laboratory tests that might have saved his patient's life.

✵   ✵   ✵

When Dylan Thomas returned to Laugharne in June 1953 he was seriously sick, but none of his complaints were life-threatening. Their overall impact was compounded by the cortisone injections and his regular use of benzedrine, and we have no way of knowing whether or not Thomas was able to bring drugs back from America – although it seems likely, as these were medically prescribed for him. There is also a curious use of words in his only published letter to Reitell, in which Thomas says, 'For all the customs-men cared I could have packed my bags with cocaine and bits of chopped women.'[7] This begs the question: was he telling her in some kind of code that he had either smuggled something through customs or, more simply, not been challenged? In any case, if Thomas was unable to maintain his use of cortisone and benzedrine once he returned to Laugharne, he would have suffered withdrawal. That in itself would have further exacerbated his lethargy, depression and sense of desperation over the state of his marriage.

Money always lay at the heart of his problems, and particularly his relationship with Caitlin, whom he used to accuse of wanton improvidence. Friends believed it was her spending that plunged the family into debt, but the truth seems more complex, for there is firm evidence that Thomas was highly paid in the last six or seven years of his life, earning roughly the equivalent of £100,000–£120,000 a year by today's prices. He was as secretive about his earnings as his health, constantly borrowing from people who earned less than he did and denying Caitlin the money she needed to feed and clothe the family. Despite this they managed to maintain both The Boat House in Laugharne and a flat in Camden Town, North London, paid the rent for Thomas's mother's home in Laugharne, sent their two eldest children to private, fee-paying boarding schools, always employed domestic help in the home and enjoyed a luxurious lifestyle on their frequent visits to London. Thomas bought expensive clothes and shoes, though his appearance tended to deteriorate as the day wore on, spent large sums of money on expensive dentistry (his teeth were in an appalling condition after so many years of constant consumption of sugary sweets), belonged to two London gentlemen's clubs and enjoyed visiting the theatre, going to nightclubs, dining out at expensive restaurants and ending up at private drinking clubs, all of which he assiduously kept as quiet as he could for much the same reason that he never told Caitlin about the night he broke his arm in New York. His life was a tapestry of petty lies and deceits, with money – or, rather, overexpenditure – its one constant thread.

During his third American tour, Thomas again earned several thousand dollars but returned home penniless, owing money to the tax authorities, facing school bills for Llewelyn and Aeronwy that he could not pay, and making Caitlin feel so helpless that she had yet another abortion. (There is some confusion about Caitlin's abortions, but she had at least four; the couple did not use contraceptives and she was, in any case, taking other lovers by this time and was by no means certain the child was his.)

Thomas even had debts in the United States, where he had earned so much. These included money borrowed from Reitell and minor sums owing to Feltenstein for his drugs, pills and services. Some of these are mentioned in a letter from Reitell to Brinnin:

> Lover-Boy
>
> Milton and I have worked out the sum of $30.00 for Dylan's medical treatment. $20.00 of this was for drugs and medications and the rest is just sort of a token. So – will'st add $30.00 to the $232.00 – making $262.00 the sum of Dylan's personal debt to me.
>
> Have any more checks come in? Or how long do you think it will be before you can reimburse me? This is asked for planning reasons and not for any Shylock ditto!
>
> Are you going to Europe this summer? When are you coming to N.Y.? (I asked this yesterday.) Here are some 50 clams for the two extra engagements. Thunderous love
>
> E[8]

And yet, despite problems that would have daunted most men, Thomas was soon back in his daily routine, pottering about in the morning, visiting his mother and having a lunchtime pint or two at Brown's, between placing that day's bets on the horses and having his usual game of cards before returning to his workroom on The Cliff. There was only one major interruption, and that came when Brinnin arrived from New York, accompanied by Rollie McKenna and the American writer Bill Read, who later wrote the first (and one of the best) of all the biographies, *The Days of Dylan Thomas* (1964). It was not a happy visit, for Thomas was quietly trying to manoeuvre Brinnin into arranging a fourth US tour, which Caitlin was determined to stop, while doing all she could to bully, wheedle or cajole Brinnin into telling her all he knew about Pearl Kazin, with whom Thomas had had a brief affair two years earlier. Caitlin clearly sensed there was another woman in his life, but knowing nothing of Reitell kept pressing Brinnin to talk about Pearl – and when he would not, made sure he felt the full fury of a woman scorned.

'He will not go back to America,' she said, well aware that this was precisely what Thomas intended to do, intervening noisily whenever he tried to discuss detailed arrangements, and only temporarily pacified when Brinnin suggested she might go as well.

Originally, the plan was for Thomas to spend a month touring the States delivering lectures, reading poetry and making enough money to spend a second month with Stravinsky in California. Their hopes of being funded by Boston University fell through, but Stravinsky was so committed to the project that he built an extension to his home to accommodate the Thomases. There was another reason for going, too. The agent and promoter Felix Gerstman offered to arrange lecture tours for Thomas with a $1,000 weekly guarantee. This would have ended Thomas's dependence on Brinnin, but first he had to go to New York to finalise the deal.

As the date for Thomas's departure drew near, Caitlin could feel herself being excluded from his plans. With no money coming from Boston, his publishers unwilling to make further advances and no bank manager willing to lend him money, Thomas decided to make his own way to New York, cashing post-dated cheques in Swansea with the bookseller Ralph Wishart and friend Dr Daniel Jones, and quite probably borrowing more funds in London, although this is undocumented.

'I'll send you the money and you can come out and join me in California,' Thomas told Caitlin, but she did not believe it, sensing she was being left alone on purpose with her husband having other reasons for wanting to return to New York without her.

'I was suspicious about his infidelities,' she said,[9] 'and I was sure all that touring was damaging his health . . . He may also have been yearning for his lady-love, because I realise now that he was far more serious about Liz Reitell than he had been about anyone else, but I didn't know it at that time, so I didn't know what was upsetting him . . . I could see Dylan was very unhappy; it seemed to me that we had lost all contact, and the marriage wasn't working at all.'

✻   ✻   ✻

Throughout that summer there were continuing indications that something was seriously wrong with Thomas's health. This worried his mother, but she had precious little influence upon him, and Caitlin was far too preoccupied with her own anxieties – the children, her abortion, the family's lack of money and her general feeling that the marriage was dead in all but name – to give much thought to a husband who kept insisting there was no need for him to see a doctor.

Thomas showed increased signs of being a sick man who suffered from some mysterious ailment that made no sense to anyone. This clearly was not alcoholism, for once he was back in the Brown's Hotel Thomas bought only beer and, like many of its other customers, drank slowly, letting a pint last half an hour and more. 'He was never a heavy drinker,' locals insist. Some noticed he often drank hardly at all. When Brinnin, Read and McKenna were staying in Laugharne, he took them over to the other side of the River Taf to see the farms and chapels that had been home to his mother's side of the family for several generations, and they noticed he did not suggest going into a pub at all.

However, there was clearly something wrong with him, for when he did drink his behaviour was marked by uncontrolled urination. Excess consumption of liquids (polydipsia) and excessive urination (polyuria) are not only indications that someone is drinking too much; they are also classic signs of diabetes. Likewise, there is anecdotal evidence that Thomas suffered occasional blackouts – on trips to London, in Laugharne and when going to the cinema on 8 October 1953, the night before he left for America. This was another indication that something was wrong with his blood sugar levels, as was his constant craving for bottles of fizzy pop, chocolates and boiled sweets.

Further anecdotal evidence comes from Mrs Minnie Dark, who cut Thomas's hair on the eve of his departure. As she loosened his shirt collar to tuck in a towel, Mrs Dark noticed a profusion of angry red boils across the back of his neck and between his shoulder blades. Thomas offered no explanation, but it is more than likely that these were a superficial skin infection known as carbuncles and furuncles that results when the body's immune system is depressed by diabetes. Doses of cortisone would have worsened this. If Thomas was not used to bathing daily (which he was not, because all the family had at The Boat House was a tin bath that they used to fill with kettles of water), such a skin infection was almost inevitable in someone already debilitated.

Earlier that same day (8 October), Thomas welcomed an old Swansea friend, the artist Fred Janes, who brought another artist, Ceri Richards, over to discuss the possibility of their collaborating on an exhibition at the Glyn Vivian Art Gallery in Swansea. Dylan told them he was not looking forward to the journey to America and felt 'very tired', but does not appear to have been the least bit suicidal (as some commentators later claimed), for he was already making plans for Christmas.

Despite having difficulty scratching money together, the Thomases spent the last night in Wales going to the cinema in Carmarthen, and it just so happened that the family's doctor, Dr David Hughes of St Clears, was sitting in front of them with his wife. 'Dylan has been having terrible headaches,' said Caitlin, explaining he was leaving for America in the morning. Hughes agreed to drive them back to his surgery in St Clears when the movie finished and said he would give Dylan an immediate examination, but by the time the lights went up Dylan was nowhere to be seen. He slipped away from the cinema to a local pub and the doctor went home without seeing him again.

There is no suggestion that Dylan's medical problems were due solely to diabetes, but headaches at night which are relieved in the morning by food is another common symptom. The blood sugar of diabetics will immediately start to sink if they go too long without food, and then starts to rise again when they absorb more carbohydrates and complex sugars. Had Dr Hughes given Thomas a thorough examination that evening, taking blood and urine samples for laboratory testing, the events that unfolded over the following month would not have happened.

✳ ✳ ✳

The next morning, Dylan and Caitlin carried their bags to the bus stop in King Street, just across the road from Brown's Hotel and only two doors away from Pelican, the house where his mother lived. The bus came up Wogan Street, turned the corner in front of the castle and stopped to pick them up. Dylan Thomas went back three times to kiss his mother.

As the bus gathered speed along King Street, he turned to wave for the last time and then turned back in his seat to begin the journey. Later, his mother would say he must have had a premonition of death, for she had never known him to kiss her like that before. However, there is no great significance in her comment, for Mrs Thomas was a woolly-minded storyteller, much given to dressing up her tales – a habit that infuriated both her husband and her son.

✳ ✳ ✳

Even though they had hardly any money in their pockets, the Thomases hired a taxi as soon as their train arrived in Swansea to take them to the home of Dr Daniel Jones. There was no way Dylan or Caitlin would struggle on a bus or through the streets of Swansea carrying baggage. It was not their style. How much they borrowed, either in Swansea or in London, will never be known, for Thomas was an assiduous debtor, never telling one friend what he owed another. When he died, most of them were far too distressed (and gentlemanly) to think of laying claim against his estate.

During their stay with Harry and Cordelia Locke, his relationship with Caitlin deteriorated even further, but the Lockes were loyal friends who refused to discuss the situation, realising the Thomases were on the point of separation.

On Monday 13 October, Thomas spent several hours at Philip Burton's apartment, reading *Elegy* and extracts from *Under Milk Wood* and working on the outline for *Two Streets*. Suddenly, Thomas asked Burton if he could lie down. Dylan was experiencing another blackout. It was the second that day. After an hour or two, Burton tried to shake Dylan awake but was unable to do so. Burton was about to call a doctor when Dylan finally stirred from a deep sleep, passing it off as part of his normal routine. Burton always remembered the incident with alarm, and it took on more significance with the poet's unexpected death three weeks later.

Dylan's blackouts and sudden mood swings from somnolence to elation were typical of a poorly controlled diabetic. As the body and the brain's supply of glucose rises and falls in wide swings, so too does a diabetic's moods, and if the glucose level drops low enough the level of consciousness approaches near coma. Many diabetics go to sleep or pass out when their blood glucose falls to around 25 per cent of its normal levels. This is part of their defence mechanism. By slowing down the brain and body activity, glucose and insulin are preserved and allowed gradually to reaccumulate. When given glucose or sugar, their levels stabilise; some miraculously awaken as if from the dead.

Despite this unexplained blackout, Burton found Thomas full of future plans and projects worthy of the mature talents of a great writer. 'I've got another 20 or perhaps 25 years to live. I've got to try new things. This is the beginning,' said Thomas, who was not the least bit suicidal, but seemed to dread the thought of more exhaustion in America, while talking excitedly of his plans to work with Stravinsky.

Thomas went to Broadcasting House on Thursday 15 October to meet the BBC Third Programme radio producer Douglas Cleverdon, handing over the completed manuscript, which Cleverdon arranged to have duplicated by his secretary, Elizabeth Fox, so that Thomas could take clean copies to New York. As he was leaving the BBC to call at the local pub, The George, his wartime friend Constantine Fitzgibbon saw Thomas's familiar bulky figure further up the street and hurried to catch him up.

'He suggested that we avoid the BBC pubs and go somewhere where we could have a quiet drink together,' wrote Fitzgibbon.[10] 'We were both entirely sober. We found a bar in which I had certainly never been before, nor I think had he. I do not know what it was called, nor in which street it lay. It was one of a thousand colourless saloon bars, almost empty at that early hour, and we drank two or three pints of beer together . . . I noticed how subdued, even sad, he seemed. He told me that he had no wish to go to America so soon again for he was, he said, very tired. On the other hand, he was clearly proud that Stravinsky should have chosen him to be his librettist, for Stravinsky was one of the great . . . we talked, amiably and calmly, about this and that, trivia mostly, while strangers drifted in and out of the dark bar. He certainly did not seem to be at all suicidal in his attitudes, though others who saw him during these days have told me that he talked, almost willingly, of his impending death – but then he had been doing that, in one way or another, for 30 years.'

✳   ✳   ✳

Early on the Monday evening (19 October), Cleverdon caught a taxi down to Victoria to join Dylan and Caitlin, the Lockes and Margaret Taylor in the airport terminal bar. He arrived with three duplicated copies of *Under Milk Wood*. 'Thank God for that. You've saved my life,' said Thomas, who was planning further readings of the revised work in New York.

The drink was flowing. Harry Locke and Dylan were telling stories. Cordelia Locke and Margaret Taylor were trying to comfort Caitlin, who was nursing her private fears. As Dylan went out to the bus that would take him to Heathrow Airport to catch the 7.30 p.m. plane, Locke walked by his side and stood watching as Thomas sat down near the rear of the bus. As the driver pulled away, Thomas turned and gave a thumbs-down sign, but his wife was not looking. That night, Caitlin walked aimlessly on her own through the streets of London, more distressed than ever, convinced their marriage was over, already composing in her mind one final, dreadful letter that would haunt her for the rest of her days.

2

A Sickly Child with an Iron Will

traveller to the western edges of South Wales can still find Dylan
Thomas Country. This is their name for it now. Posters, pamphlets,
guides and bus timetables decorated with the poet's image are
distributed far and wide, but despite all the tourism trade's tomfoolery they
have a point. There really is a landscape in the far west that now has the same
kind of ringing literary resonance as Thomas Hardy's villages or the windswept
beauty of the Brontë moors. The poet may have gone, but you can feel his
presence, for Thomas lifted the imagery of his surrounding landscape, and
there they are around you: the herons and water birds, the church built like a
snail and the castle brown as owls.

Little has changed in 60 years since Thomas first began to feel this was
home, for Laugharne, with surrounding woods, hills and valleys defining all its
boundaries, found an ideal size when the Normans arrived shortly after the last
millennium. They built a castle on a low-rising cliff to defend the estuary where
the River Taf's tidal waters mingle with the clean, fresh River Corran, flowing
down from springs in the Carmarthenshire hills. This was probably why the
Normans settled here, just like the Beaker People 6,000 years ago, for the Taf
provides a twice-daily harvest of salmon, sewin, mullet, eels and flatfish, while
the Corran keeps its fertile valley rich in crops, sheep and dairy cattle. Even
today, the population is well under a thousand, centred on this tiny, eccentric
township, cradled between the hills and sea, which has been self-governing
since a Norman manorial lord, Sir Guy de Brian the Elder, gave its people their
land and a unique constitution that has survived every local government
reorganisation. The electors are called Burgesses. The chief civic officials are

the Portreeve, the Recorder and the Foreman of the Jury. There is a bench of Aldermen, four Constables equipped with traditional wooden truncheons embossed with ancient seals, and two Halberdiers, who escort the Portreeve on public occasions carrying pikes.

These may sound like characters out of Gilbert and Sullivan or *The Hunting of the Snark*, but they are real flesh and blood, and as soon as Thomas came to know them all, with their feuds, booze and cuckoldry, their prim maids, laughing children and wise old aldermen, he knew this was home, and one day captured their daily blend of mayhem, or some of it, in *Under Milk Wood*. Laugharne gave him an ideal backdrop, but more than that this was literally his ancestral doorstep, for the Williamses (his mother's family) farmed fields less than a mile away on the other bank of the River Taf, while his father's aunts and uncles, brothers and forebears were scattered across Carmarthenshire, with one grandfather living across the river in Llanstephan and the other originally coming from Johnstown, then little more than a hamlet on the western edge of Carmarthen, the county town.

By road, Laugharne is less than 15 miles from Carmarthen, but this was always a winding road and the crow would fly over the River Taf, across the Williamses' fields and the villages of Llanybri and Llangain, and over the rooftops of Llanstephan. This very sense of being so near and yet so far away is all part of Laugharne's peculiar magic. 'They're funny people down in Laugharne, always getting drunk and fighting with boathooks,' they say in Carmarthen, while a magistrate in St Clears, only four miles away in another direction, once told a defendant, 'Go back to Laugharne. We don't want people like you in St Clears.'

And so it was in Thomas's day, when only the winding road or a tiny ferry, no bigger than a dinghy with a ferryman both deaf and dumb, kept Laugharne in touch with the outside world. Laugharne had been like this for centuries: remote and self-contained, self-governing and self-sufficient, ignoring any laws that were inconvenient – especially those to inhibit drinking – and wholly determined to stay that way. When Thomas arrived, the family that ran Brown's Hotel also owned the electricity pumping station – and turned off the town switch any night fighting broke out. There were few inside lavatories or houses with bathrooms, people went to bed with candles, radio sets were beyond the reach of most inhabitants, television had never been seen by anyone, and the township shared something else that set them apart from surrounding villages. They spoke English, not Welsh.

Coming from the other side of the River Taf, both the Williamses and the Thomases were Welsh-speaking and had been so for centuries, but already their rural roots were a generation gone. Dylan's paternal grandfather and other male members of the family found employment on the Great Western Railway, the line that linked West Wales with Paddington. By the time the first Welsh university was opened at Aberystwyth in 1872 and Dylan's father began his own school career, the family embraced the conventional thinking of the day that English was the language of the British Empire and industrial expansion, the language that had to be spoken by any aspiring Welshman anxious to find his own tidy niche in middle-class society.

✳   ✳   ✳

Dylan's father, David John Thomas, was known as Jack to his wife, family and closest friends, and as 'DJ' to his pupils. He won a scholarship to study English literature at Aberystwyth and graduated with a first-class honours degree in 1899. He was, by all accounts, far more radical as a young man than he appeared in later life, turning his back on the right-lipped chapel culture of West Wales, choosing atheism rather than Sunday observance, enjoying the company of fellow beer drinkers and expressing advanced ideas on modern literature and sexual behaviour. This open refusal to live by the norms of conformity may have blighted his prospects. Jack thought he was destined to be a poet and would have preferred to combine a writer's life with a professorship in English literature, but it was not to be.

Instead, he settled for a career far below his expectations and spent 36 years teaching in the English department, eventually becoming senior master, at Swansea Grammar School. He used to go off drinking during the school lunch-break, developing a pronounced beer belly, which can hardly have helped if Jack ever thought of applying for jobs elsewhere or rising further up the educational ladder to become a deputy head or headmaster, for he would return from the pub red-faced, blustering and inclined to shout. One of his students, Wynford Vaughan-Thomas, recalled 'old DJ' hurling books at his pupils when they chattered and hitting them hard around the back of the head. 'At times he could be terrifying,' said Wynford. Within the home, his sense of grievance and non-fulfilment left him gruff and inward-looking, finding no real enjoyment until Dylan succeeded where he failed. 'He was embittered, the unhappiest man I ever met,' said Caitlin, and there can also be little doubt that 'old DJ' positively disliked, if not despised, most of his pupils for whom he frequently showed open contempt, and yet between father and son there developed the tenderest and most remarkable of bonds, one steeped in love, intellect and literary aspiration.

That there was also a more lively side to his personality is shown by the fact that Jack met his future wife, Florence Williams, at an annual funfair on the village green at Johnstown, just across the road from The Poplars, the Thomas family home which is now a public house with the same name. Her father also worked on the railways, moving to Swansea before she was born, but there were still grandparents, aunts and uncles living in the tiny villages and hamlets between Johnstown and the Taf, the area known as 'the Llanstephan peninsula', occupying cottages that had been in the family for generations, either farming the land or working as tradesmen. By the time the couple married – on 30 December 1903 – Jack was already established at the Grammar School and Florence employed as a seamstress in a Swansea drapery shop.

Their first home was in Sketty, then a village on the edge of Swansea, but shortly before Dylan was born the family moved to the Uplands, buying the newly built house at 5 Cwmdonkin Drive that became his childhood home, with Cwmdonkin Park, setting for the famous poem *The Hunchback in the Park*, just a few minutes' walk away.

With his mother, the young, precocious Dylan, blessed with a winning, angelic smile, wondrous eyes and a mass of blond curls, enjoyed a totally different relationship. The frustrated schoolmaster was teaching his son poetry when the boy was barely out of nappies, encouraging him to recite Shakespearean speeches, while Florence took the child by the hand on Sundays to hear his uncles Tom (the Revd Thomas Williams, her brother) and Dai (the Revd David Rees, who married her sister Theodosia) singing praises to the Lord and offering salvation at their suburban chapels. Despite his rejection of religion, Jack was wise enough not to make this an issue between them as parents and Dylan thus grew up both steeped in classic and progressive literature and equally familiar with the rolling rhythms of the Bible and the great hymns of Wales, forever conscious of both strands in his family background.

In a strongly visceral sense, the Thomases never left West Wales. Even though Dylan and his sister Nancy were both brought up as English speakers, their parents spoke in Welsh across the family dinner table and Mrs Florence Thomas, a short and stocky Welsh Mam, brought the customs of her background to the kitchen, baking bread, making cakes and jams, and bottling her preserves, forever surrounded by like-minded friends and relatives, gabbling away in Welsh as they kept each other up to date with as much scandal and gossip as their memories could absorb. Although he apparently enjoyed a sexual life with Florence into their sixties, this incessant chatter drove Jack to distraction, and whenever he came home from the Grammar

School to find them all gabbling around the kitchen table, he would retreat to his book-lined study with much grunting, grumbling and slamming of doors.

There is some kind of tension in every home, for this is in the nature of the male–female relationship, but the atmosphere within 5 Cwmdonkin Drive seems to have been an odd one, with the crusty old schoolmaster retreating there to escape the noisy teenagers whose crudities he could not stand, never taking his hat off even within the house for fear someone might comment on his growing baldness, and withdrawing further within to his inner sanctum where he would shut himself away to avoid his wife's incessant gibbering.

'She was the kind of woman who couldn't walk past a sideboard without trying to dust it, and then had to tell you what she had done,' Caitlin commented, but Florence was also kindly and protective in a distinctly Welsh way, guarding her children against a plague of illnesses both real and imaginary, making sure they wore their winter woollies and sending them back west whenever there were holidays or family occasions to celebrate. Florence thought Dylan was tubercular, rheumatic, asthmatic or whatever ran currently through her mind, and part of this conviction lay in her belief that he would soon get better if he went back to the family farmsteads, enjoying fresh air and vegetables. Dylan therefore not only returned west for family reunions, but also because his mother believed it was the cure for every minor ailment, and its landscape became ingrained upon his heart.

✲ ✲ ✲

The visitor to Wales can easily trace the landmarks of Dylan Thomas's childhood and the homes of his maturity, for much of the terrain remains unscarred. Often, literary pilgrims from around the world arrive at Heathrow Airport, hire a car and drive straight down the M4 motorway to Laugharne, planning to spend a day or two tracing Dylan Thomas's poetic background before driving on to Fishguard and catching the ferry to Rosslare, to pick up the trail of Brendan Behan, James Joyce or W.B. Yeats. For them, the contrasts in Thomas's background become far more immediately apparent than they are to the Welsh themselves, secure in their own little corners of the principality.

The road beyond Cardiff, past the steel mills of Newport and Port Talbot and the docks of Neath, down through the once heavily industrial Swansea Valley, could just as easily be the New Jersey Turnpike, but then, several miles beyond Swansea, the countryside opens up, the hills are greener, flocks of sheep can be seen in the distance and there are often buzzards circling high above. This is the beginning of Dylan Thomas Country, the land to which he returned with his mother throughout his childhood, going back to the family farms and cottages, attending market in Carmarthen and eventually discovering for himself this strange English-speaking enclave, just across the Taf, with its ancient customs of beating the bounds, mediaeval strip fields handed down from one generation to the next, a church more like a mini-cathedral, a garage that was once a chapel (and has part of its roof missing) and one of the tiniest town halls in the world, with a prison cell on the ground floor (no longer used, unfortunately) and just one room above not much larger than a one-car garage.

Here was the normality in Dylan Thomas's life, off and on, for nearly the whole of his adult life. Here, he kept regular hours, ate and slept properly and drank beer in moderation. Away from these roots, he drank too much, talked too much, did no serious work and ate and slept like a man on the run. His poetry and his health were as intimately tied to this landscape as a baby to its mother's breast. Those who met him in city bars, telling smutty stories, singing lewd songs, crawling across the floor nibbling girls' ankles after claiming to have seen a mouse, rarely sensed this hinterland.

'Dylan on his native hearth was a different being from the extravagant buffoon I had met five years before in London,' observed his close friend John Davenport, who co-wrote *The Death of the King's Canary* and took the Thomases into his home at Marshfield in Wiltshire during the war. 'I realised for the first time, the intense seriousness which lay beneath the social exterior that was a mixture of Puck and Panurge, with more than a touch of Falstaff. It was essential for him to work off his puppyish sociability on extravagant trips to the despised but necessary London; but his real self was under the shadow of Sir John's Hill at Laugharne, where the stilted herons and grave cormorants fished in the estuary, the melancholy cry of the curlew haunted the air and the night was brushed by the white owls' wings.'[1]

* * *

Today, people remember Dylan Thomas by his physical identity – the round face and bulky figure that left him with almost a waddle; those sad eyes and the surprising pugnacity that made one wonder whether this was a man who was wholly happy within his frame – but he was not always like that. When he first came to Laugharne, Thomas was trim and slight, a little fey, bouncy on his toes, and undersized. (He liked to say he was 5 feet 4 inches tall, sometimes 5 feet 5 inches, but he invariably wore shoes with built-up heels and was more probably 5 feet 2 inches to 5 feet 3 inches tall, and the inches clearly mattered.)

Dylan Marlais Thomas was born on 27 October 1914, his first name taken from the Welsh classic legend *The Mabinogion*, the second from a river in the Carmarthenshire hills (this was also used by his great-uncle William as a bardic name). Dylan was a small baby, weighing less than 7 lbs, and his mother seems to have been unusually anxious about his survival. She had good reason to be worried. In the dim and distant past, Jack and Florence had had to marry because she was expecting a baby (which would have been a scandal at the time), and the child died in her womb. After the birth of Dylan's sister Nancy, Florence suffered another frightening pregnancy when a boy child was stillborn, so there can be no doubting that she was fearful when Dylan arrived.

Neither Dylan nor Nancy was healthy as a child or an adult, but, so far as one can tell after two generations, there was nothing in either Florence's or Jack's family background to suggest that their son and daughter would suffer ill health throughout their entire lives and both die prematurely. There was some evidence of heavy drinking in the Williams and Thomas families, and Florence appears to have had a lifelong fear of tuberculosis, which was a much more common (and deadly) disease in her day than it is now with the availability of antibiotics.

Florence complained that her father died of tuberculosis, although the death certificate states that the cause of death was pneumonia. There is no evidence, apart from her recollections; but one of the dangers from tuberculosis was that it destroyed lung tissue and left it vulnerable to infections, including pneumonia, so there may have been some truth in her memory and this may be an indication of genetic weakness.

Underweight at birth, Dylan was from the start behind in life in a number of ways and remained well below average height. Forever fussing, and quite probably affected by the loss of two children in pregnancy, Florence kept him away from school for much of his early childhood, certainly until the age of seven, insisting this was necessary because of his weak chest and asthma. (Nancy suffered from similar problems, but Dylan's seem to have been worse.)

'Dylan used to get asthma very badly as a little boy,' Florence told a Swansea friend, Ethel Ross.[2] 'If one of the masters spoke sharply to him at the Grammar School he'd come home gasping in the middle of it. So they knew that if they checked him he'd be home for a week with a bad attack. In the end no one checked him and he got away with everything . . . as a child he would collapse while playing with his toys. Often I'd find him lying on the rug. He suffered from acute anaemia.'

These are all indications that Dylan, like his maternal grandfather, had a weakness in the lungs, and in later life there are reports that he suffered from 'lung haemorrhages'. Unfortunately, whenever he talked dramatically about problems like these, making himself the centre of attention, he thoroughly enjoyed the experience, claiming that the specks of blood he sometimes coughed up were signs of tuberculosis when it is quite clear from the X-rays that were taken of him as an adult that he had clear, non-tubercular lungs. However, the history of asthma – which is not the same thing at all – did become significant, and by smoking he may have exposed himself to the virus that possibly triggered diabetes when he was 18.

Thomas started smoking when he was 11 or 12 years old, and by the age of 15 was smoking 40 Woodbines a day – the worst possible habit for someone with lungs sensitive to pollens and pollutants in the air. When an asthma attack occurs, the lungs suddenly close off large portions of their interconnected air spaces and the person literally cannot breathe. Desperate for air, the person further undergoes a severe anxiety or panic attack which, if left unchecked or unrelieved by oxygen or drugs, can easily lead to instant death.

Because of these asthma attacks, the walls of the lungs, where the vital exchange of oxygen into blood occurs, become markedly weaker. Smoking further breaks down remaining lung tissue, decreasing the capacity to breathe. Dylan could easily have suffered lung haemorrhages as a child from weakened areas of his lung walls. As an adult, his episodes of coughing up blood were the result of broken blood vessels in thinned regions of his lungs caused by smoking and exacerbated by severe bouts of coughing. His diabetes may well have been caused by an autoimmune reaction triggered initially as a response to a simple, respiratory viral illness or 'cold'.

More will be said about this later, but there is statistical evidence that diabetes was more common in rural Wales and England than the towns because of prior viral illnesses, with both children and adults having less-developed immune systems. They were more susceptible to winter colds, but instead of turning off after fighting a cold, the immune system would attack cells in the lungs and in the pancreas with similar surface markers where insulin was made. With enough destruction of the pancreas or alteration of the body's insulin receptors by an autoimmune process, the body would lose its ability to store and regulate sugar, glucose, and the development of diabetes would be the inevitable result. This is what may have happened to Dylan Thomas, because of his history of asthma and smoking.

Other aspects of his childhood health are also disturbing. By the age of 12, he had had more than his share of accidents. One day, when Dylan was five, he was playing and fell or, perhaps, was pushed, and broke his nose. There were no serious consequences except that Dylan's nose became a distinct physical trademark. Such things happen to adventurous boys, getting up to their normal degree of mischief, but when something like this happened to Dylan the consequences were always more complex than one would expect. A broken arm in a healthy child would heal at home in four to six weeks, but Dylan needed a month in hospital and two operations – an altogether higher and more intensive level of care, indicating he did not recover from a simple broken arm in a normal way. This was a pattern that would be repeated often during the course of his life.

Dylan was put in a man's ward and, according to Florence, his doctor told him to practise writing with his left hand while his right hand remained in a cast following his discharge. His parents gave him paper and pencils and one day Florence glanced out of the window and saw him in the garden, 'feet up on the table, not writing at all, puffing away at a cigarette. That's what came of being in that ward of old men.'[3]

Despite his bouts of ill health and broken bones, there were also events in Thomas's childhood that demonstrated his potential. His ability to recite Shakespeare by heart at the age of six or seven, winning a mile race for 15-year-olds when he was only 12, and seeing his first poems in print at 14, all of them unusual talents for one so young, suggest a strong sense of determination that underlines more than it condemns his complete failure at school in every subject but the one he enjoyed: English.

When Dylan's belongings were returned to Caitlin after his death, his black leather wallet contained a yellowed newspaper clipping from *The Cambria Daily Leader* with a photograph of him after winning the race, a memory he clearly treasured to the end of his life. Because of his reputation for ill health, he was given a 100-yard head start. Nevertheless, he hung on to win, arriving at the end scratched and bloodied from bushes along the course. The event demonstrated that Dylan could achieve a goal once he set his mind to it, and was one of the few occasions in his life when he chose to do something which was also good for his health.

The extraordinary willpower that he demonstrated was seen again and again during his later reading tours in America. Exhausted or hungover from travel and late nights, Dylan would rally and deliver a performance of memorable proportions. This kind of physical strength contrasted throughout his life with bouts of real sickness and provided a central contradiction in the character of Dylan Thomas.

3

A Life in Denial

The conflicting traits in his character of both strength and weakness came through in Dylan Thomas's poetry in both a literary and a physical manner. His history of sickness gave him a precocious awareness of bodily frailty, and its growth and decay became a central image repeated throughout his writing with visions of death. For Dylan Thomas, the body was a symbol of both earth and universe.

However, he was no dilettante. Not for him the cultivated aloofness of T.S. Eliot or the tireless backscratching of the Audens and Spenders. This was a poet who thought himself no better than any other working man, choosing their company rather than his literary peers and looking upon the process of writing as a hard physical vocation. The many surviving drafts of his poetry offer a glimpse of his methods. If he changed a single word in a poem or altered its punctuation, Thomas would start again from the beginning, rewriting every line so that he could see for himself how its structure stood upon a page. Sometimes this compulsive search for perfection would make him rewrite a poem more than 200 times until he was satisfied that what he had before him was the finished article – and, even then, he would often return to a poem weeks, months or sometimes years later to change a word or a comma that still offended him. The routine he followed was unchanging: pottering about in the mornings ('I'm a great one for pottering about,' he used to say) before a lunchtime pint of beer, concentrating at his desk throughout the afternoon (almost invariably from 2 p.m. to 7 p.m., with several bottles of lemonade and a large bag of boiled sweets at his elbow), and then back once more to the pub. According to

Caitlin, this timetable was immutable; not once in all their years together did he ever spend an evening at home.

His writing and health were inextricably linked from the very beginning. Swansea and West Wales were shrouded in rain for long periods of the year, leaving children susceptible to colds and winter infections. Florence knew Dylan was weaker than his friends, especially in the lungs. With her simple wisdom she devised a subtle way to keep her son inside during the inclement weather. 'The only way we could keep him in, when it was wet or anything, was to give him plenty of notepaper and pencils. He would go into his own little bedroom and write and write and write.'[1] At Swansea Grammar School he contributed poems to the school magazine which he went on to edit, and at the age of 15 wrote a critique, *Modern Poetry* (*Swansea Grammar School Magazine*, December 1929), that demonstrated a wide grasp of the entire range of current literary opinion.

Thomas left school in 1931 at the age of 16 without passing in enough subjects to matriculate (his only pass was in English). Any hopes his father might have had of him going on to Oxford or Cambridge were out of the question. For nearly 18 months he worked as a trainee reporter on the local newspaper, *The South Wales Evening Post*, before being sacked, apparently for bringing the newspaper to the brink of a libel action. (Thomas suggested in a lively review that Nina Hamnett's book *Laughing Torso* had been banned, and it had not. Another story about his dismissal suggests he wrote a review of a concert that he had not attended and the pianist took offence!)[2]

Thereafter, apart from working for a film company during the war, Dylan Thomas never had another paid job. Instead, he stayed in his bedroom at Cwmdonkin Drive, writing poetry and short stories, smoking Woodbines, drinking bottled beer or fizzy lemonade, eating meals brought up by his mother on a tray, and only leaving the house (usually with money given by his parents) to drink with friends, walk across the cliffs on the Gower peninsula or perform with an amateur dramatic group, the Swansea Little Theatre. It was a strange routine that he followed for the rest of his life with only minor variations, and without it he was unable to write.

✳　✳　✳

When this pattern began at Cwmdonkin Drive, with Florence thoroughly enjoying the opportunity to fuss over her teenage son as if he was still a little boy, Dylan experienced a period of stability in his health. He wrote over 200 poems, eating less, drinking more and smoking far too much, but only in relative terms, for he remained dependent upon his parents for money and they had little to give. This does not seem to have worried them overmuch so long as Thomas was writing and working at his poetry, and was, in any case, the fairly normal flowering of adolescence.

However, during this period there were two major events in Thomas's life which can be dated from his long correspondence with the future novelist Pamela Hansford Johnson, whom he met when they both won poetry prizes in *The Sunday Referee*. They sustained a courtship through the mail that nearly ended in marriage, but foundered and is memorable mainly for the glimpses of character and attitude, method and ambition that shine through his letters. Fortunately, she kept many of his; the ones she wrote to him do not survive and were probably thrown away.

To Johnson, Dylan wrote about his father's first attack of cancer. Firstly, an ulcer was found in his father's mouth when he visited a dentist and this turned out to be cancer of the tongue, which required painful treatment at University College Hospital, London, with radium needles pierced through the tongue. This affected Jack's powerful speaking voice, through which his son learned the resonance of words, and for many months it was feared he might die. During this same period, while his father was travelling up to London for treatment, Thomas went to see a doctor (November 1933) and was told he had diabetes and bad lungs and would only live another four years, unless he changed his habits.

Like most young men, Thomas was too busy enjoying life to give much thought to mortality, but a few months earlier he had been brought face to face with death for the first time when his aunt Ann Jones died, also of cancer, prompting one of his finest poems, *After the Funeral*. Now here it was again, staring him between the eyes.

Had they been more ordinary men, unskilled in literature or the arts of self-expression, the blows would have been hard enough, but father and son were unusual in their sensitivity, and the impact of these twin events upon Dylan was to prove profound. He was already a poet, a fine one for his age, but now began to acquire the depth, range and texture that turns a provincial writer into a great one.

From his letters to Pamela Hansford Johnson, it seems that Thomas went to see his doctor because he was feeling unwell and found it difficult to sleep due to constant headaches. The doctor must have given him a thorough bodily examination, testing both blood and urine, for otherwise he would not have had the information available to suggest Thomas had diabetes and was susceptible to tuberculosis. Thomas was obviously worried, so much so that he would rarely visit another doctor – but he also tried to glamorise his condition, telling Pamela Hansford Johnson how many days he had to live, but not saying how unwell he really was. In just a few months, his weight went down from 122lbs to 112lbs, a 10 per cent loss of body weight in an otherwise fairly healthy 18-year-old with asthma. This might have gone unnoticed but for the headaches that troubled him at night, disappearing in the morning after breakfast. These were so bad that he barely slept at all for a fortnight early in November 1933. 'These 12 November nights have been 12 long centuries to me,' he told Johnson, describing how he lay in darkness through the night staring at 'the empty corners of the room'.

Later in the same letter, after wondering whether his 'consumption' affected his ability to write, Thomas thanks Johnson for her faith in his 'power to write', saying, 'This is one of the few things that makes me deny that twice-damned diabetic doctor.'[3]

✳ ✳ ✳

It is possible to reconstruct what happened when Dylan went to the 'diabetic doctor', probably more than once, since his tests would have been analysed and treatment monitored, because of these references to insomnia, headaches and loss of appetite. The doctor would have asked, 'How long have you been suffering from headaches?'

'Several weeks,' would have been the probable reply, making the doctor wonder what other neurological signs or symptoms there might have been.

'No blurred vision or vomiting?'

'No.'

'No blood in your sputum?'

'Not recently.'

'But you have had it?'

'Yes, ever since I had asthma as a child.'

'Do you smoke?'

'Yes.'

'How many cigarettes a day?'

'About 40.'

'Well, that explains your coughing. Do you drink as well?'

'Yes.'

'How often do you go drinking?'

'About four nights a week.'

'Four nights a week! Drinking what?'

'Beer, mostly . . .'

That would have been enough to alert the doctor to Dylan's habits, without him necessarily volunteering the information that he rarely ate proper meals at the right time, and consumed abnormal quantities of sugary sweets. This was another significant clue. His appetite for sweets was noticed by friends to the point that many commented upon it later. Both Bert Trick, the Swansea friend who introduced him to politics, and Constantine Fitzgibbon, who knew him in London during the war, described it as 'a craving'. When sweets were rationed, Fitzgibbon used to let him have his coupons, likening this to giving a child presents at Christmas.

Dylan would also hide chocolate bars under his pillow, and sometimes travel halfway across London 'to a certain public house that was next to a place that sold ice-cream. He would buy an ice-cream cone, take it into the pub and then put the ice-cream into a fizzy light ale.'[4] This was Dylan's preferred breakfast. Diabetics who suffer chronic shortages of blood sugar crave sweets as the fastest solution to their starvation. In Dylan's case, eating sweets and drinking beer kept him alive. The sweets gave him instant sugar. The beer contained enough carbohydrates from the grains of barley and hops to provide basic nutrition that he would never have had from wine or whisky. Later, when he began substituting whisky for beer in America, his health quickly deteriorated.

The Swansea doctor must have talked to him bluntly. Not only was Thomas stunned and frightened by what was said but he also developed an illogical hatred for doctors. Again, we can reconstruct what happened. The craving for sweets, weight loss and headaches would have been caused by inadequate sugar levels in his blood. This would have been identified by analysing blood and urine samples.

'Young man, you've got to take yourself in hand,' the doctor said. 'These things are curable, but you will have to change your way of life . . .'

The words 'twice-damned diabetic doctor' indicate that Dylan received two pieces of bad news. Not only did he have diabetes, but his weak lungs combined with smoking and drinking made him vulnerable to tubercular infection, although that can be eliminated now. Chest X-rays conducted in London after the war revealed no evidence of TB scars on his lungs and no evidence was found when the post-mortem was conducted after his death in New York in 1953, but the doctor would have been right to point out the risk even without the help of tuberculin skin tests which did not become widely available until the 1940s. People with pre-existing lung problems were more prone to TB and that association remains today. The doctor's concern also dovetailed perfectly with Florence's fear of TB, her claim that

Dylan's grandfather died of it, and Dylan's own awareness that D.H. Lawrence, a writer he admired, also suffered from the same disease.

In 1933, treatment of diabetes and TB was expensive, time-consuming and required constant attention by the patient and his or her family under the supervision of a doctor. Thomas was not the man to submit himself to such a rigorous regime and was not in need of insulin, the cure for diabetes discovered in 1922 and made available to hospitals by the end of that decade. Its discovery by Banting and Best in Toronto earned them both the Nobel Prize. Thousands of lives were instantly saved, but diabetes took several forms, and if he was unsure of the precise nature of Dylan's diabetes (which seems probable), the doctor would also have had within his armoury the methods for treating diabetes that were commonly used in earlier years. Long before the Banting and Best breakthrough, it was realised that diabetes was a disorder of carbohydrate metabolism in which the body could not conserve complex sugars or glucose for storage and later use. Scientists suspected some missing factor prevented storage. What Banting and Best realised was that this was insulin, which is present in a normal pancreas but absent in that of a diabetic. But before that, for well over a century, the symptoms of diabetes were known by all physicians.

At the time Thomas was diagnosed in 1933, two general types of diabetes were recognised, based on age of onset: juvenile and adult. The classic picture of a young diabetic was an emaciated, underdeveloped, cachectic, cadaveric-looking child with flat facial features. Their problem was an inability to make insulin which left them with no stores of glucose in the body. They could eat and eat and eat, but without insulin to store the glucose all the sugar passed straight out of their bodies in urine. Their lives were saved by Banting and Best's discovery, and juvenile diabetes became known as insulin-dependent diabetes.

Adult diabetes occurs differently, often gradually. Obesity is often the first visual sign. Instead of lacking insulin, diabetics with this form of the disease often have variable insulin levels with wide swings in the level of body sugar. The symptoms are similar to juvenile diabetes, but in milder forms like polydipsia, polyuria, glucosuria and hyperglycaemia. This used to be called chemical, latent, borderline, subclinical, asymptomatic or occult diabetes, but today all these terms have been replaced by the phrase non-insulin-dependent diabetes.

Dylan was 18 years old when he saw the Swansea doctor. We have already mentioned his symptoms of polydipsia, polyuria, weight loss, lassitude, headaches and insomnia. While these might suggest juvenile diabetes, it seems more likely he actually had a form of non-insulin-dependent diabetes, for he later became obese, putting on four stone in weight, during Caitlin's first pregnancy. One cannot be sure what triggered it off, but stress, poor or non-existent eating habits, smoking, a cold, alcohol or even too much sugar have all been known to cause diabetes — and all were present in his lifestyle.

What would have upset him more than anything else (and probably accounted for his subsequent attitude to doctors) was that in those days diabetics were required to follow a strict living regime that would have restricted most of his pleasures in life. They had to monitor their intake of food, quantifying the nutritional value of every food type in the same way that dieters count calories. In addition, they were advised to engage in 'correct living' — a calm mental life, active daily exercise, light woollen underwear to preserve body heat, a daily bath, at least nine hours of sleep and frequent teeth brushing.[5] Smoking was not allowed and alcohol strictly forbidden, since it was preferentially metabolised by the liver and caused blood sugar levels to rise dramatically.

So it is not surprising that Dylan Thomas reacted the way he did . . . there was no way he was going to let a doctor stop him smoking, drinking and staying up late at night! However, he did briefly give up Woodbines for a pipe. Fitzgibbon noticed he was also prescribed 'valerian', a natural root used as a sleeping pill.

Luckily for him, Dylan Thomas was non-insulin-dependent. Had it been the other way, he would have been unable to live without insulin and would have died even younger, in his teens rather than at the age of 39. He would have needed injections between four and seven times a day, special diets and frequent visits to the doctor, and the price of insulin would have been a burden upon the family in those pre-war years before the introduction of a National Health Service.

Having ruled out the more severe forms of diabetes, we can also eliminate the possibility that Dylan was told by his doctor that he already had tuberculosis. The doctor would have pointed out his vulnerability, but had there been any evidence of the disease he would have been required to take further action to protect the community at large. TB was a major public health concern in the '30s. Doctors had to report all cases to the local health authorities, and patients with the disease were sent off to sanatoriums for extended periods of rest and recuperation, forbidden by law to continue living at home until there was no further risk of infection.

What Dylan's admissions tell us, then, is that he had a mild form of diabetes and was warned that with his particular weaknesses he faced the risk of much more serious infections — i.e. would only live another four years — unless he pulled himself together. One also has to face the possibility that he took some satisfaction from the warning, for there had long been a romantic association between genius, especially literary genius, and tuberculosis, exemplified by Lawrence, Keats and Byron, and Dylan had a tendency to draw such comparisons. He was able to get away with this because those who heard him whingeing about his health sensed it was all an act; the tragedy was that he had been given a warning without appreciating its seriousness.

✻   ✻   ✻

Father and son faced death in different ways. For Jack, his cancer was like a slow death sentence. He fell into despondency, continued to drink and smoke and took pleasure only in his son's success. Dylan fell back into his old bad habits once his crisis point passed, but his letters to Pamela Hansford Johnson reveal a new focus in his concepts of poetry. Dylan always claimed there were only two kinds of writers: those who believed in the wisdom of the mind and those who preferred the flesh.

While the prim and priggish Pamela considered the human body hideous, Dylan disagreed. The body was 'a fact' as much as death, disease or trees. What he admired in John Donne's *Devotions* was the quality of earthiness:

> All thoughts and actions emanate from the body . . . Every idea, intuitive or intellectual, can be imaged and translated in terms of the body, its flesh, skin, blood, sinews, veins, glands, organs, cells or senses.[6]

In the same letter, Dylan described his own body as 'a bonebound island' through which he learned all he knew. The scenery of this island was used as a symbol of all his thoughts and feelings. There was never a more explicit statement of his literary beliefs than this, but Johnson would never have seen that. She was far more prosaic. 'Letter from Darling Dylan, which was morbid,' she noted in her journal.

Dylan's correspondence with Johnson continued until they realised they were not suited for each other; she could not reform him, no matter how she tried, but the letters show that all the elements of the eventual Dylan Thomas legend were in place remarkably early.

When his willpower demanded it, he was capable of physical feats, whether winning a race or walking 18 miles home after being stuck all night by high tides on The Worm, a rocky promontory overlooking Carmarthen Bay, but he played the sick genius for all it was worth. After being diagnosed as diabetic, he completely ignored his condition. In medical parlance, borrowed from the language of psychoanalysis, Dylan was in denial. He simply refused to acknowledge that he had any serious health problems and continued to lead a stressful life, drinking, smoking and eating improperly. And he remained in denial until the end of his days.

4

The Flaws and the Gift

As Dylan Thomas approached his 20th birthday, there were plenty of reasons for him wanting to leave Cwmdonkin Drive and put Swansea far behind him. Home was no longer home, and he was no longer a provincial dreamer with hopes of being noticed, but an up-and-coming poet already featured in newspapers and magazines like *The Sunday Referee, New English Weekly, Adelphi, The Listener, Criterion* and *New Verse*. Recognition came swiftly to him, and as the prize for winning a poetry competition in *The Sunday Referee*, his first collection, *18 Poems*, was published in book form.

Having grown up under his father's tutelage, reading the literary magazines that came through the letterbox (there were many more of them in those days, and Jack kept up with them all) and following trends in literature as much as he read the classics, Thomas knew that fame was not to be found in Swansea suburbs. He had to go to London, meet the editors who published his work and make himself known to other writers and critics.

The first time he made the journey, Thomas was too nervous to leave the precincts of Paddington Station. That may have been in 1932, for a Swansea friend, Trevor Hughes (who really was tubercular and had already moved to London), said Dylan stayed with him in Bloomsbury, while the poet and translator George Reavey claimed to have met him then in a well-known writers' and painters' pub, the Plough, also in Bloomsbury, near the British Museum. Reavey insisted that he showed Thomas around the museum and also took him to the Fitzroy Tavern, another familiar watering-hole for artists only a few minutes' walk away in Charlotte Street. Fitzgibbon could find no one else to corroborate his story, but the point barely matters.

Nancy and her first husband, Haydn Taylor, were married in May 1933 and made their home upon a houseboat on the River Thames at Chertsey. Dylan spent a fortnight there, travelling up to town by train to meet editors like A.R. Orage (*New English Weekly*), Sir Richard Rees (*Adelphi*) and possibly Geoffrey Grigson (*New Verse*). Still only 19 years old, Thomas visited London several more times, sometimes staying with Pamela Hansford Johnson and her mother in Battersea, before moving in with Fred Janes, with whom he shared a room at 5 Redcliffe Street, on the borders of Earls Court and Chelsea, from November 1934. The artist Mervyn Levy, a childhood friend of Dylan's, had another room in the same apartment, and he and Janes had great difficulty persuading Thomas to come up with his share of the rent, even though Florence was sending him £1 a week to cover such necessities. (£1 went a long way in those days, before the ravages of wartime inflation and the even greater price-rises that followed; many houses could be rented for less than £1 a week – and it was enough to buy 30 pints of beer!) Just as he later tried to fool Caitlin, Thomas would insist he had no money to pay them – so they would grab him, turn him upside-down and give him a good shake until the coins rattled out of his pockets.[1]

Although unreliable in any relationship that involved money or repaying a debt, Thomas never missed an opportunity to find a new market for his wares. A personal meeting with an editor would be swiftly followed up with a letter and the enclosure of poems or short stories; he was already a consummate salesman, and therein lies another contradiction.

Selling anything is hard work, demanding concentrated energy – and selling oneself is possibly the hardest work of all – but there can be no doubt that Dylan Thomas maintained a high sales pitch, never allowing any editorial door to go unknocked upon, and constantly monitoring each minor breakthrough. When it came to promoting himself, he was indefatigable. And yet, between 1934 and 1949, Dylan was sick an astonishing number of times, with several major illnesses which required hospital treatment, and numerous minor ones. Many of these problems were due to his untreated diabetes. Whenever he was away from home for any length of time, he always returned sick and this became such a feature of his life that one can see, retrospectively, that his later illnesses in the United States were inevitable. He went to America for much the same reason he first visited London – to make his name and earn money – and in both situations his life followed a similar pattern.

In the 15 years between leaving Swansea in 1934 and making his first American tour in February 1950, Thomas experienced almost 50 periods of illness. These can be dated by analysing *Dylan Thomas: The Collected Letters* (1985).

There was only one year in which he did not describe ill health, 1942, and even this may be misleading, for that was either a year in which he wrote few letters or one from which few survive. For a young man between the ages of 20 and 35, this was an astonishingly poor health record. At least six of these illnesses were serious enough to require hospital treatment or medical care, and they include one period of two months' semi-isolation after a diagnosis of venereal disease. His health paralleled his lifestyle and his habit of running from one debt to another, and it was often from his bed that he wrote pleas for money, dramatising his illnesses with bogus premonitions of death.

The key to understanding his deterioration in 1953 lies in piecing together information on his health and habits. The range of clues is bewildering, but the whole truth is rarely told, for Thomas often dissembled, avoiding telling the whole story about any one situation. He was a compulsive liar, deceiving himself as much as he misled his family. There would be noisy complaints about broken bones, the flu, headaches or hangovers, but he was conspicuously silent about visiting doctors or spending time in hospital, perhaps anxious not to revive memories of the 'diabetic doctor'. The lying began with his letters to Pamela Hansford Johnson and became a habit that cost him dearly in the end.

✳   ✳   ✳

The state of Thomas's health in 1934 can be pieced together with remarkable accuracy through the intense documentation provided by his letters to Johnson. These have often been acclaimed for their insight into his intellectual development, but to a doctor they also give precise indications of the way his body was reacting to various illnesses. It was the only period in his life that Thomas gave so much away.

Their relationship began with a letter. They were both sending in poems to the Poet's Corner section of *The Sunday Referee*, and she wrote to congratulate him after reading *That Sanity Be Kept* (3 September 1933). Thomas replied enthusiastically to anyone who complimented him upon his poetry, and she duly received the first of a long series of letters that often ran to many pages. Those published in *The Collected Letters* were mostly written between September 1933 and October 1934, totalling around 60,000 words, but they may represent less than a third of his total outpouring. Johnson, who later married the novelist C.P. Snow, once claimed to have received over a hundred letters from him yet only 30 survive. Most are now preserved in the New York State University Library at Buffalo.

The letters became surprisingly intimate long before they first met, towards the end of February 1934, when Thomas visited her at home in Battersea Rise. Thereafter, as they wondered whether or not to marry (and were briefly engaged), Thomas frequently wrote about himself in a way that he rarely did to anyone else. His letters to Caitlin, for instance, gave away little personal information, possibly with good reason – she was by nature intensely jealous.

Having told Pamela he loved her (in a letter that is among those that have not survived), Thomas went on to write about an illness that was troubling him in March 1934, four months after the warning from the 'diabetic doctor'.

'I've been too ill to write, to do anything at all but sit fatalistically by the fire, sipping Turkish tobacco out of a most exotic pipe . . . now I am regaining vitality,' he wrote.[2] Later that same month, he boasted that he had smoked only two cigarettes recently after being a chain-smoker for five years, and was also going for morning walks. Clearly, he heeded the doctor's advice.

Within two months Thomas was ill again, reporting the same symptoms of headaches, insomnia and weight loss. 'I am ill, ill as hell. I have had a headache for a fortnight, and haven't slept longer than that. I've lost all hope of ever going to sleep again,' he said,[3] adding that he was taking a course of tablets, sometimes tripling the dose to find some relief.

These episodes of ill health, and especially the one referred to in the last paragraph (May 1934), bear striking similarities to his later illnesses in New York. On both occasions he claims to have made an effort to cut down on smoking and drinking and followed a more healthy nutritional regime, but, nevertheless, continued to feel unwell, requiring several weeks' recovery. This begs the question: what went wrong? And one can answer that with clear evidence from the letters to Pamela. In one of his letters to her, he writes, 'I can't get up, I'm sleeping no better, I've done everything that's wrong, I daren't see a doctor' (27 May 1934).

In other words, he knew what he needed to do to restore himself to good health – and ignored his doctor's advice. His refusal to accept fully his fundamental susceptibility to illness was a deep sign of immaturity. Dylan Thomas did not accept responsibility for his own life and death, even though as a poet he, more than most, made life and death the constant themes of his work. It was a fatal flaw in his character.

✻   ✻   ✻

Thomas's refusal to recognise his own problems or listen to his doctors was reinforced by his superstitious nature and serious ignorance of basic medicine. In that same letter to Johnson, he admitted embarking upon a three-day drinking spree and claimed to have slept with a friend's fiancée. As if that was not enough to shock a woman he was hoping to marry, Thomas added, 'I'm just on the borders of DTs, darling.'⁴ This claim was sheer nonsense. If he really did have the money to spend three days drinking beer (which is unlikely), that would not have been enough to give him delirium tremens. He might have had a hangover, but that would have been all, and it is significant that he subsequently made similar boasts to other friends, especially Liz Reitell, during his last days in New York.

The signs and symptoms of delirium tremens have been known since the early nineteenth century. The popular misconception about delirium tremens was that it was associated with heavy drinking. This is not the case. Delirium tremens occurs after a prolonged period of heavy drinking has ceased and following a period of abstinence of between 48 and 72 hours, although some authorities believe the period can be between 72 hours and 96 hours after the last drink. The major symptoms are 'tremulousness, hallucinations, agitation, confusion, disorientation, fever, tachycardia and profuse perspiration'.⁵ The patient is usually very sick, requiring constant supervision by medical personnel, and DTs may lead to death if there are coexisting diseases connected with the heart or lungs that are not being adequately managed. It would be virtually impossible for someone in true DTs to be writing letters to friends.

We can therefore say with certainty that Dylan Thomas was not suffering from DTs in 1934 – or in 1953 when Feltenstein was called to his bedside. When he drank too much, especially in those early years, it was almost always beer that he drank, and he simply went to bed with a bad hangover from which he recovered after a day or two like most social drinkers. Had Dylan suffered from DTs while still living at home with his parents, it would have made his other illnesses pale by comparison, but there is no evidence of this. Florence tended to underplay his drinking bouts, calling them 'the flu', because it was her experience, just as it had been during his father's more boisterous drinking, that Dylan always recovered with simple bed rest and his favourite antidote: tiny cubes of bread soaked in milk.

✳   ✳   ✳

In London, with few possessions, only a few clothes to his name and virtually no income apart from his parents' handouts, Thomas led a restricted life. If he did go drinking, it was hardly on a prodigious scale because he did not have the money. The few portraits, photographs and personal descriptions of him that survive show him to have been a rather smart young man, without the slightest trace of raffishness.

Thomas and Janes were often unable to go out because of lack of money. Since Dylan was incapable of cooking, his only daily nutrition came from a breakfast of 'beer, cake and perhaps an apple'.[6] He did no serious work in London, producing no poetry, but continued his correspondence with Pamela Hansford Johnson, whom he could not see during the day because she worked in a bank. His main preoccupation was exploring the pubs around Chelsea, Soho and Charlotte Street, where other writers and artists also congregated. The American writer Kay Boyle met Thomas during this period, observing:

> He would climb up on the bar and tell the press of people from there what the hills and the sky were like where he came from, and how far away he was from the place he wanted to be.

Already, Thomas was finding he could not settle down to a serious writing schedule 'out of his country in that alien place where he was'. In a letter to Bert Trick, the Swansea grocer who befriended him, Thomas admitted, 'I really do need hills around me before I can do my best with either stories or poems.' [7]

His first attempt to live away from home collapsed within little more than a month, and Dylan returned home to Cwmdonkin Drive in November 1934 with advance copies of *18 Poems* to distribute to his friends. There is some evidence that he collapsed with exhaustion, for he wrote to another friend in South Wales, the poet Glyn Jones, that he was taking a holiday, while Johnson was informed more precisely, 'I've retired home, after a ragged life, for a few weeks' rest before I go to the country for the summer.' [8]

That begs the question: why did he need a rest after no more than four or five weeks in London? Drinking may be part of the explanation, but one has to be wary of that, for Dylan Thomas was always inclined to exaggerate his intake. This is all part of the 'boyo' culture of South Wales, where being able to sink ten or 12 pints on a Saturday night – preferably after a tough game of rugby football – is thought to be proof of manhood; you are an even bigger hero if you also down ten or 12 pints the night before the game! Thomas grew up with this ludicrous preoccupation with excessive drinking. His father was like that, and the offices of provincial newspapers have long been notorious for the same boring habits. Another feature of Thomas's immaturity was that he liked to convey the impression of being 'one of the lads', whereas at least three of them – Fred Janes, Mervyn Levy and Dan Jones – have confirmed that Thomas had such a low threshold that he would invariably be the worse for wear by the time they were on their third or fourth drink.

So, perhaps he was suffering the ill effects for someone of his limited physical resources of having just two or three drinks; or was there something else? Although he produces no detail to back up the implication, Fitzgibbon comments that 'benzedrine began to be taken in the late '30s. Opium, cocaine and the like were too expensive.'[9] We know of no other supporting evidence for this suggestion, although many reports confirm that Thomas was taking benzedrine in New York, was sometimes seen swallowing pills by the handful, and may easily have fallen in with the community of writers, artists and musicians in Greenwich Village, where a wide selection of drugs was available and the Beat Poets were just beginning to make their first impact.

Thomas's history of asthma would never have accounted for the exhaustion of a young man of 20 after only four or five weeks away from home, but the probability that he was suffering from exacerbations of diabetes does. The Swansea doctor's advice was to reduce or give up drinking and smoking, eat regularly, get proper sleep and exercise frequently. In London, Dylan did none of these things and his body was forced to rely upon his inadequate reserves of glucose. Once they became depleted, he felt exhausted, experienced more headaches, could not sleep, became susceptible to infections and suffered stomach pains. As soon as he returned home, however, and was safely tucked up in bed at night, eating regularly and topping up his glucose reserves, his health snapped back – which was clearly evidenced by his renewed ability to write.

As soon as he felt better again, Dylan would return to London – and then the symptoms would come back. The following spring (1935), Dylan stayed at the Hampstead home of Geoffrey Grigson, author and editor of *New Verse*. He arrived 'in a filthy and squalid condition. My wife got his clothes off and got him into the bath, then found he was covered in a pink rash.'[10] Worried that Dylan might have a venereal disease, the Grigsons took him to a doctor near the British Museum who allayed their fears. However, this rash or superficial infection was another powerful clue. Such disorders are common in diabetics who do not eat properly or keep themselves clean, for their diabetes suppresses their immune system and leaves them more susceptible than most people to infections.

Later that same year, Dylan did catch gonorrhoea, 'the clap', a common sexually transmitted disease. Before the introduction of antibiotics, rest and avoidance of sexual contact for six to eight weeks was the usual treatment. Dylan went home to Swansea and managed to keep the infection secret from his mother, but alluded to it in a letter to Grigson: 'I drank the night custard of the gods, but they must have been the wrong gods . . . I have to stay indoors for six to eight weeks, during which time I feel sure I'll be able to work hard and well.'[11] He later boasted to friends in London that he had caught a dose of the clap. This may have been exacerbated by his depressed immune system, but its cause was obvious: he had slept with a woman who carried the disease.

In all these stories about his earliest visits to London there is nothing to suggest alcoholism, and even those later stories of his excessive drinking refer to how he behaved after drinking, not to the quantities consumed. Despite 'The Legend of the Drunken Poet', there is no firm evidence that he drank much more than anyone else, only that he consumed more than his body could process – which was not much at all.

✿　✿　✿

Alcoholism and drunkenness were at the time considered different conditions. Like many men, Dylan often got drunk, but this was always in a social setting, a pub, which was an integral part of daily life. In London Dylan's day would start with beer for breakfast, but he would go long periods in Wales when he hardly drank at all. Unlike the poet Hart Crane, Dylan rarely drank heavily when he was writing and did not need to drink to produce his best work. An alcoholic, on the other hand, drinks because he absolutely must. Often, he dislikes the taste and despises himself for the habit, but the craving overwhelms his life and becomes the only antidote to the severe psychological anxieties that plague him. Within the guidelines of this distinction, Dylan Thomas was not an alcoholic.

In *Portrait of the Artist as a Young Dog*, Dylan described his feelings for beer:

> I liked the taste of beer, its live, white lather, its brass-bright depths, the sudden world through the wet brown walls of the glass, the tilted rush to the lips and the slow swallowing down to the lapping belly, the salt on the tongue, the foam at the corners.[12]

He started drinking when he was about 15 years old, shortly before he became a reporter on *The Swansea Evening Post* (which later changed its name to *The South Wales Evening Post*) and began appearing regularly in amateur productions at the Little Theatre in the Mumbles, a Swansea suburb. Having a drink after work or following rehearsals was part of his daily life, and this was the way it continued; as a writer, he was a solitary figure by day – but a man who loved social drinking at night. 'It helps me sleep,' was a frequent explanation, and he told the poet and cricket commentator John Arlott that he drank 'because it's different every time'. He was not the first writer, nor will he be the last, to allay loneliness with alcohol. It is a frequent trait in the characters of writers, and one which was possibly overemphasised in Thomas's case because he enjoyed the company of people who drank far more than that of others.

His behaviour was noted carefully by Pamela Hansford Johnson, for she was wondering whether or not to go ahead with their marriage. Thomas had several unattractive habits, not least his indifference to money and bodily hygiene, but she declared in her memoirs, *Important to Me*, that she did not consider him alcoholic despite him turning up for their first meeting with a bottle of brandy in his pocket. 'Drinking was, for him, one of the great romantic necessities of the poet's image; he fantasticated his drinking. The other two necessities were to become tubercular and – extremely odd – to get fat.'[13] (This is probably another reference to the advice of the Swansea doctor, who would have told him that he had to put on weight. At that time, weight loss was thought to indicate that diabetes was out of control.)

✡ ✡ ✡

By the time he met Caitlin Macnamara in the spring of 1936, Dylan Thomas was already a minor celebrity in literary London. His first book, *18 Poems*, had been reprinted; his second, *Twenty-five Poems*, was awaiting publication; his book reviews appeared regularly in *The Morning Post*, and over 40 of his poems and short stories had been published in magazines ranging from *New Verse* and *New English Weekly* to T.S. Eliot's *Criterion*.

He was a popular figure around the pubs of Soho, Chelsea and the area between Oxford Street, Charlotte Street and Fitzroy Square that became known as 'Fitzrovia' because he was always good for a joke and had a vast fund of shaggy-dog stories. The first person to mention his name to Caitlin was Augustus John. 'He's a bright young spark,' said John, who became a central figure in both their lives and was a close friend of her father, Francis Macnamara, a minor poet and writer and part of Southern Ireland's Protestant gentry. Her grandfather was High Sheriff of County Clare, and during 'The Troubles' in 1916, Republican rebels shot at the family mansion at Ennistymon (which is now a hotel), leaving its walls pitted with bullet holes.

At one time the Macnamaras owned the whole village of Ennistymon, with a large acreage of farmland, a river with a series of waterfalls and a wooded glen. However, when Francis inherited the estate it soon dribbled through his fingers. Although he graduated in law at Oxford, Francis managed to avoid all forms of serious work and devoted much of his energy to womanising. Like Augustus, he believed in free love and does not appear to have been too bothered when Augustus slept with his wife, Yvonne, during a family holiday at Doolin on the west coast of Ireland, where the Macnamaras owned another house.

The two families remained close after Francis and Yvonne were divorced, with Augustus occasionally employing Francis as a tutor for his children and Yvonne taking their son and three daughters – John, Nicolette, Brigid and Caitlin – to live in a rambling old house that was once a pub at Blashford near Ringwood, Hampshire, not far from the Johns' family home at Fryern Court.

Throughout their childhood, the Johns and Macnamaras were in and out of each other's homes, riding horses, hunting and competing in gymkhanas, sitting down for supper wherever they happened to be and often staying overnight. For a long time Caitlin was deeply in love with Caspar John, who later became an admiral, First Sea Lord and Chief of the Naval Staff. 'My mother warned him off because he was ten years older than me,' said Caitlin, who never forgave her. 'That was a terrible thing for a mother to do,' she added, harbouring a sense of regret until the end of her life. 'I never quite got over it. If Caspar had come back into my life while I was married to Dylan, I would have gone off with him. He was the most beautiful man . . .'

Even more problematic was her relationship with Augustus, who asked her to pose in his studio when she was in her mid-teens. When he finished work for the day, Augustus suddenly leapt upon her, ripped off her pants and raped her – which often happened to society women who wanted their portraits painted, but was quite a shock to this young virgin who had known him since she was two. Afterwards, he got up, readjusted his trousers and ran out of the room while Caitlin put on her clothes and went home, without saying a word to her mother. The next day, Caitlin returned – and was raped again. 'I had to go back,' she said, 'because he hadn't finished the painting.'

To say they were lovers is not quite true, for love never came into it, but they became close and Augustus would take Caitlin up to London, wine and dine her, and introduce her to his friends, many of whom wondered whether she was really his daughter, while he continued to exercise something akin to *droit de seigneur* whenever he felt like it. Caitlin was curiously passive about all this, and the arrangement did have compensations; Augustus regularly stayed at the

Eiffel Tower Hotel in London and Caitlin was able to book herself in there too, signing costs of food and accommodation to his account.

✳ ✳ ✳

Dylan and Caitlin first met on 12 April 1936. Until that day he was living with someone else, the American writer Emily Holmes Coleman, who suffered a mental breakdown after the birth of her son, described the experience in her famous novel *The Shutter of Snow* (1930) and became an important literary figure in Paris in the '20s and London in the '30s. Thomas tended to gravitate towards women like this, widows or divorcees with a central London home of their own and independent financial means: it avoided paying for bed and breakfast or the expense of renting a flat.

✳ ✳ ✳

They met in the Wheatsheaf, another of the literary pubs in Fitzrovia. Caitlin was sitting on a stool at the bar when Dylan walked in and began telling stories. Their eyes did not meet, but she became aware of his voice saying 'You're beautiful', 'I've been looking for a woman like you all my life', 'I love you' and 'We must get married', and before she knew what was happening he was kneeling beside her with his head in her lap, and she felt an immediate closeness. No man had ever said he loved her before, and it all felt good and right.

When they left the Wheatsheaf, Caitlin took control of the situation, held him by the hand and walked to the Eiffel Tower for the night. They stayed a week, charging the bill to Augustus John, who never noticed.

It was one of the strangest weeks of her life. When they went to bed for the first time that night, she noticed he was smelly – and his trousers so thickened by dirt and sweat that when he stepped out of them, they stood up beside the bed. She also noticed he did not wear underpants. According to Paul Ferris, Thomas was sexually undersized. 'I never knew what made Ferris say that,' said Caitlin caustically. 'Dylan looked perfectly normal to me ...'

Stranger still was the lack of food. Thomas was now in London mode, living on beer and reluctant to waste good drinking money (of which he had little) on breakfast, lunch or supper. 'We didn't have anything to eat all week and by the end of it I was starving,' she said. 'This didn't seem to bother Dylan. He was anxious to introduce me to all his friends, so every day was spent going from pub to pub, with Dylan saying proudly, "This is the woman I am going to marry ... I have been searching for her all my life".'

Caitlin was bowled over. The fact that they had no work, money or anywhere to live barely crossed their minds. So what? They were in love. That was enough. She could have been a successful dancer, and appeared in several London shows, but that was all abandoned. Thereafter, she devoted herself totally to Dylan.

It may seem silly to those with a practical mind, but Dylan and Caitlin were happy, drifting from one friend's home to the next, their days spent walking through fields hand in hand, picking bluebells or riding bicycles down country lanes, talking merrily of all the wonderful things they would do when he became rich and famous. She never doubted this would happen. Neither did anyone else. They could all see that Dylan Thomas had 'The Gift'.

✳ ✳ ✳

Further bouts of ill health plagued Thomas throughout 1936, usually after visits to London where he drank too much and ate too little. He and Caitlin were not together all the time. Sometimes he would go home to Swansea, and she was still posing for Augustus John. In a letter to one of his closest friends, the Swansea bank clerk and minor poet Vernon Watkins, Thomas summarised one of these London forays:

> promiscuity, booze, coloured shirts, too much talk, too little work . . . I had a spot of rheumatism . . . I left London with Life No. Thirteen's headaches, liver and general seediness, and have by this time fully recovered.[14]

This time, instead of remaining in Wales, Dylan accepted an invitation from Wyn Henderson, another of his 'bed-and-breakfast women' (as Caitlin called them), to stay in her cottage at Porthcurno, near Land's End, Cornwall, and later at Mousehole, where she co-owned a guest house, the now-famous Lobster Pot restaurant. Thomas spent most of his days writing, and Henderson (who later became close to Caitlin) fulfilled the role of host, mother and nurse, trying to keep him out of the local pubs where he claimed to be able to drink 40 pints of beer a night.

Such a ludicrous boast would barely be worth mentioning but for an incident that happened there. One night, his need to urinate after drinking became so urgent and unstoppable that he urinated all over himself before he could get to a toilet.[15] Mrs Henderson was unshockable. She took off his clothes, washed him like a baby and put him to bed in clean pyjamas. The significance of this event is that it happened again and again in the years that followed. During his American tours, he would sometimes start to urinate before he could reach a lavatory. Once it happened on stage – and there was one wonderfully funny night (for everyone else!) when he distressed Charlie Chaplin by urinating all over his potted plants.

This is another indication of diabetes. An uncontrollable urge to urinate is a classic symptom. What was happening to Thomas in Cornwall in 1936, just as in America 15 years later, was that his beer intake overloaded his bloodstream with carbohydrates that were not absorbed by his liver because of his low level of insulin. Their high concentration acted like a diuretic, causing a massive fluid overload to which the body responded by flushing out enough glucose through his urine to maintain a normal level of carbohydrates. Before leaving Cornwall, Thomas also complained of headaches, a swollen throat and asthma.

✵ ✵ ✵

Thomas's other travels during 1936 are not well documented. He and Caitlin continued their strange courtship, sleeping wherever a friend would provide a bed, rarely going out socially other than to drink (they did not have enough money to go to the theatre and Dylan would never dream of spending what little he had on food), retreating home whenever they were penniless.

From a literary standpoint, his reputation was growing. That September, J.M. Dent and Sons Ltd published his second book, *Twenty-five Poems*, which was acclaimed by Dame Edith Sitwell in *The Sunday Times*:

> The work of this young man (he is 22 years of age) is on a huge scale, both in theme and structurally – his themes are the mystery and holiness of all forms and aspects of life. He writes of the brotherhood of man with the mineral and vegetable world . . . of the splendour and inexorability and fatefulness of spring
>
> > Beginning with doom in the bulb, and
> > the springtime marvels.
>
> In all these poems, so strangely young in their strength and vitality, all things are identified with God, Who is present in 'the sensual root and sap', and where
>
> > the summer blood
> > knocked in the flesh that decked the vine.

The form of many of these poems is superb. The eighth poem, though not a sonnet either in rhyme, scheme or shape, yet, by its particular motion, gives the impression that here, alone among the poets of the younger generation, is one who could produce sonnets worthy of our great heritage . . . I could not name one poet of this, the younger generation, who shows so great a promise, and even so great an achievement.

✳   ✳   ✳

Thomas returned to Cornwall in 1937, this time with Caitlin – and they were married by special licence at Penzance Registry Office on 11 July. The wedding was postponed at least once because money set aside to pay for it was spent on drink. In the end, Wyn Henderson paid for the licence and the young couple were duly married, he wearing a tweed jacket, corduroy trousers, check shirt and no tie and she in a simple blue cotton, flowery dress that she could remember in detail for the rest of her life. 'I was amazed how soon it was all over,' she used to recall, admitting that it was Thomas who pressured her into marriage; she could not care less about such scraps of paper.

5

The Happiest Days of Our Lives

The Thomases lived well during the first three years of their marriage, with Dylan's reputation growing and Caitlin happily entwining her life around him. Initially, they stayed with their parents. Jack retired from the Grammar School, moving to a smaller house at Bishopston, and, despite telling Dylan that he thought it utter foolishness to marry without money or anywhere to live, he and Florence helped the couple generously. So did Mrs Yvonne Macnamara, providing Dylan with a writing room through the winter of 1937–38.

In the spring of 1938, they returned to Wales to look for somewhere to live in Laugharne, where the poet, novelist and short-story writer Richard Hughes, already internationally famous through the success of *A High Wind in Jamaica*, was firmly ensconced at Castle House. 'High Wind Hughes', as Thomas called him (every acquaintance was known to them by a nickname, many of them insulting), helped them find Eros, a tiny furnished fisherman's cottage facing Gosport Street, with a back garden leading straight down to the Taf estuary and overlooking Laugharne's ancient castle. Eros has been extended and modernised in recent years, but was then tiny with only two bedrooms and no bathroom. The Thomases claimed it was damp, even in summer, and quickly began to describe it as 'ugly' and 'poky', disliking its ageing velvet curtains and creaking Victorian bed. But it was home – their first home – and Dylan soon resumed his daily rhythm, depending upon his bottled beer, lemonade, boiled sweets and cigarettes while he wrote, with Caitlin following the local custom of picking cockles and stabbing for flatfish.

Laugharne was a poor town with no industry, but a rich harvest of millions of cockles lay just an inch or so beneath its sandy riverbed. At low tide, these could be picked with a hand-rake. The legendary gatherers – the 'web-footed cocklewomen', as Thomas described them in *Under Milk Wood* – developed enormous hips through constant bending, filling as many as 30 or 40 half-hundredweight sacks on every tide. Some would be sold as they were and sent to other towns and others were boiled and bottled in their own brine, but locally, when picking cockles for their own consumption, the townsfolk would fatten them up overnight by feeding them on oats and dousing them in salted water, a process that encouraged the cockles to clean themselves in their shells before being boiled alive the following morning. People ate them fresh from their shells with a sprinkle of pepper and a dash of vinegar, fried them in fat with breadcrumbs or baked them with other fish in a pie. Likewise, Caitlin soon learned how to walk through the river when the tide was out, stabbing with a fork an inch or two ahead of her toe, spearing flatfish.

The town may have been poor, but no one went hungry. The river was also rich with salmon, migratory trout and mullet. Ducks and geese wintered along its banks, and in the hills around rabbits abounded. Some nights there was pheasant, and there was always someone knocking at the door with a bag of potatoes or swedes, a bundle of runner beans or a cauliflower. More than that, the town was totally devoted to drink in a way that suited the Thomases down to the ground. If the mood was right, the pubs stayed open all night, with the landlord manning the bar while his wife went to bed. During the day those with a job would call in for a pint before going to work, call back again late morning if they happened to be passing through (sometimes leaving tractors outside with their engines running), and return for an early-evening pint before going home to supper. What held them together was talk. There was a constant exchange of gossip and news – particularly news of horses running that day at 3.30 p.m., with more tips traded across the bar in Brown's Hotel than anywhere else.

There were other attractions, too. The town was ancient, built around its castle, with fine domestic architecture and that strange form of local government. It was, in effect, frozen in time, refusing to grow or acquire modern habits, while other places like Cardiff, Swansea and Llanelli metamorphosed into industrial conurbations.

Being so compact and self-reliant, Laugharne was a world in itself with its tradesmen, shopkeepers, churchgoers and English immigrants living in the Upper Town, in the fine houses and better cottages around the castle, and its fishermen and cockle-gatherers in the smaller cottages down in the Lower Town, also known as The Docks, despite no ship worthy of the name having been seen there in two generations. These two communities lived uneasily side by side, separated by a short hill. On bank holidays, primed by drink, their young men would clash, fighting with fists, knives and boathooks. And yet, despite all this, Laugharne was outward-looking. With no other income but cockles, its people travelled far and wide in search of a wage. Some went to sea and captained boats; others lived in improbable places like Russia, Canada, Australia and South Africa, but always came back, giving Laugharne a strangely cosmopolitan feel for a small Welsh township.

This was strengthened by the occasional presence of High Wind Hughes and his wife Frances, who divided their lives between this out-of-the-way, some might say forgotten, backwater and their other home, a palace in Morocco. In Laugharne, Hughes leased the fine Georgian mansion Castle House and entertained on a scale that was grand by the standards of rural Welsh life, inviting writers and painters down from London, employing servants, dressing formally for dinner and maintaining a cellar of fine wines.

Hughes was related by marriage to one of the county families of Carmarthenshire, and so when the Thomases moved to their tiny fisherman's cottage, with its damp-stained wallpaper and external earthen closet, they also found themselves dining with the local gentry at Castle House. Within three months, and with a little extra help from Hughes, they moved up the social scale to a rather grander house at the posher end of town. They rented Sea View from the Williams family, who also owned Brown's Hotel, the electricity generator and the local bus company. The weekly rent was ten shillings, or fifty pence.

Sea View is strangely imposing: double-fronted, one room deep but three storeys high. Augustus John thought it looked like a doll's house, and he was right. On the ground floor there was an old-fashioned kitchen with a solid fuel stove, and the Thomases largely lived upon cockles, flatfish and Caitlin's perennial pots of broth. Hopelessly undomesticated, she knew that if one threw diced root vegetables and meaty bones into a pan of water and simmered it, there would be something to eat in two or three hours' time. 'We hardly ever ate anything else,' she used to claim, which may have been an exaggeration, although she added convincingly, 'Bones were cheap and meat was too expensive, and people were always giving us vegetables . . . I'd keep reheating the pot for days, until it turned blue, but Dylan didn't mind. He was forever telling people I made very good stews.'

The Thomases were happy, for there was a room at Sea View for Dylan to work, another where Caitlin could practise dancing and two spare bedrooms to accommodate guests. Soon they acquired enough good furniture to decorate them all, French provincial style, when one of Caitlin's aunts died and the family decided to let them have the contents of her house.

Enough money was coming in for them to live reasonably well. Dylan's short stories and poems were being published in leading British literary magazines like *Life and Letters Today, Seven, Criterion* and *Twentieth-Century Verse,* translated into French and published in book form both in Britain and the United States. His poems also appeared in the US magazine *Poetry* (Chicago) and regularly in anthologies; he was sometimes invited to broadcast for the BBC, and earned fees for reading not only his own works but also other contemporary poets.

'It was the happiest period of our marriage,' Caitlin confirmed, and it was also the most orderly. They regularly saw their parents, frequently invited friends down from London, and spent many summer afternoons alone in bed, as Dylan lay back on pillows reciting poetry as she cradled in the fold of his elbow, her head laid across his chest, wrapped in the sound of his voice. 'That's what I remember more than anything else, hearing him reading, especially Shakespeare, and reading it just for me,' she said.

* * *

Shortly before they moved to Sea View, Caitlin found herself expecting a baby, and this seemed to trigger another diabetic episode. Over the course of several months, Dylan's weight went up by almost 30lbs and within a year the increase grew to around four stone. This was highly unusual for a man of his age, only 22, and provides a further clue to Dylan's abnormal metabolism which was ignored by all, including the poet himself. What happened was probably that the stress of the impending birth caused Dylan to accelerate his drinking and craving for sweets, so that he ballooned in size and weight. It was an extraordinary phenomenon in a man who was, at the most, only 5 feet 4 inches tall.

* * *

The Thomases returned to stay with Mrs Macnamara in November 1938 when Caitlin was seven months pregnant, remaining at Blashford for several months after the baby was born, No one warned Caitlin how painful childbirth could be and she found the experience traumatic. 'I had a frightful time and was terribly shocked, and afterwards felt stripped of all my flesh, like Christ crucified,' she said.[1] Llewelyn Edouard Thomas was born at Poole General

Augustus John in his prime. When he raped Caitlin, she said it was like being attacked by a goat

Caitlin practising eurhythmic dancing on a riverbank near her mother's home, circa 1935

Dylan at his mother-in-law's home in Blashford, circa 1938

Caitlin cradles Llewelyn in her arms, 1939

Dylan and Caitlin at Brown's Hotel in Laugharne, circa 1939

Dylan and Caitlin in the rear yard of Brown's Hotel, circa 1946. Left to right: family friend Mabley Owen, Caitlin, Ebie Williams (landlord of Brown's Hotel), Nicolette Devas (Caitlin's sister), Dylan, Ivy Williams (wife of Ebie) and Bill McAlpine, close family friend

Dylan Thomas in his workshed
at The Boat House, Laugharne,
summer of 1953

The famous photo of Dylan
Thomas during a reading in
New York (© Rollie McKenna)

The Boat House as it was when the family lived there. This photograph was taken circa 1954, shortly after Dylan's death

Portrait of Caitlin in her old age, taken in Sicily in 1986

OPPOSITE
TOP LEFT: Aeronwy greets mourners at her mother's funeral, August 1994 (© Ralph Carpenter)

TOP RIGHT: Stewbags, the solicitor with whom Caitlin was locked in combat for nearly 40 years, joins the family mourners at her funeral at St Martin's Church, Laugharne (© Ralph Carpenter)

Aeronwy and Caitlin on the doorstep of the house in Delancey Street, Camden Town, London, where the family had a flat in the early '50s. The plaque was unveiled by Caitlin

Aeronwy, Francesco and Llewelyn at their mother's funeral (© Ralph Carpenter)

Brown's Hotel, Laugharne

Sea View, Laugharne, where Dylan and Caitlin lived shortly before the Second World War

Hospital on 30 January 1939. He was a small baby, weighing less than 7lbs. Caitlin's mother hired a nanny to look after him while Caitlin recovered from an ordeal that she tended to overdramatise.

Many of her memories about this period are unreliable. She insists in her memoirs that Dylan was nowhere to be seen when the baby was born, and this was probably true. Men seldom sat by their wives' bedside during childbirth in those days. However, Caitlin dresses up the story by claiming he preferred to spend the night with 'Joey the Ravisher', an 'ostentatiously flashy piece of goods' whom she had known at dancing school. The story seems unlikely, for his letters show that Dylan was at Blashford all the time.

What is undoubtedly true is that both of them started behaving jealously, with Dylan feeling neglected now that all her attention was concentrated on the baby and Caitlin suspecting him of infidelity. It was the beginning of a major stress in the marriage that did not become apparent for several years. Outwardly they seemed happy enough, returning to Sea View in April 1939 and settling back into their familiar routine. Compared with their later reputation, they lived conventionally. Dylan made sure Llewelyn was christened at St Martin's Church with Augustus John, Richard Hughes and Vernon Watkins as godfathers, and whenever he and Caitlin left the house, especially on Wednesdays when they caught the bus into town to visit Carmarthen market, he insisted she be 'properly' and not immodestly dressed.

Their life would probably have continued to be like this, overcoming the first hints of jealousy, with demand for Thomas's work increasing and no reason whatsoever for anyone outside the marriage to suspect unhappiness. In August 1939, J.M. Dent published *The Map of Love*, including both poems and short stories. Four months later, New Directions brought out an American collection of his works, *The World I Breathe*, and Thomas also completed a volume of autobiographical short stories, *Portrait of the Artist as a Young Dog*. But just when he seemed to be on the threshold of international acclaim, the outbreak of the Second World War ended all their hopes.

✻ ✻ ✻

Many families were ruined by the war. Lives were lost, homes bombed and marriages broken. For the Thomases, the impact was on a different scale, but no less destructive. Book sales plummeted, so there was no income to be had in royalties or new publishers' advances. Restrictions were imposed on the production of newsprint and other forms of paper, so newspapers shrank in size and magazines closed. Thomas found himself with fewer outlets for his work, and no means of earning enough to pay the rent on Sea View or feed and clothe his family.

As their income fell and they ran heavily into debt, Thomas was totally preoccupied with finding a way of avoiding military service. Some explain this by saying he was a coward; others suggest he was by nature incapable of killing another human being. Whatever the truth, and we suspect Thomas lied about this just as he did about many other aspects of his life, the hard facts remain that Thomas was afraid of pain and death and felt no responsibility towards his country. 'My one and only body I will not give,' he told Davenport early in the war.[2]

Initially, he tried to join a unit of anti-aircraft gunners formed by Victor Cazalet, enlisting the aid of Sir Kenneth Clark – not because he particularly wanted to shoot down aeroplanes but simply that anyone who tried to do so was exempted from further military service. Thomas also explored the possibility of registering as a conscientious objector, but abandoned that when he realised most of them were the very worst kind of Welshmen: mean-mouthed, small-minded men who were willing to wriggle and squirm before the appropriate tribunal in the hope of saving their skins with false allusions to God.

Instead, Thomas took the fake Army medical route, claiming disability. This required an appearance before a tribunal in Llandeilo. The night before, he tanked himself up at the Brown's Hotel with a cocktail of whisky, sherry, gin, port, beer and whatever else he could lay his hands on. This brought him out in spots and gave him the sweats, and next day he was duly classified Grade Three and given exemption on medical grounds. Afterwards, he celebrated his escape from military service by getting drunk at Brown's Hotel. 'Many of his friends were envious,' said Caitlin, remembering them asking how he managed it because they, too, wished to avoid the draft. Caitlin was not impressed. 'It was a cowardly thing to do,' she said.

Although he told the story many times, not everyone was amused. The men of Laugharne were going off to war, leaving their wives and children behind, and the sight of Thomas boasting and drinking angered other customers at Brown's Hotel. One night, he was taken outside and given a hiding.

Soon after that the Thomases fled, unable to obtain any more credit, owing money to the butcher, grocer and milkman and rent to their landlord, with a large bar debt unpaid at Brown's. Their immediate refuge became The Malting House, a fine Georgian mansion at Marshfield, Wiltshire, where John and Clement Davenport were welcoming friends anxious to escape the nightly air raids on London. Other guests included the composers Lennox Berkeley and

Arnold Cooke, musician and critic William Glock, poet William Empson and novelist Antonia White, all living together in genteel harmony, for the Davenports used their inherited fortunes to furnish the house with fine paintings (including works by Tanguy, Roualt and Picasso), not one but two grand pianos and a fine library of books. There was also a substantial wine cellar.

Thomas and Davenport spent much of each day either shut away in the study working on a spoof crime story, *The Death of the King's Canary*, or drinking in the pubs of Marshfield, and Caitlin soon felt ignored. Initially she took to dancing alone, and then to the piano accompaniment of Glock, who was everything Dylan was not — tall, slim, handsome and urbane, with neat blond hair. Glock, who was later knighted and became Controller of Music for the BBC, flattered her with compliments, and after much secret whispering (noticed by everyone but Dylan) they agreed to meet for a night of adultery at a Cardiff hotel.

The couple left The Malting House separately, with Caitlin saying she was going to stay with Dylan's parents while she returned to Laugharne and disposed of the furniture and other possessions left behind at Sea View. As it was, nothing happened — she and Glock did end up in bed, but both were too embarrassed to make the first move, and lay side by side through the night, looking at the ceiling. When she returned to Marshfield, Caitlin found Dylan in a rage. His mother had told him she had not spent every night at Bishopston. While he may not have been a cuckold, Dylan felt like one, and his anger was compounded when he realised everyone else at The Malting House knew what was going on. There were many tearful scenes. He threw a knife at Caitlin and refused to sleep with her, eventually sending her back with Llewelyn to stay at his parents' home (which she thought 'a very low trick') while he went off to London.

That could have been the end of their marriage, and very nearly was, but Caitlin would not let go. Instead, she returned to Ringwood and left Llewelyn with her mother and sister Brigid, virtually abandoning the child while she went off to rejoin her husband.

'It was a terrible thing to do to a child,' Caitlin admitted in her old age. 'We didn't see him for several years, and the poor boy suffered terribly. He began to feel I didn't love him, which wasn't true, and never really got over it. After that business with Glock, I felt that if I didn't stay with Dylan I would lose him, and I couldn't bear the thought of that.'

✲　✲　✲

Thomas arrived in London with several introductions to film directors and producers, provided by Davenport who worked in Hollywood before the war, and was soon engaged by Donald Taylor to work on documentary scripts for Strand Films Ltd, who were producing documentaries for the Ministry of Information as part of the war effort. He was paid £10 a week.

Taylor was flexible and easy-going. He did not bother too much about keeping office hours, providing scripts were ready on time and his writers available for last-minute work on location. This left Thomas free to pick up commissions from the BBC, and he soon found himself with these two basic sources of income and freedom to live out of town whenever air raids resumed, but little time for writing poetry.

The Thomases' main home during the war was a studio apartment at Manresa Road, Chelsea, which was where they were living when their second child, Aeronwy, was born on 3 March 1943. They also travelled frequently, briefly renting a house at Bosham on the Sussex coast, sometimes staying with Taylor at Hedgerley Dean, near Reading, and often returning to West Wales, either to join Frances Hughes at Castle House (Richard Hughes was at the Admiralty in London), to visit his parents who were now living at Llangain to escape the air raids on Swansea, or to live with Vera Killick, a childhood friend of Dylan's, at Talsarn, Cardiganshire.

Caitlin spent more time in Wales than he did, for Thomas had to go off to London for script meetings or to join film units on location. This gave him the opportunity to pursue other women, and there is some evidence that he did. Several of his letters survive to an actress, Ruth Wynn Owen, who rebuffed him, and another Swansea friend, the broadcaster Wynford Vaughan Thomas, remembered meeting Thomas during the war with two other girlfriends, who both insisted Dylan never went to bed with them. However, he was undoubtedly flirtatious, which may have been as far as it went, for there are no other incriminating letters and no evidence of paternity suits or claims to be his child.

'I heard the rumours,' said Caitlin, 'but could never really believe it whenever anyone tried to tell me he had been unfaithful. You only had to look at him. Whoever would want to go off with a man who looked like that?'

✳　✳　✳

During these war years, Thomas suffered more than his share of winter maladies, often confined to bed for days or weeks at a time. 'I've got laryngitis or bronchitis or asthma or something; a complaint, whatever it is, that makes your chest like a raw steak, prevents breathing and produces a 'food-losing cough,' he told Donald Taylor on one occasion in 1943.[3]

The American writer William Saroyan, who was also published by New Directions, met Thomas in London 'swollen by sleeplessness, nervousness, boredom, bad eating and general poor health'.[4] Saroyan also thought Dylan was dirty and in need of a bath and clean clothes. They met during the morning and drank tea, not alcohol, yet he still thought Dylan's behaviour bordered on the bizarre, as he maintained a monologue that was 'wild, funny and grim all at once'. Saroyan was confused by this behaviour, and later felt guilty, wondering whether he was partially responsible for encouraging it. 'He was moving swiftly towards exhaustion and collapse,' Saroyan observed.

Other, older friends of Dylan's, such as Hugh Portems, who had known him since the '30s, were appalled by the change that came over him, and horrified by his 'grossness'. There was clearly something seriously wrong with his health, but this was not the sole reason for his reduced poetic output. There were a number of explanations for that. Filmwork now occupied most of his time, and, more importantly, he was unable to write consistently when detached from his landscape. As Virginia Woolf once noted, artists and writers often need a room of their own, somewhere safe to work. Such a place did not exist in London for Dylan Thomas, but when he returned to Wales, especially after he settled in New Quay in 1945, he would write as confidently as ever.

At New Quay, the Thomases rented a bungalow called Majoda, high on the cliffs overlooking the Irish Sea, with its own footpath down to a private beach. To avoid Aeronwy's bawling, Thomas also rented another room nearby for concentrated bursts of writing, winding up most evenings in the bar of the Black Lion Hotel.

With Taylor's payments providing a regular income, work still coming in from the BBC and frequent company when friends in the documentary film industry came down to help develop current projects, Thomas was soon following the same daily routine he had in Laugharne before the war. Out of this came the first of his narrative radio scripts, *Quite Early One Morning*, a precursor for *Under Milk Wood*, the film scripts for *Twenty Years A'Growing* and *The Doctor and the Devils*, and several key poems that lie at the heart of his reputation, including *Poem in October*, *Holy Spring*, *Vision and Prayer*, *A Winter's Tale*, *The Conversation of Prayer* and *A Refusal to Mourn the Death, by Fire, of a Child in London*. Perhaps his most famous poem of all, *Fern Hill*, was written soon after the Thomases felt compelled to leave New Quay for reasons every bit as dramatic as their earlier departures from Laugharne and Marshfield.

✳   ✳   ✳

Vera Killick's husband, Captain William Richard John Killick, returned from serving with the Commandos behind enemy lines in Greece to find his wife spending much of her time with the Thomases who, as usual, had friends down from London. There was a fracas at the Black Lion, where Killick was said to have made an anti-Semitic remark to a Jewish girl; this led to a fight between him and Dylan, and the others throwing Killick out of the pub. He disappeared for about 40 minutes, before suddenly arriving at Majoda with a submachine gun and firing two bursts of bullets through its asbestos walls. As everyone flung themselves on the floor, Killick burst in through the door, looking very wild, wearing dark glasses, holding the gun in one hand and a hand grenade in the other.[5]

'Don't be a fool,' said Dylan, trying to calm him down.

'There are two babies in the next room,' added Caitlin, as Killick fired another round of bullets into the ceiling, shouting 'You're nothing but a bunch of egoists' and 'You haven't seen anything yet'.

The police arrived soon afterwards, and Killick was charged with being in possession of a machine gun with intent to murder. Within days of the case going to trial and the captain's acquittal being widely welcomed in the press and throughout North Cardiganshire, the Thomases left New Quay. This was inevitable. The Killicks were their landlords.

✿ ✿ ✿

After two or three months at his parents' cottage in Llangain, with the war now over and normality returning to life in the capital, the Thomases made their way back to London, briefly renting flats in Twickenham and Chelsea. Outwardly they appeared to be thriving, for Dylan was now broadcasting regularly for the BBC, his work was attracting the critics' attention and his latest collection of poems, *Deaths and Entrances*, was about to be published by Dent, but privately their finances were as muddled as ever. No matter where they lived, even at New Quay where their outgoings were low, they always spent more than they earned, borrowing to make up the shortfall and then wasting whatever cash came into their hands rather than paying off debts. They were not poor in the sense of having no money and not knowing how to live, but whatever short-term funds Thomas managed to raise would always be spent on drinking, expensive meals and other forms of entertainment like visits to the theatre and nightclubs, even when Caitlin was left alone in the country without enough left to pay for food or other essentials.

A few days before Christmas 1945, they arrived on the doorstep of the historian A.J.P. Taylor in Oxford, Caitlin holding Aeronwy by the hand and carrying a suitcase that held all that was left of their current possessions, and Dylan with his arm in a sling. Homeless and penniless, they had taken care not to say they were coming, for Taylor would have closed the door on them, whereas his wife Margaret was known to be a very soft touch.

✻ ✻ ✻

That winter, Thomas spent four days in St Stephen's Hospital, Westminster, suffering from 'alcoholic gastritis'. There was a full medical examination. Thomas once told Wyn Henderson that X-rays of his lungs in 1936 or 1937 showed no trace of TB, and once again the X-rays indicated that his lungs were still clear. According to Fitzgibbon, a urine test provided no evidence of diabetes. This is not necessarily conclusive; a negative urine test would not be unusual in a diabetic who was non-insulin-dependent, given the usual vacillations of the disease. Dylan complained of exhaustion and there was a report that he had high blood pressure, or hypertension. 'I drink so that I can sleep at night,' he told his doctors, which was an excuse he had been using since the early '30s. Dylan was rumoured to have sought medical help for his drinking in 1945 and again in 1950, but this has not been substantiated. However, the fact that he spent this time in hospital suggests he may have thought his drinking was out of control.

Fitzgibbon argues that Dylan could not have had diabetes on the grounds that if he had, he would have told either him or someone else. This underlines the difficulties Thomas presented to any doctor, for he clearly preferred to say as little as possible about his medical history. Diabetes was then a disease that carried a stigma, and Thomas wished to avoid that. We have not been able to verify all the details of Fitzgibbon's account because the medical records for the period at St Stephen's Hospital have long since been destroyed, but the safest thing that can be said is that no excess glucose was noted in this one spot check upon Thomas's urine in 1946. Events in America in 1953 were to tell a very different story.

6

Beggars, Debtors and Thieves

Thomas had known the Taylors since long before his marriage. The introduction came through one of his wealthier friends, Norman Cameron, who studied with Taylor at Oriel College, Oxford. Cameron was nine years older than Thomas and made his money writing advertising copy for the international agency J. Walter Thompson. An accomplished but under-recognised poet, Cameron was one of the first to acknowledge Thomas's unusual gifts, inviting him to stay at his home in Chiswick and introducing him to many other literary figures of the '30s. The two remained close, but that did not deter Dylan from making passes at his wife.

Taylor, then an active Communist (as were several of Dylan's friends), became a lecturer in Modern History at Manchester University, living with Margaret at a cottage in Disley, high in the hills on the border of Cheshire and Derbyshire. The couple met in Vienna, where Margaret, a lapsed Catholic, educated at an English convent, was studying German and the piano. Dylan first went to stay with them in April 1935, helping to paint the cottage's external walls and being paid in beer. At that time the relationship was friendly enough, with Thomas reading Rabelais and reciting poems to Margaret, and joining them at the local pub in the evenings, although Taylor was to claim in later years, embittered by the break-up of his marriage, that he disliked Dylan from the start. That may well have been true, for he probably knew even then that his wife was what we would now call a 'groupie'. Just as some women cannot resist rock musicians or men in uniform, so Margaret Taylor constantly chased poets and writers. Her pursuit of the author and broadcaster Robert Kee[1] and Dylan Thomas are both well documented. There were several others, and Dylan probably knew of her weakness when he arrived on their doorstep, claiming that their landlady had thrown them out and his arm had been broken when he clambered in through a broken window trying to regain their possessions. Whatever reservations her husband might have had, Margaret invited them in.

By now, Taylor was a Fellow of Magdalen College, Oxford, and lived at Holywell Ford, a large house of mediaeval origins owned by the College. It had extensive gardens and was tucked away in the centre of the city behind high walls, where the Taylors reared ducks and hens, grew their own vegetables and watched otters hunting for fish in the river. For the first three months, the Thomases lived in the house itself, sharing the Taylors' Christmas dinner and seeing in the New Year, but in March 1946 they moved out to a large, timber-framed summerhouse on the bank of the river. This became their home for the next 12 months, even though it had no running water, an earthen closet, and only a stove to cook on. Rather than thank the Taylors for their charity, the Thomases continually cursed the grumpy historian for casting them out into the cold while he, for his troubles, found himself the butt of endless stories about his meanness, told by Dylan in the city's pubs and across its dinner tables.

Night after night, wrote Taylor, 'there would be a row with Caitlin. Dylan would cajole her in a wheedling Welsh voice, and Caitlin would succumb. Margaret became more involved. Here at last was the congenial company which university wives had not provided. Every night she went off drinking with Dylan and Caitlin at some local pub. She laid on literary and artistic dinner parties for them where I felt out of place. She pushed Dylan on the Oxford literary clubs. She even induced me to take Dylan into dinner at Magdalen High Table ...'[2]

Worse was to come. When the Thomases moved out to the summerhouse, Alan Taylor found himself left alone in the main house with his children while Margaret spent both day and night organising the Thomases' lives. After an evening's drinking, she would turn up on their doorstep, drag them out of bed and announce her plans for their day. 'Bloody woman,' they would sometimes say to each other, but not too loudly or in her presence, for she was readily running through her cash reserves to keep them fed and clothed.

The drain on the Taylors' finances was not to end there. Margaret was a relatively wealthy woman in her own right, and invested some of her inheritance in fine paintings, including a Utrillo. These decorated the walls of Holywell Ford. Now, Taylor started to notice them disappearing. They were Margaret's to sell, but he deeply resented his home being stripped while she raised more and more money to fund the Thomases' insatiable lifestyle.

In a desperate attempt to end the drain on the family resources, Taylor himself produced £2,000 to help Margaret buy them somewhere further away from Oxford, the Manor House at South Leigh, near Witney, believing this might encourage her to spend more time at home with her husband and children. The arrangements were made between April and August 1947 while the Thomases were out in Italy, this time funded by the Society of Authors, who awarded Dylan a travelling scholarship at the behest of Dame Edith Sitwell, who chaired the appropriate committee.

As the Thomases travelled on from Rapallo to a villa outside Florence and then to the island of Elba, Margaret set to work on the Manor House, which was then no more than a dilapidated three-bedroomed cottage with two rooms downstairs, kitchen and wash-house. She installed water and electricity, bought them a bathroom suite, applied for a telephone and even began buying furniture. They thanked her, of course – but still wrote to say they were running short of funds in Italy. Margaret sent money there as well, perhaps not realising what a trail of debts they left behind in Florence and Elba.

Any hopes Alan Taylor might have had of seeing more of his wife were dashed when the Thomases returned from Elba in August 1947, constantly complaining about their lot, with Dylan also appealing for Margaret's sympathy because he had broken his arm again.

✵　✵　✵

This was his fourth fracture since breaking his nose as a child and his wrist as a youth. In December 1948, Thomas broke his arm and fractured several ribs – and there were to be other similar injuries.

Such a strange propensity for breaking bones, rare in a man who was still in his mid-thirties, is another important medical clue, suggesting an underlying calcium deficiency as a result of his sporadic diabetes or poor nutrition. Diabetics lose important electrolytes in their urine because of high concentrations of glucose. Sodium, potassium and calcium may also be lost through the excessive diuretic effect of glucose-laden urine. Chronic loss of calcium would cause brittle bones. Blood levels may not appear grossly abnormal in people with low calcium, but bone reformation, which is a continuous process, does not occur with the same tensile strength each time. A person of Dylan's age would not have broken bones so frequently without such an underlying metabolic weakness.

Dylan was not alone in his poor health. Llewelyn continued to suffer from incapacitating bouts of asthma and Florence broke her hip which required three months in hospital. Extra bills were now falling upon Dylan's shoulders, and on top of these family responsibilities came a tax bill and other debts. He began looking to America as the solution to all his problems, asking his US publisher and other friends there how he should go about securing an invitation to work in the United States.

✿   ✿   ✿

Instead of staying at home with her family, Margaret Taylor began travelling over to South Leigh by train, often pursued by the great historian on his bicycle. It was a ludicrous situation, made even worse by her willingness to satisfy each new demand from the Thomases. When Dylan spent all their money on drink, horses and pleasure, Margaret would come up with funds for Caitlin to buy food or a new dress. While these dramas were going on inside the house, Alan Taylor would be whining on the doorstep, having caught up with her on the bicycle, imploring his wife to come back home. Eventually, he would depart tearfully and Margaret would wind up the day with the Thomases in the village pub.

When Caitlin complained that Dylan could never get enough work done with all these distractions, Margaret came to the rescue again, buying him a gypsy caravan, which Thomas kept in the garden and used for writing. This caused even more strife. Margaret continued travelling over from Oxford, going straight to the caravan and shutting the door behind her. One day, Caitlin became so angry that she turned the caravan over with them both inside it.

'I don't think Margaret ever slept with Dylan,' said Caitlin.[3] 'I was always asking myself (and him) that, but whenever I brought it up he would shudder. Some time later, I did find a letter that she'd written to Dylan in which she said, "To sleep with you would be like sleeping with a god." *That* told me they hadn't got very far with it.'

Thomas could have earned enough himself to maintain his wife and family had he had the slightest inclination to accept personal responsibility for their welfare. In the immediate period after the war, he became one of Britain's most acclaimed writers. *Deaths and Entrances* was well received by the critics and reprinted four times, and its success led to more and more commissions from the BBC, with Dylan travelling regularly up to London by train (and never forgetting to claim his expenses). These were invariably well paid, for he was a recognised writer and performer who could command good fees for his scripts, stories or poems, with separate fees for performing them and further fees whenever their text appeared in written form in magazines like *The Listener.* He also earned repeat fees when his work was broadcast a second or third time (which happened frequently) and extra money when his work was published in American magazines.

He also began to receive script commissions from friends in the film industry whom he worked with during the war, often for better money than he was paid by the BBC, and these should have been enough to put the Thomases' overall finances upon an even keel, but it was not to be. No matter how much came in, they always exceeded their income, often with silly spending. Rather than catch the train back to Oxford or South Leigh after a day at the BBC, Thomas would hire a taxi and return back home penniless, with the return rail ticket still in his pocket.

Meanwhile, Caitlin would remain all day at the Manor House, chafing at her fate and with no opportunity whatsoever to be unfaithful, for Dylan now brought his parents to live nearby and Llewelyn returned to the family. Since leaving him at Blashford early in the war, the Thomases had often gone many months without seeing their son, but on moving to Oxford and then South Leigh, they retrieved him after an absence of nearly six years. Caitlin was stricken with conscience when she found Llewelyn a bundle of nerves, suffering from asthma and walking with crabbed movements as if something was wrong with his muscles.

'I am more ashamed of that than anything else,' she said many years later, admitting that this was still troubling her conscience. 'I should have stayed with him rather than Dylan. Llewelyn never recovered from the way we treated him, and even now he recoils from me when I see him and doesn't want me to touch him.'

✳   ✳   ✳

Within months of moving in to the Manor House, the Thomases were anxious to leave. They felt too crowded, with the children, Dylan's parents, Margaret Taylor and a village girl called Mary who helped them around the house getting under their feet all day. Impractical as ever, Dylan suddenly thought one morning as he travelled up to London in the buffet car (where he always stood so as not to be without a drink) that he did not enjoy train journeys like this in the company of 'egghead dons, smelling of water biscuits . . . cowlike girls in, may be, hessian . . . and furtive small damp physicists'.[4]

In that moment, he said, he decided to go back home to Wales – but there could have been more to it than that. South Leigh was too close to London for him. There was a direct train service from Witney, and he was tempted away too often. Sometimes, his excuse was going up to London to discuss his latest film projects,[5] or he might have meetings at the BBC that developed into bibulous lunches or long drinking sessions at Soho drinking clubs the Gargoyle and the Mandrake, or equally lengthy but more gentlemanly sessions at the Garrick, the Savage or the Arts Club. (Thomas himself was a member of the National Liberal Club, which he always referred to as the 'National Lavatory', and applied to join the Savage soon after moving to South Leigh.)

More often than not, Caitlin was left at home in the bowels of Oxfordshire, bitterly complaining as she bundled their clothes into a copper boiler and hung them out to dry, sharing her ironing with Mary and trying to grow vegetables for her family. She was deeply unhappy. Rows now happened frequently, triggered by her lack of money for everyday essentials. Twice she took the children to stay with her mother at Blashford, threatening not to come back. 'If I had ever had enough money to provide them with a home myself, I would have left him,' Caitlin said. 'But that's the bugger of it for so many women. We know what we ought to do, but we haven't the money, the freedom to make the right decisions, and I couldn't go back to my mother permanently. That would have been too demeaning, with its confession of failure.'

Thomas promised their lives would improve for the better if only they could return to the familiar surroundings where he had written so well and they had been so happy in the first blush of marriage. In Laugharne, without the allure of London hovering over his workdesk, Dylan thought he could divide his year evenly, with six months set aside for money-earning film scripts and the rest of his time devoted to poems, short stories and perhaps his unfinished novel, *Adventures in the Skin Trade*. Once again, they turned to Margaret Taylor, who agreed to sell the Manor House and use the money to set them up in Laugharne.

Initially, after hearing from Richard Hughes that he was planning to move away, they hoped to lease Castle House. Margaret went down to Laugharne, expecting to reach agreement with its owner, Miss Starke, whose family had owned the house and the castle since the eighteenth century (and still do), but Miss Starke decided to move back into the house herself. A few weeks later, Margaret heard that The Boat House was available and that pleased them even more, for it stood just a few yards from The Ferry House, overlooking the tidal waters of the River Taf and the fields and farmhouses Dylan had known since childhood. Within days, Caitlin found herself pregnant again and, temporarily, a note of optimism returned to their lives.

✿　✿　✿

The long-suffering Alan Taylor reluctantly agreed to help his wife buy The Boat House, believing that with the Thomases 140 miles away some normality might return to his marriage. Since the beginning of the war, when she first began chasing writers, Taylor endured 'a decade of intense, almost indescribable misery' which left him 'crippled and stunted emotionally, a person useless to God or man',[6] but he still thought their relationship might be saved. Although he did not give her any more of his own money, Taylor helped Margaret rearrange her finances, enabling her to buy The Boat House for £3,000 and install water and electricity. At the same time, Taylor wrote to Dylan saying that he hoped there would be no further drain upon the Taylor family finances. Dylan replied with a postcard, telling him to 'FUCK OFF'.

So long as she was prepared to help them financially, Margaret continued to be almost a part of the Thomas family. 'Maggs wasn't a stupid woman by any means,' Caitlin said, 'but she could be tiresome' – but that was something they were willing to tolerate, for Dylan was always dry-eyed about benefactors, sensing what they wanted in return, which, in Margaret's case, was to be taken seriously as a writer herself and to be able to share in his success. She might have wished for a sexual relationship too, but Thomas probably shied away from that, anxious to avoid its complications, the risk of being cited or having to assume responsibilities that were alien to his nature. She was much more useful as a milch cow.

✵   ✵   ✵

The Thomases returned to Laugharne early in May 1949, with Dylan renting part of a house known as Pelican, almost opposite Brown's Hotel, for his parents. The Boat House came complete with a wooden garage, standing on stilts beside the cliff path, that had once housed Laugharne's first motor car. There were still patches of oil on the floor but these could easily be covered with a carpet, and the installation of a coal stove and two windows looking out across the estuary towards Llanybri in one direction, and to Sir John's Hill in the other, turned it into 'the workshed' that was to become the nerve centre of Dylan's creativity for the remaining four and a half years of his life.

Every morning, Caitlin would light the stove. By the time Dylan slowly adjusted to the rhythm of his day, reading novels (especially detective stories), answering letters, calling at Pelican to finish *The Times* crossword with his father, and crossing the road to Brown's Hotel for a couple of pints and a game of dominoes with Ivy Williams, the workshed would be warm and ready for him to settle down around 2 p.m. for five hours of concentrated writing. This routine rarely varied and he could not work without it.

Only days after their return to Laugharne, a letter arrived that was to change their lives and lead, more or less directly, to Dylan's death. It came from John Malcolm Brinnin, the newly appointed director of the Poetry Center at the Young Men's and Young Women's Hebrew Association in New York. With a budget at his disposal, Brinnin invited Thomas to participate in a series of readings, adding that others might also be arranged elsewhere in the United States. For just one reading, he offered a fee of $500 plus travelling expenses.

Thomas was already known in the United States, if only within the relatively narrow world of literary criticism. In 1938, he won the Oscar Blumenthal Prize for Poetry and, subsequently, New Directions published four collections of his poems and short stories. For several years, Oscar Williams, an anthologist and minor US poet, helped Thomas place his work in American magazines and also found buyers for his original manuscripts, providing a useful form of extra income.

With these credentials, Thomas had asked Williams to enquire about the possibility of him lecturing on screenwriting in the States, knowing that writers there were often better paid, underpinning their lives financially with university appointments that brought in regular fees in return for a limited number of annual lectures, but this invitation from Brinnin came out of the blue from a total stranger. 'I feel extremely honoured to be the first person to be invited from abroad,' Thomas replied, saying he would like to come the following February for three months, but had no private resources of his own, 'and therefore must, by other arrangements made by you, make money immediately'.

✳   ✳   ✳

Brinnin was two years younger than Thomas, and had been aware of him since the '30s, when their poems were published in the same magazines. There were some similarities in their backgrounds. Both their families had a history of illness, perhaps explaining the way the grand themes of life, love and death ran through their poetry; both had roots in small communities where births, weddings and funerals loom large in everyday life.

There may also have been some similarity in their emotional backgrounds, for Brinnin, who was born in Halifax, Nova Scotia, and partially raised in Boston, was deeply bonded with his mother. Her only other child, Brinnin's sister, died suddenly at the age of nine, leaving them emotionally dependent upon each other. He entered graduate school in Michigan, planning to study for a PhD in English and starting to write a thesis on Marcel Proust, but this came to grief when his tutor thought he was being too ambitious. Strongly disagreeing, Brinnin thought of starting his own poetry magazine, but found the costs too prohibitive and ended up working in bookshops before being given another opportunity to enter academia. After studying at Harvard, Brinnin taught at Vassar College, lecturing on the poetry of Dylan Thomas as early as 1942, considering him as early as that to be the finest poet of his generation.

Physically, the two men could not have been more different. Thomas had lost none of the body fat that he acquired during Caitlin's first pregnancy, and was now thick set and jowly. Brinnin was of average height, thin, prematurely balding with clean-cut Ivy League clothes, and a heavy drinker and smoker. His health was somewhat fragile with chronic stomach problems, including bouts of gastritis that occasionally required hospital treatment.

✻   ✻   ✻

Ironically, in the same letter as that in which he accepted Brinnin's invitation, Thomas also complained of being unwell. 'I've had influenza, and am full of injections,' he wrote. This illness not only delayed his reply but also prevented him finishing a radio script for the BBC for which he had already partially been paid.

Within weeks of returning to The Boat House, despite their low rent and outgoings, the Thomases were again in financial difficulties, with Dylan trying to augment his income by writing begging letters to Margaret Taylor, John Davenport, David Tennant (owner of the Gargoyle Club and a prominent friend of the royal family) and now Princess Marguerite Caetani, an international socialite otherwise known as the Duchess of Sermoneta, who lived in Rome and paid generously for contributions to her literary magazine, *Botteghe Oscure*.

One letter to Davenport suggests that the real problem was that the Thomases were continually overwhelmed by the normal expenses of everyday life, no matter what money they had coming into the house – and at that time Thomas had fees due in stages from Gainsborough for a film script based on *Vanity Fair* – for he says the butcher would not supply them with meat, no coal could be bought from the coalman, four cheques were returned by the Savage Club, and he was being summonsed for not paying rates. 'We are – for the first time in years – literally without one shilling,' Thomas wrote, realising that such a plea would immediately produce a five-pound note.

The strain upon Caitlin was continuous. When she needed money, Caitlin was told they had none. She knew about their debts all right, and would be told whenever Margaret Taylor sent a few pound notes in a registered envelope to relieve some immediate crisis, but Caitlin never realised Dylan was already one of Britain's better-paid writers. When he had money to spare, as he frequently did, Thomas hid it. Caitlin retaliated by rifling through his pockets when he was drunk and frequently calling him names. 'This morning I had a toadstool for breakfast, and Caitlin called me a guttersnipe, though there seemed to be no connection,' Thomas told Davenport with a levity that suggests he was indifferent to her distress.

Caitlin gave birth to their third child, Colm Garan, at the hospital in Carmarthen on 24 July 1949. Like her other babies, Colm (the Welsh name for heron) weighed only 6lbs. Childbirth never came easily to her, and she returned home thin, weak and debilitated, with no one to look after her. Llewelyn and Aeronwy were too young, Florence was still recovering from her broken hip, and Dylan's health was sinking again. He was already suffering from gout and it was hurting him to urinate. Left on his own to take care of himself, he survived on beer, smoking, sweets and erratic half-meals, with predictable results. His lung infections recurred, showing he was still extremely susceptible to illness.

The complaint of pain on urination (made in a thank-you letter to David Tennant, who sent him some money) was a new one and a bad sign. This kind of pain is usually due to inflammation of the lining of the penis duct, the urethra, and was an ominous symptom that Dylan's weakened immune system permitted a recrudescence of his gonorrhoea. While these bouts of illness – flu, gout and recurrent gonorrhoea – were not direct symptoms of diabetes, they most definitely were caused by a chronically weak immune system which was a classic problem of diabetes. The implications of Dylan planning an ambitious three-month tour of the United States while he was sick were lost on all the parties involved.

✶　✶　✶

Plans for the tour took shape rapidly over the last six months of 1949. Brinnin had enough academic contacts to arrange a schedule of 40 readings across North America. No formal contract was ever signed, but it was agreed that Brinnin would act as Thomas's lecture agent and take a 15 per cent commission, which was less than most commercial agencies would have charged. This lack of any agreement caused confusion later. Dylan expected to have free use of Brinnin's apartment in New York but instead found himself having to pay hotel bills, and he was similarly disappointed when he found that for some of his engagements there were no separate travel expenses, which meant he had to pay the fares himself.

Initially, Caitlin was expected to accompany him, but the birth of Colm left her nervous and weak. Thomas told Margaret Taylor he thought the tour would be 'difficult, expensive and bad for her', but was unable to raise funds from New Directions to pay for Caitlin to go on holiday to Elba.

So, with Dylan going away and Caitlin far from well, The Boat House was not a happy home as the departure date drew near. With her broken hip, Florence was barely able to move around and look after Dylan's ailing father, who was suffering from pneumonia, and Llewelyn's recurrent asthma and bronchitis were so worrying that Caitlin took him to see a specialist.

With more broken bones gently mending (this time his ribs), Thomas prepared for the journey, leaving his wife behind with the children and the promise of £10 to be sent each week by his agent while he borrowed the fare to Cardiff from his mother. There he borrowed enough money to take him to London, where he cashed a post-dated cheque with a friendly bank manager against his future earnings, producing both his plane ticket (airmailed in advance by Brinnin) and his US visa as proof that he really was going to the United States to undertake this series of public readings.

7

Old Tricks in a New World

Over a thousand people crowded into the Kaufmann Auditorium, New York, on the night of Dylan Thomas's first American reading, largely drawn by Brinnin's promotional tag that this was a rare opportunity to witness living genius, the finest poet of the twentieth century, reading his own work.

This was a higher reputation than Thomas enjoyed in Britain, where he was still largely known as a regular performer on the BBC Third Programme, reciting his own poetry, sometimes narrating books in serial form, like W.H. Davies's *The Autobiography of a Super-Tramp* or Milton's *Paradise Lost*, reading classic writers like Byron, Blake or Keats, or his own selections from the works of more modern poets such as Dame Edith Sitwell, Vernon Watkins, Wilfred Owen or Edward Thomas. Such regular radio appearances gave Thomas a high profile within literary London, but he was by no means a household name and when reading to literary societies in his own country seldom drew an audience of more than 30 or 40 people. So that first appearance at the Kaufmann, for the Young Men's and Young Women's Hebrew Association, came as as much of a shock to him as to the audience taking their seats with a bristling sense of expectancy; they did not know what to expect any more than he did.

Forty years later, the Kaufmann still has the same sense of intimacy as on 23 February 1950. The walls are heavily panelled with warm, dark wood. The balcony and floor seats are close to the stage. There is the feeling of being in someone's living-room or the privacy of a club.

That night, the empty wooden podium was illuminated with a single column of light. The curtains shifted at the side of the stage and a short, portly figure in a dark blue suit and bow tie emerged from the wings. He produced a sheaf of poems, all written out in his childlike longhand script, and placed them on the podium. One was immediately struck by the high, shining forehead, the curly, tousled hair, the dark-pooled eyes, pug nose and round, full cheeks.

A hush fell over the audience, and as he began to read they were immediately transported by the deep, billowing, rolling 'organ voice' (as Thomas sometimes described it), with its perfect pitch and resonance, like the depths of the earth and the endless sky speaking through the crucible of a single man. Recordings that he made in America preserve the sound with all the richness in range and power of a great Shakespearean actor, a Richard Burton or a Laurence Olivier. None of the audience had heard anything like this before, for New York does not have the same repertory tradition of classic theatre. As his first reading came to a close, the applause was thunderous. People sprang to their feet, clapping and cheering, and as Dylan left the stage, sweating and exhausted, a large crowd pressed forward, eager to shake his hand or be given his autograph.

'I felt a very lonely, foreign midget, orating up there, in a large hall, before all those faces,' he wrote to Caitlin,[1] telling her of his first impressions of the 'furiously polite and hospitable' New York poets, writers and critics, adding (no doubt to reassure her) that he was terrified of skyscrapers, hated the speed and the noise and would never go there again without her.

✻　✻　✻

Right from the beginning, his letters home cast an illusion. Thomas downplayed any incident that might prompt his wife or parents to ask too many questions, hardly mentioned the money he was earning, and avoided saying anything too revealing about his health. Always an evasive man, he was now surrounding himself with a veil of secrecy. The truth about any one occasion is seldom easy to establish.

All subsequent accounts of Thomas's first American tour have been based either upon Brinnin's largely secondhand reportage, *Dylan Thomas in America*, or, in more recent years, Thomas's family letters[2] which tell a totally different story. Neither can be relied upon, although both contain useful clues.

Whether or not he was pursuing a fast buck, Brinnin produced a compelling tapestry of alcoholic excess, bizarre behaviour and rampant promiscuity, interwoven with a record of on-stage brilliance. The family letters reveal a lonely man left to his own devices in a strange land, somehow managing to cope with each new stress laid upon him. Other accounts, describing Thomas's performances at different times in the itinerary, convey another impression altogether, of a sober, considerate but frequently sick performer determined to fulfil his commitments.

Significantly, his letters home to Laugharne make no mention of illness, and yet there is ample evidence that Thomas was unwell throughout much of the tour and continued to exhibit symptoms of occult diabetes and depression. His drinking was frequently heavy, and it was now bourbon whiskey, which was as socially acceptable in American society as beer in Britain. Thomas was only following the age-old principle 'when in Rome, do as the Romans do', but his body could not cope with the chemical change, and he was exacerbating its problems by popping pills to sleep when he was tired and to perk him up when a performance loomed.

In London, Dylan's cycles of too much drinking, smoking, no food and little sleep or rest were broken by Caitlin when he returned home. In New York, he had nowhere to retreat. From the moment he arrived, a pattern developed of minor, bordering on major, diabetic crises. It shows great strength of character that he survived at all.

As he stepped off the plane on 21 February, two days before his first reading at the Kaufmann Auditorium, Thomas immediately steered Brinnin into the airport bar. In Manhattan, after checking into the Beekman Towers Hotel, Dylan persuaded Brinnin to introduce him to the local bars, often coughing violently to the point of retching and claiming that this was due to cirrhosis of the liver. Brinnin treated this as a genuine complaint, but any doctor would confirm this was absurd. The coughing was due to Dylan's insistence on smoking despite knowing full well that he suffered from asthma and, after 20 years of continuous smoking, chronic bronchitis and emphysema. Bronchitis is inflammation of the main bronchi or airways of the lung. Emphysema is over distension of the terminal airspaces which can cause breakdown of the lining of the lungs, resulting in infections, productive coughs or bloody sputum. These were all conditions Dylan suffered from before arriving in America.

Friends from London visited him in New York and were shocked by the change in his physical appearance. The thin youth from Swansea was now a puffy, overweight exaggeration of his former self. His coughing and retching were alarmingly frequent, often daily events. After drinking, he would fall asleep in Brinnin's car, waking up two hours later, revived and mentally fresh, completely sober. This was clearly due to his blood sugar levels being driven up by alcohol, and then back down again when his glucose levels normalised.

The day of that first reading, Dylan was sick throughout. He vomited in the street, managed to eat some oysters and then went through another bad coughing attack minutes before walking out on stage. Despite fortifying himself with beer, he was sober, anxious and morose. He sweated profusely before and after the performance. The stress must have been overwhelming. Remember: he was in a strange country and had never spoken to an audience of this size before. At the last second, his spirit rose to the occasion and he gave a memorable reading, like an actor conquering first-night nerves. This pattern of stress and fear, mood swings and bouts of illness interspersed with drinking was repeated throughout his four American tours, although not so starkly when Caitlin was present on some occasions during the 1952 tour.

On his third day in New York, Thomas transferred from the Beekman Towers Hotel to the Midston House, where Brinnin called in the hotel doctor who 'prescribed medications which soon put Dylan into a deep sleep',[3] the first time he had slept properly since his arrival. Thomas clearly needed rest and the chance to revitalise, but there were inherent problems in this kind of quick-fix treatment. This was a doctor who had never seen him before, coming to his hotel room and prescribing medicine without undertaking laboratory tests, physically examining his patient or being given full details of the patient's history. This is not necessarily absurd, but in Thomas's case it set a dangerous precedent.

✶   ✶   ✶

If someone is ill enough to require immediate medical treatment, most doctors visiting a hotel room would follow the same guidelines used when treating a patient in his home. The patient's health would be stabilised and then, if necessary, he would be transferred to hospital. In Thomas's case that did not happen, but all went well. He was given relief and everyone was happy, but the precedent was established that Dylan Thomas would not be treated as a normal patient. After all, he was (if only in Brinnin's eyes) the most famous poet in the world. Such men did not go to doctors. The doctors went to them.

Brinnin and Thomas both fell prey to the dangerous phenomenon of 'celebrity patients'. They may simply be wealthy, or movie stars, famous poets or powerful politicians. Elvis Presley suffered as a celebrity patient, as has, more recently, the Russian President Boris Yeltsin. In all these situations, when the doctor is practising without his usual protective back-up of laboratory tests and detailed physical examination and/or reference to the patient's medical history, there is always a greater risk of something going wrong. As long as a simple treatment is used, and there are no serious, underlying, pre-existing conditions, patient and doctor are usually safe. However, there is always a risk, because of the awe in which the patient is held by either his friends or the doctor, that an important part of the usual follow-up procedure will be missed. The patient may not be referred to a specialist when he should have been, or some crucial test may be overlooked. Somehow, the rules do not apply with celebrity patients – and secrecy is often all-important. Confirmation of illness can be damaging to any businessman, performer or politician, and had it been known that Dylan Thomas was diabetic, his tours of America would have been very different. There would have been constant care instead of continual attempts to put just one more drink in his hand.

Dylan's reputation as a heavy drinker and clown began those first few days in New York, with friends and strangers vying to encourage him. One such incident occurred at the home of Oscar Williams and was noted by the critic John Gruen. Williams was married to the poet Gene Derwood, and they occupied a cavernous loft in an office building on Water Street in the shadow of Brooklyn Bridge, one block from East River.

Gruen was invited to a dinner party there with his wife, the painter Jane Wilson, and arrived to find Dylan fast asleep on a couch. He collapsed after not eating and slept for about two hours. Williams placed four bottles of beer near the couch, and encouraged Thomas to start drinking again as soon as he woke up. Immediately, Thomas launched into a detailed, rhapsodic description of Laugharne and The Boat House. At first his speech was clear, but as he continued drinking the beers it became slurred. As the other dinner guests arrived, Williams continued giving him more and more to drink, until Dylan started trying to entertain them all with his London pub repertoire, reading his poems with the book upside-down and falling down on his hands and knees to look underneath a woman's dress until, inevitably, he collapsed. The evening was judged a roaring success.[4]

Beyond the swirl of constant parties was a gentler, saner side to Dylan's new friendships which has received far less attention than the stories of Brinnin and Williams. Thomas discovered for himself the Artists Club on Eighth Street in Greenwich Village, and there met other writers, artists, painters, sculptors and printmakers who belonged to The Atelier 17 studio. Its director, Peter Grippe, introduced him to the Greenwich Village bars, including the White Horse Tavern, Julius's and the Cedar Street Tavern, where artists and writers met every night of the week, often talking until 3 or 4 a.m. With no one trying to get him drunk, Grippe noticed that Dylan was in his element, talking for hours and drinking slowly.[5]

Thomas was always happier in this environment of working craftsmen. He was uncomfortable with the New York literati and chose, instead, to be among those who worked at the coalface. Several collaborations that receive no mention whatever in *Dylan Thomas in America* came from this. Isaac Rosenfeld of *Partisan Review* and his wife, Vasiliki, arranged for Thomas to give a private reading at the Cherry Lane Theater especially for local artists and writers, something Brinnin discouraged because Thomas asked for no fee.

Similarly, Thomas collaborated with Grippe on two projects. The first was a portfolio of original etchings paired with handwritten poems by different writers, to which Dylan contributed *The Hand that Signed the Paper.* This is now a highly prized collectors' item. Dylan's second project entailed visiting Grippe's studio on Second Avenue, between Sixth and Seventh Streets, where he posed for a sculpture and bust that captures his exuberance, tousled hair and pug nose, with a totally different physiognomy from the death mask that Dave Slivka prepared in November 1953 when he looked bloated, fat and unrecognisable, just hours after death. These two sculptures, which are unfamiliar to most readers of Thomas's work, tell a poignant story of physical deterioration. Within four years, he was a dying man.

✻　✻　✻

Over the next three months, Dylan Thomas crisscrossed the United States, driven to engagements close to New York by Brinnin, taking journeys further afield alone by train and sometimes by plane. He visited over 40 universities, slotting in extra performances on an ad hoc basis as he went, often being interviewed for radio and recording his poems both commercially and for the Libraries of Congress and Harvard.

Each reading was as informal as he could make it, beginning with a chatty introduction that would enable him to bond himself to the audience, and then ranging over not only his own work but also favourite poems by other writers, including Thomas Hardy, Wilfred Owen, W.H. Davies, Edward Thomas, Alun Lewis, Vernon Watkins, Robert Graves, T.S. Eliot, W.H. Auden, W.B. Yeats, Walter de la Mare, Dame Edith Sitwell, John Betjeman and D.H. Lawrence.

Sometimes Thomas read poems straight, but on other occasions he would give them extra depth by changing his vocal pitch or interspersing different accents, as in Henry Reed's *Naming of Parts*, where the use of two voices at once explained what the poem was all about. News of this ability to employ humour, wit and humility, or subtle changes of pace, travelled fast, with organisers of one reading phoning the next to report how he enjoyed mingling with the audience afterwards, talking, signing autographs or entertaining small groups of students, usually young women, with scatalogical jokes and short stories.

This was all fairly harmless, but sometimes (and especially when primed with American bourbon whiskey) Thomas would work through his repertoire of bawdy stories, peppered with four-letter words, or begin playing pub games, squatting down on his hands and knees, barking like a dog, or pretending to have seen a mouse run up a woman's leg, which was always an excuse for a noisy, fumbling attempt to peep up her skirt. People were used to such ribaldry in London's pubs. It kept the drink flowing and was all part of their atmosphere, but in New York (and elsewhere across America) Thomas came face to face with something he had never encountered before: the grim, po-faced, wooden respectability of the US college establishment, and the prim and proper professors for whom a university post provided a house, a car, a secretary and social status.

A wiser man than Dylan Thomas would have played them at their own game, honouring their sense of gravity and flattering them with civility, but he was never like that. It was not in his nature. When asked to explain the meaning of his long poem *The Ballad of the Long Legged Bait*, he said it was 'the story of a monumental fuck'. When described as a genius, he would reply, as if talking about someone else, 'no fucking genius, he', and he managed to silence one particularly dull dinner party by announcing in his best stage voice, 'I wish we were all hermaphrodites.' Just as expected, someone asked him why. 'Because then we could all fuck ourselves!' he replied. Any dumb academic who sought the poet's attention by a learned analysis of his verses would be told 'Fuck off!' while Thomas proceeded to rattle off music-hall jokes or sing his favourite songs.

This behaviour amused some and appalled others. Thomas made many friends, who recognised him as the genuine article, a man with rare gifts and, even rarer, true humility, but he also laid down the seeds of a reputation that was to be grossly magnified in death, for Thomas was right about literary America, '50s-style. Academics *could* secure lectureships and other sinecures with minimal talent and achievement, but the downside was that they duly expected to be treated with unnatural respect, like all men promoted beyond their true abilities, turning up for his readings in their trim Ivy League suits and polyester bow ties, sipping their drinks with caution, never quite seeing the point of a joke.

On one level, this was the most successful tour of the United States by a British writer since Charles Dickens or Oscar Wilde, even possibly surpassing them as he travelled the length and breadth of the country, aided by such modern tools as the plane, radio and microphone. On another level, it was a personal disaster, with Dylan Thomas now looked upon as both an international celebrity and a clown. Tales of his drunkenness grew with the telling, and 'The Legend of the Welsh Lothario' was born.

✻   ✻   ✻

None of this was known to Caitlin or even to the British press, who were as ill-informed on the achievements of Dylan Thomas as they were of the success in America of British actors, writers and musicians in the '60s, '70s and '80s. And there was no way tales could get back to Laugharne with so little news from America in the daily newspapers. Thomas was travelling alone from city to city, with only his schedule, plane or rail tickets and a few clothes in a bag. There was no satellite television to beam the news, there were no tabloid newspapers to report his progress, and even phone calls from the States in those days were long delayed, hard to arrange and expensive. Thomas did not call home once – and Caitlin would have thought it odd if he had.

✻   ✻   ✻

Over the first month of the tour Thomas gave 16 readings, which took him from Boston to Washington DC and out to Chicago and Iowa. At each stop, more stories were told of his ribald behaviour and famous drinking bouts. These tales mostly came from Brinnin, whose account built 'The Legend' brick by brick. However, another story lies beneath the myth. The tour required stamina and out of it all, Dylan Thomas emerges as a strangely ambiguous character. On the one hand, his body tolerated constant travelling, lack of proper rest, relentless drinking and continual stress. He missed meals, and fell back upon his old, familiar diet of cigarettes, sugary sweets and beer. But during his readings, Thomas became a different person from the clownish Welshman in the bar, performing with absolute assurance. 'It was the poetry that gave Dylan the confidence to perform on stage to large audiences on those American tours,' wrote Caitlin. 'It was the only area of his life where he was totally sure of himself.'[6]

Afterwards, Dylan often stayed up all night, talking, telling shaggy-dog stories, reciting limericks – anything that would amuse his hosts. But the clowning had a frantic, desperate quality. He was clearly as insecure in the small town colleges and larger universities as he was among the literary gentry of New York. About this sense of intellectual inferiority Bill Read wrote wisely, 'Dylan was a frightened youth who found it difficult to accept his great gifts and feel equal to his celebrated peers. A great deal of this came from lack of formal education; he just never learned how to handle intellectuals . . . They knew they were his inferiors but he didn't.'[7]

Little of this was witnessed by Brinnin, but he wrote as if he was there even when his reports were based on hearsay. What Brinnin reported as fact was often not, but many years were to pass after publication of *Dylan Thomas in America* before anyone came up with the contradictory evidence. It is clearer now that Brinnin found himself torn in several directions. He was attracted to Dylan on one level, but appalled by him on another; he enjoyed the social invitations that came his way as Dylan's agent, but resented the demands this role placed upon him (especially by Dylan himself). He looked upon himself as major-domo and 'The Poet's Best Friend', but there was some jealousy, too.

At Bryn Mawr, Thomas was sick before and after his reading. The symptoms were familiar — violent coughing, exhaustion, more drink, no food, little sleep. After a few beers during a car journey to Washington, Thomas revived. Several days later, on his return from Virginia, Brinnin picked him up in New York. John Cage and Merce Cunningham were also in the car. Brinnin describes this in revealing detail:

> It was on this occasion that I first became aware of a fact about Dylan for which I still cannot account — the fact that, without liquor at all, or with but a glass or two of beer, he would often move into a state of euphoria precisely like that state of uninhibited gaiety common to people who depend upon liquor.[8]

This was passed off as another example of Thomas's eccentric behaviour. The truth was that as a diabetic, Dylan would have been subject to wide mood swings, depending upon his glucose levels. They would have ranged from sleep and exhaustion to uninhibited euphoria, often within hours, sometimes more than once a day, and as often as not related to his pattern of drinking.

Dylan ended his first month in Iowa, where he stayed for two weeks before going on to the West Coast. Ray West, his host and a member of the university faculty, wrote a lengthy description of Dylan's visit, recalling him collecting bottles of beer from the ice-box before going to bed, coming downstairs for more beer during the night, and then starting the day with beer, a bottle of milk, a daily burst of vomiting and pills which Thomas insisted were 'my pregnancy pills' — he claimed they were usually prescribed for pregnant women and were meant to cure morning sickness.[9]

The main reason for Dylan spending two weeks in one place was to have some repair work done at the Iowa School of Dentistry; his teeth were rotting, ruined by cavities from all those years of eating sugary sweets and poor hygiene. West says a dentist took one look inside Thomas's mouth and 'began almost visibly to tremble'. When told Thomas would only be in Iowa another ten days, the dentist said: 'Impossible – we would need at least a month to six weeks.'

Throughout the fortnight, Dylan drank mainly beer. West was in no doubt that this was what he preferred, but twice Thomas was offered whisky – and both occasions ended in disaster. The first time, Dylan had offered to take the Wests out to dinner to thank them for their hospitality. Mrs West was all dressed up for her evening out, but Dylan arrived back several hours late, very drunk and fell fast asleep. 'He had met a woman, he told us, who invited him to her place to read her poetry. She had given him Scotch, keeping his glass full while she read her poetry to him. He couldn't remember her name, all he could tell us was that she lived somewhere over by the river. The poetry, he said, was perfectly dreadful, but the Scotch was good. He had drunk, he guessed, about 12 glasses . . . He didn't say anything about the dinner we had missed until the next day, when he suddenly remembered and was so filled with remorse that we couldn't stay angry with him.'

The other occasion when Dylan was given whisky was much more embarrassing. This time he was at the home of the chairman of the English department, Baldwin Maxwell, where a doctor's wife listened to him claiming what wonders were performed by Britain's new National Health Service, which was regarded by many Americans as a semi-Marxist innovation.

'You don't know what you're talking about,' she suddenly said angrily.

Thomas exploded with rage, calling her a 'bloody fucking bitch' – and following this with 'the most elegantly strung-together sequence of obscenities'. This was all too much for the doctor's wife, who 'collapsed in tears onto her husband's starched white shirt front'. That was the last time Dylan Thomas was invited to Iowa.

✳   ✳   ✳

From the Mid West, Dylan flew to the West Coast where he gave eight readings, remarking to the Wests as he waited for his plane at Iowa Airport that the scenery was beautiful 'so I must be sober' (which suggests he was well aware of the image he was creating for himself). He enjoyed San Francisco and Hollywood the most. The natural beauty of the areas, especially in San Francisco, the warm sun, the food and the people all seemed a world away from Britain's post-war austerity. His readings were well received, and he spent a warm, friendly evening with Salvador Dali in Sausalito. But several incidents indicated all was not well. In California he seemed to be drinking more and eating less, which prompted the University of California at Berkeley not to go ahead with their plans to invite him to spend a year there as a visiting professor. From San Francisco he cabled the University of Florida to say he would have to reschedule a reading because he was ill.

In Hollywood, he spent an uproarious evening with Marilyn Monroe and Shelley Winters which began with dinner at their apartment, with him drinking Martinis through a straw, polishing off a bottle of white wine and a bottle of red and then finishing off a six-pack before climbing into their car to drive to Charlie Chaplin's house.[10]

'Where's the bloody steering wheel?' he shouted.

'It's over here on the left, where I'm sitting,' said Winters.

'Every fucking thing's backward in this country,' said Thomas, pretending he could drive. On the way, he bought another six-pack from a supermarket and then produced a bottle of gin from the inside pocket of his jacket. When he did try to steer the car, it ended up on Chaplin's tennis court, tangled in the nets.

Monroe and Winters managed to persuade him to leave the beer and the gin in the bushes, and Oona Chaplin quickly found him an armchair and a cup of black coffee after taking one look at the 'stoned leprechaun' wearing 'strange brogues with flapping tongues that seemed to flap in unison with his belt and tie and his real tongue'.

Thomas soon found a bottle of brandy, and made no attempt to speak to any of the other guests who included Marlene Dietrich, Lotte Lenya, Greta Garbo, Thomas Mann and Katharine Hepburn. Sensing disaster, Winters thought the only way to keep him under control was to sit on his lap, but that did not stop him grumbling, 'Isn't that bloody genius ever going to talk to me? That's why I came to California. He's ignoring me like he's the governor and I'm the colonial . . .'

Moments later, while Chaplin was sitting at his piano playing the theme from *Limelight*, Thomas jumped to his feet and Shelley Winters fell off his lap onto the floor. Chaplin crashed his hands down on the piano and hissed, 'Even great poetry cannot excuse such rude, drunken behaviour . . .' With as much dignity as he could muster, Thomas stalked out into the conservatory and was last seen urinating on Chaplin's plants.

✳ ✳ ✳

Dylan did eventually fulfil the booking in Florida and over the next three weeks gave 14 readings from Massachusetts to Michigan and Indiana. In all, this first tour was a remarkable test of stamina. He travelled over 15,000 miles and did not miss one of the 40 readings. It was more like a presidential campaign than a literary reading tour, and by the end of it he was without doubt the most famous poet in the Western world. The only hint that he had done too much came in a letter to his parents in which Thomas said the travel and weather changes left him 'too exhausted to do anything'.

Throughout the tour Dylan continued to exhibit signs of diabetes and depression, which were not only ignored by his friends and hosts but passed off as behaviour caused by too much alcohol. None of these highly intelligent, well-educated and sensitive professors of literature seems to have imagined for a moment that the hard-drinking genius-poet, with his whimsical flights of humour and wayward habits, might have serious medical problems. They cheerfully kept him supplied with alcohol and cigarettes, and noticed that all he seemed to eat was sweets. Most passed this off as a quaint, endearing habit, possibly left over from an overindulgent childhood.

✳   ✳   ✳

The most critical factor in diabetics' lives is keeping their energy level constant. Their energy is tied tightly and unforgivingly to their glucose or sugar level, and without proper self-management, the difference between good days and bad, consciousness and coma, life and death is a fine thread easily snapped. All diabetics fear the repercussions of a low sugar level. They may have half the energy for work. They may be continually sleepy and easily exhausted. Dylan not only exhibited polydipsia, polyuria and candy cravings, but his sudden collapses, abrupt recoveries and periods of euphoria and depression fitted the pattern of an undiagnosed and untreated diabetic. The suddenness of his collapses and recoveries also indicates that Dylan responded to alcohol and stress in a significantly different way from his peers. While some of these collapses were associated with alcohol, there were just as many episodes when there was no alcohol involved at all. Another important clue is that they also happened within a few hours of eating food.

In Dylan's case, these clues, symptoms and episodes provide a pattern that can be reconstructed like a medical history. His refusal to take better care of himself made it difficult for anyone to help him.

✳   ✳   ✳

Thomas returned to New York from his tour of the West and Mid West during the second week of May. He was booked for poetry readings at Vassar College and Princeton University on Tuesday 9 May and Wednesday 10 May, with a prose reading at the Kaufmann Auditorium on Monday 15 May, reciting short stories from *Portrait of the Artist as a Young Dog*.

In ten weeks, he had earned several thousand dollars. The precise sum is not known, for he would readily add extra readings to his schedule, pocketing the cash, and even the itinerary published as an appendix to Constantine Fitzgibbon's *Life of Dylan Thomas* is incomplete. Three of his readings were for Brinnin, with whom he established a going rate of $500, and he is unlikely to have earned less when addressing large audiences at major universities like Yale, Harvard, Chicago, Kenyon, Cornell or Columbia, though Brinnin observed that he was willing to add extra dates for as little as $50. Whatever the true total, whether it was a gross income for the ten weeks of $5,000 or $10,000, Dylan now started to spend it as rashly as ever, happily picking up bills for dinner parties, visiting burlesque shows and winding up most nights at his favourite haunt, the White Horse Tavern in Greenwich Village. This was another strange part of his character. When Dylan had no money, he borrowed aggressively – but with plenty in his pocket, he was always an easy touch.

✲ ✲ ✲

His last two weeks in New York are barely documented by Brinnin, who admits not seeing Dylan for ten days, hinting that the poet was engaged in two affairs, one with a woman whom he calls 'Doris' and the other with a woman known as 'Sarah'. Brinnin prefaces this revelation with the words, 'The sexual life of Dylan Thomas was already as much a source of legend as was his fabulous capacity for alcohol. Reports from Boston to Los Angeles suggested he lived by lechery, fondling girl sophomores and the wives of deans with an obsessive disregard for anything but his own insatiable desires . . . uncovering sexual imagery in the poems of Dylan Thomas had already become a national undergraduate pastime. The precise, obscene references and the four-letter ejaculations of his drunken talk, his often lascivious retorts to civil questions, and his lewd attention to details of the female anatomy were repeated and embellished . . . stories cropped up everywhere, along with rumours of fantastic sexual prowess and a sexual preoccupation indicating satyriasis. While the extravagance of Dylan's social behaviour made these true in tenor, in their details they were almost always spurious.'[11]

Brinnin admits that all he really knew about this side of Dylan's life, until then, was the frequency with which he expressed a preference for 'naked girls in wet mackintoshes' or 'a little woman just my size', but these words were harmless enough to anyone who knew that *double entendre* was a popular part of the British comic tradition. Thomas had been saying things like this for 15 years, with as cheery a leer as Max Miller.

Likewise, in observing that Dylan's approaches to pretty women at parties 'showed not so much sexual aggression as a kind of puppy-dog appreciation for the physical attractions he might snuggle up to', the thought never seems to have crossed Brinnin's mind that this was as far as Dylan went, despite his admission that these approaches were nearly always rebuffed. 'He would end up sulking about his ugliness and mumbling about the cruelty of women as he drank on into the night,' said Brinnin, adding that, 'More than one of the women ... told me ... that he did not really want them to respond, at least not to the point of commitment.'[12]

Doris and Sarah may have been a little more encouraging, humouring the poet when he was in his cups, responding cheerfully to his harmless banter (as many women would in similar situations), but there is little evidence to suggest anything more than that.

The more serious relationship was with 'Sarah' – Pearl Kazin, a dynamic, au courant New York publishing executive. Dylan may have been a slovenly, ribald, hard-drinking, self-educated poet with a beer belly and rotten teeth, but a genuinely strong attraction developed between him and Kazin, whose background was closer to his than her sophistication might suggest.

Kazin's family and cultural background as the daughter of immigrant Jewish, Polish parents were eloquently and lovingly described by her brother Alfred in his 1951 memoir, *A Walker in the City*. Their grandfather died from pneumonia caught in a picket line on Manhattan's Lower East Side and was buried in an anonymous mass Jewish grave for the poor. Their father, as early as 1908, worked as a railroad car painter, then as a painter in New York. Their mother, from Dugschitz, Poland, became a dressmaker at the age of 13. The family eventually left the Lower East Side, and Alfred and Pearl were raised in Brownsville, Brooklyn, where their whole world was contained within five blocks. By attending New York universities and distinguishing themselves, Alfred and Pearl became university teachers. Alfred also became a distinguished literary critic, while Pearl rose in the publishing world. Alfred wrote that they came from 'a place that measured all success by our skill in getting away from it'.[13]

Despite their success in their chosen careers, Dylan Thomas and Pearl Kazin remained outsiders, conscious of their backgrounds, but sharing a love of words.

Brinnin, who never married and was always reserved with women, could not help wondering 'how he managed to keep his two loves apart' – and then tells us that on Thomas's last day in New York, both these 'loves' turned up at Thomas's hotel and joined him and a large party of friends at a farewell dinner at an Italian restaurant, before repairing to Pier 90 to escort Dylan up the gangplank of the *Queen Elizabeth*. Somehow this simpering account of Thomas's departure does not ring true. Do 'true loves' ever engage in joint farewells? Do they share such moments with a rival?

As Thomas sailed for home and family, his emotions were mixed. This first American tour proved a tremendous success, but there was a price to pay. Thomas had done no serious literary work for several months and had been ill on every leg of his American journey. He was now in love with two women, Pearl in New York and Caitlin in Wales, and was still in debt despite all the money that passed through his hands. But he knew two things for certain. He had to get back to writing, and he stubbornly held on to the belief that America was still the answer to all his problems.

8

In Love with Two Women

Dylan returned home from New York a changed man. He went there hoping to make money, expecting to read to rather more audiences than usual but with no idea of the travelling that would have to be done, and found himself facing large crowds of a thousand and more, honoured and fêted by universities, invited into the homes of film stars, to meet America's most distinguished editors and Congressmen and even future presidential candidates Adlai Stevenson and General Dwight D. Eisenhower. The penniless poet from Wales was treated as an international celebrity wherever he went, with writers like William Faulkner, e.e. cummings, Nelson Algren and Christopher Isherwood welcoming him as a friend.

And now, after three magical months of acclaim and whisky, he was arriving back, laden with gifts but little money to show for it, to a wife who would never really understand the change in his literary standing.

Caitlin travelled up to London to meet him off the boat train, and wanted to wine and dine and go shopping, which was the last thing on his mind. 'I was having a lovely time, and all he wanted to do was get back to Laugharne,' she said.[1] 'He had been to a million parties in America, and found all the old friends an awful nuisance . . . I could sense the thrill – all that lecturing, all that applause, all those students gathering around him afterwards; he felt that all the things he had been working for over the years had now been recognised, and that his beloved poetry was now being understood . . . the contrast with London must have been painful.' Far deeper than that was the change in his self-awareness, with the realisation that he now had a live audience for his work.

Thomas was careful not to say too much. Writing from the United States he had stressed his loneliness, and now that they were back together he avoided saying how ill he had been after drinking whisky or how much money he had really earned and where it had gone, emphasising instead the contacts made and the foundations laid for the next tour. Dylan was exhausted, but when he insisted that it had been work, work, work, with no time for leisure, she 'did not believe that for a moment', but 'didn't suspect him of having an affair there, either; the occasional night of drunken sex, perhaps, but not an affair', having convinced herself through their years of marriage that 'these rich women wouldn't want to bother with him, stinking of beer and sweat and stale cigarettes, and God knows what'.

Caitlin always carried with her the consoling thought that Dylan was meant for her, and their marriage meant to be, which enabled her to withstand stresses that would have broken many wives. In a sense, it was reassuring that all Dylan wanted was to be back home in the bosom of Laugharne, bedded in the familiarity that gave his life a structure, but Caitlin quickly sensed an inner emptiness, a restlessness, a hankering for those illusory trappings of literary fame. Thomas played down the scale of his socialising. Names and places meant little to her, but Caitlin realised he was missing something, applause, acclaim and some of the more attractive aspects of American literary life, finding it difficult to settle back into a world where none of it mattered, a world in which he was bedevilled by debts and had no one to talk to.

In the past, Dylan had always been happy to 'play darts in the cheerless bar, put my flat beer on the slate, listen to talk about swedes and bulldozers, Mrs Griffiths's ulcer, what Mr Jenkins said to Mrs Prothero, who is no better than she ought to be, the date of Princess Margaret's birthday, the price of geese, Christmas coming',[2] but that was no longer enough and it bored him. Caitlin wrote to Brinnin and told him Dylan had been 'spoiled' by all the attention, still not suspecting anything deeper.

✳ ✳ ✳

Within weeks of his return, Caitlin found herself pregnant again, totally unexpectedly, and they slowly settled back into their daily routine, with Dylan walking along The Cliff mid-morning to see his parents and call in at Brown's Hotel. On such a day, he left his jacket over the back of a kitchen chair with a bundle of letters sticking out of a pocket. Curious and seldom reluctant to rifle through his clothes, Caitlin started to read them and felt herself chill to the bone; they were affectionate, friendly letters from Pearl Kazin. 'When I read them I felt absolute fury, jealousy and fury. It was pretty obvious that they had been to bed together, and I wanted to kill her,' she said.[3]

When Dylan returned from Brown's there was a tearful confrontation, but he fiercely denied any affair. 'She's just someone I met in New York. They're all very friendly over there. I got lots of letters like that after readings, and I often replied and said, "Thank you",' he insisted, maintaining that American literary people were just like theatricals everywhere, greeting each other with kisses, and writing in affectionate terms.

'You'll love it over there,' he continued. 'Next time you'll have to come with me and see for yourself.'

Eventually Caitlin believed him, for, whatever the troubles between them, he never stopped saying he loved her and accepted her just as she was, which she felt rare in a man. 'He was never nasty and never criticised me . . . I think he did look upon me as an idealised woman . . . but, of course, sex is quite different from love and there were times when all he needed was a bit of drunken sex, and if I wasn't there he got it from somebody else (and that was all I wanted when he wasn't there as well). I think Dylan always had this need for drunken sex. For one thing, it gave him a bed for the night; it was often as simple as that, because he was very simple in drink . . .'

The one possibility that never crossed her mind was that Dylan might be attracted to another woman for reasons other than drunken sex, for she remained convinced, whatever anyone said to the contrary, that there was an underlying bond between them, a mutual reliance beyond love or being parents of children. Caitlin would never claim any credit when people discussed his poetry, as if there was some invisible boundary there that could not be mentioned, but Thomas shared it with her line by line, walking into the kitchen to test a verse or a phrase while she said to herself, and not always silently, 'Why doesn't the bloody man leave me to get on with the cooking?' But he did listen to what she said, amending his work accordingly, and admitted when he was far from home, 'She's a better poet than I am . . . Oh, she's the only one for me. I adored her the day I married her and now after 14 years I adore her more than ever. When I was little she could carry me across a brook. She's stronger than I am *now*.'[4]

So the shock was all the greater when Margaret Taylor phoned in September. Dylan was in London, partly to see Brinnin, who was staying over briefly on his way to Italy, and also to discuss the possibility of being commissioned to write another movie script. Margaret said she had something important to tell Caitlin. 'I can't talk about it on the phone,' she said, 'but I'm coming down to see you straight away.'

Margaret immediately caught a train from Paddington to Carmarthen and then a taxi out to Laugharne, where she greeted Caitlin with a kiss on the cheek, following her down a flight of stairs to the kitchen, almost at sea level. There, as usual, Caitlin had a cauldron of broth simmering on the stove, and stood over it, stirring, as Margaret said, 'Have you heard? Dylan has this lady friend over from New York and is going all over London with her. She's called Pearl, and he's taking her round the pubs and introducing her to his friends.'[5]

Caitlin twigged immediately. This must be the same Pearl who had written before, and she realised from what Margaret said that there must have been other letters, too, sent to Dylan c/o the Savage Club, which showed he was being secretive about a relationship dismissed only weeks before as meaningless.

Initially, Caitlin did not respond, other than to ask what Pearl looked like, how she dressed, where she was staying, whether Brinnin had been with them, where they had been and who they had met. As the answers came she began to sense that Dylan was showing Pearl off in the pubs and restaurants where they were both well known, to people who were friends. 'The full impact was very unpleasant,' said Caitlin. 'I got the impression that she was very efficient and businesslike, one of those blue-stocking women who can do everything . . . Had I seen her I would have killed her. She had all the things I hadn't got: I only had my fury, and I just *knew* – without anyone having to tell me – that she had an efficient life, smartness, money and all that odious stuff. With all that rage inside me I was quite capable of knifing her or strangling her. I still think she behaved like one hell of a bitch: she knew I was stuck at home in Laugharne with the children.'

There was another aspect of Taylor's revelations that angered Caitlin intensely. Dylan was always claiming he did not have enough money to buy food or clothes or pay tradesmen's bills in Laugharne, but now she realised money must be coming in from somewhere. Brinnin was being driven around London by taxi, taken to favourite pubs like the Salisbury in St Martin's Lane and El Vino's in Fleet Street, and then on to the Mandrake Club in Soho when the pubs closed. In the evenings, they dined at Wheeler's, Soho's most expensive seafood restaurant, before catching the latest revue, *Les Compagnons de la Chanson*, at the London Casino, with champagne in the foyer in the interval. On other days, there were parties at friends' houses, afternoons spent at the cinema seeing the Marx Brothers in *Duck Soup* and *Destination Moon* at Leicester Square, and always more pubbing, taxis to the Savage or the Gargoyle, where Margaret Taylor joined them.

Now in her second or third month of pregnancy and still not fully recovered from giving birth to Colm 15 months earlier, Caitlin did not know what to do. Taylor told her Dylan and Pearl were planning to spend a weekend in Brighton and then might go to France. Knowing that their housekeeper Dolly Long would look after Colm and Aeronwy (who at that time was attending school in Laugharne), Caitlin thought of travelling to either London or Brighton, knowing precisely where she would find them. 'I was angry and hurt and wanted my revenge,' she said, admitting being also anxious not to lose face by allowing Margaret Taylor to become a ringside spectator or by giving Dylan an opportunity to choose publicly between her and Pearl Kazin.

'Words can't express what I felt for Dylan,' she said. 'I thought he was beneath contempt . . . I never forgave him. How could I?'

Resisting the temptation to catch the next train to London, Caitlin stayed at The Boat House, awaiting his return. She could not remember what time he arrived, whether she waited up late at night or he came back on a daytime train, only that the moment he walked in through the door, she looked at him coldly and demanded, 'What's all this about?'

There was no scope for evasion this time. Thomas could not deny that Pearl was in London or that he had been living a life few can afford. 'It means nothing,' he blustered. 'She's just a friend, someone I met in New York,' trying to explain she was an executive with one of the world's most famous literary magazines and there was a chance they might want to publish his work (all of which was true).

✢   ✢   ✢

The Thomases never recovered from this shock to their marriage. Caitlin sensed her husband was undecided, although he would not admit that in so many words. Five years later, with the publication of *Dylan Thomas in America*, she realised how close he came to leaving her, reading of his conversation with Brinnin in London, travelling on a riverboat down the Thames to Greenwich, when Dylan asked, 'John, what am I going to do? I'm in love with Pearl and I'm in love with my wife. I don't know what to do.'

'My pregnancy was the only strong weapon I had,' said Caitlin. 'I didn't have to make him feel guilty; he was guilty already; he was torn in two. If I hadn't been pregnant at that time, I'm not sure whether he would have gone off with her or not. One part of me still says he wouldn't, because he never stopped telling me how much he loved me.'

Caitlin had one other secret weapon: the knowledge that Dylan was receiving private letters at the Savage Club. She cleverly arranged for Margaret Taylor to call there every day, collect his mail and then not forward any letters from Pearl. This probably did more to kill the affair than anything else, for Pearl continued writing from France, hoping that Dylan would join her there or that they might spend a week together in London in October. Unaware of her letters, Dylan did not reply, and when Pearl arrived back in London, as arranged, all her messages went unanswered. Convinced the affair was over, Pearl spent the winter in Greece.

Meanwhile, the Thomases lurched through the autumn, tormented as always by debts, kipping down with friends in London to avoid the tradesmen and landlords of Laugharne, where Dylan had paid no rent on The Boat House or his parents' home for over a year and owed substantial sums to the milkman, coalman and chemist and other monies to a dress shop in Swansea. He was also behind with his boarding-school fees for Llewelyn. Believing their life too wretched to bring another child into it, Caitlin had an abortion – and in the midst of all this domestic chaos, Dylan Thomas completed the first 39 pages of his comic masterpiece, *Under Milk Wood*.

Their life now was a misery, and yet every night, by some means, they managed to find money for drink. Many evenings ended in rows and violence, with Caitlin tanked up with whisky, beating Dylan around the head, knocking him to the ground, straddling his chest, pummelling him with her fists, grabbing him by the hair and banging his head on the floor before he somehow managed to wriggle free and scramble whimpering to bed. Twice Dylan lost consciousness after her blows to his head.

On some nights Dylan threatened to commit suicide and, increasingly, these dramas were witnessed by friends. The composer Elizabeth Lutyens was staying at The Boat House when Dylan walked out and said he was leaving for good, only to phone up later from Swansea. A friend drove her and Caitlin over to Swansea, where they found Dylan drunk in a pub. Caitlin assailed him with words and attacked with her fists, knocking him to the ground and screaming abuse while he whined, pleading for forgiveness. 'They were having a whale of a time,' said Lutyens.[6]

In the New Year, Dylan left Caitlin alone in Laugharne while he flew to Teheran with the documentary film director Ralph Keene, commissioned to write a 'lucrative' script for a promotional film financed by the Anglo-Iranian Oil Company. He collapsed on arrival after travelling for nearly 24 hours and suffering from gout. He seems to have drunk very little, but was taking sleeping pills and also tried opium. While he was there, Caitlin wrote to say she was leaving him and took her revenge in the bar of the Brown's Hotel.

At the end of an evening's drinking, charged up to Dylan's account in 'the book', Caitlin would pick up lovers for the night without attempting to conceal her plans. Primed with whisky, which she always drank far more than he did, she would point her finger at a man and say 'I've had you', and then similarly work her way around the bar before deciding, 'You can have me to night.' News of her readiness travelled fast. One night she was sitting at a table when a man put his hand up her skirt. Caitlin immediately slapped him across the face with the back of her hand, with the unforgettable words, 'You can fuck me in The Boat House, but here you treat me like a lady.'

Inevitably, someone broke the news when Dylan returned, and that someone was Mrs Ivy Williams, who owned Brown's Hotel with her husband Ebie. Dylan confronted Caitlin, whose denial was every bit as firm as his when accused of the affair with Pearl Kazin.

'I wouldn't do a thing like that,' she said.

'No – I didn't think you would,' he replied, never mentioning the incident again – but there was no disguising the distressed state of their marriage now.

✲ ✲ ✲

Many couples would have separated in circumstances like these, but the Thomases continued to live together, threatening to leave each other and staging emotional reconciliations, with Dylan constantly driven to swear his devotion and Caitlin, by her femininity, keeping him in doubt. It was becoming an odd relationship, as Brinnin observed for himself when he visited Laugharne to discuss arrangements for the second American lecture tour. He was accompanied by Bill Read, an academic from Boston who later wrote the first Thomas biography, *The Days of Dylan Thomas.* They stayed at The Boat House, and Dylan arranged for them to be driven along the coast to St Davids and Fishguard, seldom passing a pub without stopping. As soon as she had a chance, Caitlin began bombarding Brinnin with questions about Pearl. What did she look like? How did she dress? Where was she educated? What was her job? Had she said anything to him about Dylan? When Brinnin would not answer to her satisfaction, Caitlin froze, saying, 'America is OUT!'

After riling each other for two days, arguing over where to go, which pubs to visit and what to eat, the Thomases finally came to blows over dinner in The Boat House. Playfully, Dylan flicked an empty matchbox in her direction and she threw it back in his face. 'That's unfair,' he said, but before Dylan could add another word Caitlin grabbed him by the hair and yanked. Chairs went flying in all directions, plates and cutlery flew as she began flailing him with her fists, and Thomas retreated as fast as he could to the safety of bed. For some strange reason, he knew she would never attack him there, and their fights nearly always ended with him running upstairs and wrapping himself in sheets and blankets, curled up like a baby.

Once he was out of the way, Caitlin commenced a litany of woe, telling Brinnin and Read for over an hour of their troubles and lamenting Dylan's failure to look after his family. 'All you do is flatter him and make him feel like some sort of god,' she said. 'When he came back from America his head was bigger than ever. They ought to know what he's really like in America – all those fool women who chase after him while I'm left here to rot in this bloody bog with three screaming children and no money to pay the bills he leaves behind him. He won't go to America again without me – and I shan't go, so that's that.'

Like much else in their contradictory marriage, Caitlin's word was seldom final. The next morning, Brinnin and Read came downstairs for breakfast wondering whether or not to cut short their visit. Caitlin greeted them cheerfully as if nothing untoward had happened, and happily began discussing Brinnin's proposals for another US tour which would earn Dylan enough in three months of readings for them to spend a fourth month on holiday in either Florida or California.

✼   ✼   ✼

Two hard facts confronted Brinnin when he arrived in Laugharne. Firstly, Caitlin was not his friend. Secondly, at home in Wales, Dylan Thomas was a different man from the boisterous character he met in New York. This situation put Brinnin on shaky ground, for he found himself caught up in their domestic conflict.

Understandably, Caitlin believed Brinnin knew far more than he said about Pearl Kazin; she was not to know that Dylan only met Pearl during his last two weeks in New York when he saw very little of Brinnin. As far as Caitlin was concerned, this was the man who had enticed her husband away to New York with a promise of high earnings (which, so far as she could see, had not been fulfilled), was responsible for the frenetic schedule that had left Dylan exhausted, and was now failing to tell her what really happened in America.

Another unknown factor in all this is whether or not Thomas was taking drugs during his first tour of America. There is some evidence he was. Vernon Watkins and his wife Gwen heard Thomas refer to drugs. So did Caitlin. It is known that he was using sleeping pills at the end of each day and benzedrine to perk him up, and that in Persia he experimented with opium, describing it as 'no good'. This prompts the question: compared with what? Had he tried anything else? And if he was willing to try opium in Persia, was he equally prepared to sample whatever he may have been offered in Greenwich Village?

Thomas was so secretive about his health and sexual affairs that one can safely assume he would have been equally careful in discussing a matter such as this, since many of the drugs that were being used and sold in Greenwich Village were illegal. The writer William Burroughs and the painter Larry Rivers were both active drug-takers; so were the early Beat poets, gathering in the same bars and cafés. Benzedrine, morphine, heroin, opium, marijuana and cocaine were all being used within the writing and artistic communities to which Dylan was drawn. Benzedrine, which we know Thomas used, could be obtained easily from a doctor. Students were often prescribed it to help them stay up all night preparing for exams. By 1950 the drug had an infamous history. Many high-ranking Nazi leaders had taken it, including Hitler, and a form of the original batch of methamphetamine, of which benzedrine is a derivative, made by the Nazis during the Second World War was still available in New York in the '60s, when it was known as 'Nazi meth'. Dylan's own use of benzedrine was therefore neither rare nor even unusual – and is significant mainly for what it tells us about his willingness to use stimulants.

How much Caitlin knew of this is uncertain, although she did confirm many years later that there was 'a lot of talk about drugs' after Dylan's death.

✳   ✳   ✳

Any hopes Dylan might have had of strengthening his marriage by sharing his American experiences with Caitlin were soon dashed. In theory, they had all the money they needed to make the tour a success. His US publishers were bringing out a new collection of his poems, *In Country Sleep*, to coincide with his second tour. Plans were far advanced for British and American publication of his film script, *The Doctor and the Devils*, based on the famous Scottish bodysnatching case of Burke and Hare. Likewise, the publishers Allan Wingate Ltd agreed to pay them £400 to produce a book jointly, describing their travels across the United States.

The first £100 arrived from Wingate's in time to buy their Christmas turkey and fill the children's stockings with gifts, and Wingate's agreed to release a further £50 every month to meet their domestic expenses in Laugharne while they were away: the £1 a week rent for The Boat House and its running costs, the £1 a week rent for Dylan's parents' apartment at Pelican, and £3 a week wages for Dolly Long, who was looking after Colm and Aeronwy.

With all these expenses covered on the home front, their tickets for the *Queen Mary* provided and Brinnin also paying a month's rent in advance for a small suite at the Chelsea Hotel in Greenwich Village, the Thomases should have had few worries.

Initially, their visit started happily enough. Brinnin welcomed Dylan and Caitlin to New York with some celebratory drinks in Manhattan, and then drove them out to Millbrook, NY, to stay with his friend Rollie McKenna, a photographer. Quiet conversation, regular meals, drives out into the country and moderate drinking were the order of the day. The only jarring note was Caitlin's behaviour. Rather than talk to her host or other guests, Caitlin would withdraw to her room 'to work on my journal' or sit in a corner, reading American magazines. McKenna thought this 'remoteness and rudeness' puzzling, and wondered whether she felt inhibited by strangers.

At one dinner party with some university professors as guests, Caitlin made a point of continually correcting whatever Dylan said, trying to deflate his flamboyance, and interrupted one guest with the question, 'Are they all stuffed shirts like yourself?' The party stumbled on, but the guests could see that Caitlin was unhappy, jealous and resentful at all the attention Dylan was getting whilst she was being virtually ignored.

In *Caitlin*, she also admits suffering from severe depression which is wholly understandable. She felt betrayed by Dylan's affair with Pearl Kazin, and was troubled emotionally by a particularly brutal abortion. This occurred during the sixth month of pregnancy. She was under sedation, not a general anaesthetic, and realised the foetus was being dissected in her womb and removed in pieces. This left her with a sense of guilt for the rest of her life. She was a woman in need of love and affection, and here she was in a foreign land, ignored and invisible, nothing more than the poet's wife.

With nearly all their basic costs met in advance, Dylan and Caitlin had every reason to look upon the tour as an excuse for a holiday, and a chance to restore their marriage. Even if they arrived without any spending money (which was more than likely), Thomas would have known that once the readings started he would usually be paid in cash on the night – so they borrowed hundreds of dollars from Brinnin. When that vanished, they borrowed more – until Brinnin began to realise that however kindly Providence shone upon them, the Thomases were doomed to fritter away every dollar and every cent that came within their grasp.

It wasn't only the Thomases' attitude to money that appalled their American host. As Dylan prepared to walk out on stage for his first reading, again at the Kaufmann Auditorium, Brinnin heard Caitlin say, 'Just remember – they're all dirt!' And although he only saw them once a week to hand out tickets and confirm details of Dylan's itinerary for the next seven days, Brinnin found himself witnessing a marriage in turmoil. 'The unhappiest development of their visit [came] through loud and stormy scenes at parties where their private marital war [was] needlessly exposed to view . . . their marriage was essentially a state of rivalry . . . to begin to understand Caitlin's resentful unhappiness, one would have to acknowledge her feeling that Dylan's great success in America had become just one more weight on the cross she had to bear.'7

✵ ✵ ✵

Thomas's schedule for the second tour took him back to many of the colleges and universities he had visited two years earlier. Over the first two months, February and March 1952, he read largely in New York and New England, delivering 26 performances in 47 days. This time he was not driven to these venues by Brinnin, who was becoming wary of the all-consuming nature of Thomas's demands and Caitlin's resentment.

Overall, Dylan's health was better during the second tour. Despite their daily battles, Caitlin's presence gave him a degree of stability, countering his tendency to substitute drink for food, sleep as little as possible, and talk all night. Significantly, he seemed more resilient and there were fewer reports of his suffering asthma attacks or collapsing, although it is also clear that he had alarming habits. At the University of Vermont, where Dylan read in February, arriving without a coat in the middle of winter, he was observed taking barbiturates at breakfast. Before the reading, Thomas drank several beers at a local tavern, the Sugar House, but no one thought him in any way alcoholic.

Two weeks later, Dylan visited Montreal to read at McGill University, which he had been unable to fit into his 1950 itinerary. As usual, he was uncomfortable among the professors of the English Department whom he met at the Faculty Club, but loosened up after the reading when surrounded by students and younger faculty members. Someone suggested that poetry required 'extraordinary experiences' to which Dylan replied, 'Ordinary experience should do.'8 Louis Dudek, a member of the McGill English faculty and later a friend of Leonard Cohen, considered Dylan 'the first of the celebrity Messiahs', inspiring something in his audiences that came close to a 'religious mania'. Dudek noted that Yeats, Eliot, Pound and Auden did not inspire the same response.

It was during Dylan's solo trips to places like McGill that Caitlin had her happiest times in the United States. Left behind in New York (probably to avoid unnecessary fares), she developed friendships with Rose Slivka (wife of the sculptor Dave Slivka), Rollie McKenna and Brinnin's mother, who lived in Boston, visiting theatres and art galleries and going shopping.

Brinnin noticed that when Dylan was ill he stayed in bed, and if he was suffering from a hangover Caitlin left him to recover in his own good time. He could see that Dylan looked after himself more carefully when she was around.

✻ ✻ ✻

Before leaving New York for his swing west, Dylan complained of a gum infection when a nylon bristle dislodged from his toothbrush. The bristle was removed at a doctor's surgery and then he and Caitlin were given their tickets and schedule for San Francisco, Vancouver, Seattle, Berkeley, Chicago, Salt Lake City and Columbia.

For any other literary tourists, this would have been the adventure of a lifetime, with journeys down into the Arizona desert to stay with the painter Max Ernst and his wife, across America to the Golden Gate, and down the California seaboard into Steinbeck country, to Carmel and Monterey, and to stay with Henry Miller and his wife at Big Sur. But the Thomases were not like other travellers. Wherever they went, they arrived penniless and bickering, either managing to convince themselves that it was all someone else's fault, or with Caitlin complaining with her usual bitterness that Dylan was failing her.

In Vancouver, Dylan was set up by his hosts and local reporters who hatched a scheme to get him as drunk as possible so that they could all enjoy the full force of 'The Legend'. A table was stacked with beer and a phone call faked so that Dylan would walk past it, not knowing a camera was concealed nearby to catch him downing the bottles one by one. Fitzgibbon reported that 'no reporter could believe that Thomas wanted to do anything but get drunk as rapidly as possible'.[9] The photographs were published as sick proof that the famous Welsh beer hog had been in town, and the story travelled far and wide. Once again, Thomas was disappointed when no university would offer him a visiting professorship.

While they were staying in San Francisco, all Caitlin's resentment boiled to the surface again when a telegram arrived from England to say Llewelyn had been sent home from Magdalen College School in Oxford because Dylan had failed to pay his school fees. She also learned that poor little Dolly Long, their diminutive household help, was not receiving her weekly pittance and Dylan's parents were facing eviction because the rent had not been paid on Pelican. Had Caitlin been 6,000 miles away in Laugharne, no doubt Dylan would have shrugged off the crisis with another drink, knowing *someone* always came to the rescue – but there in San Francisco, with Caitlin right beside him, knocking back tumblers of whisky far faster than he ever could, there was another crisis in the marriage, with her noisily packing her bags and preparing to fly home without him.

Frequently, her behaviour lacked logic. When Dylan tried to wheedle $1,000 for Llewelyn's school fees from a rich admirer, Caitlin destroyed their lunch with rudeness – and the promised money was lost. The day Dylan announced he was going to read selections from *Hamlet*, she sneered, '*You* read *Hamlet*? You *can't* read *Hamlet!*' which prompted him to throw a book at her. To polite enquiries about their impressions of America, Caitlin snarled, 'I can't get out of the bloody country soon enough.' And if ever she thought insufficient attention was being paid to her at a party, which happened more than once, she had the perfect question to silence every guest: 'Is there no man in America worthy of me?'

☆ ☆ ☆

Except for their week with Max Ernst, Thomas did not have a serious break from travelling in three months. He had already delivered 35 readings, and there were ten more to go. On their way back to New York from the West Coast, Dylan called Brinnin from Chicago, saying he was exhausted and ill and could not keep to the scheduled reading at Tulane University, New Orleans. Brinnin tried to push him into fulfilling the engagement, arguing that all their hard work would be wasted and their reputations damaged if he missed this one performance.

Brinnin makes much of this in *Dylan Thomas in America*, perhaps too much, for Brinnin had more at stake. Teaching in universities was his lifeblood, his primary source of income, and he needed to be sure of employment after Thomas returned to Laugharne – but even when he was ill, Thomas was stronger willed than Brinnin and flatly refused to go. It is not hard to imagine Caitlin sitting on a hotel bed, egging him on, while Dylan spoke into the phone. Brinnin then said that the least Thomas could do, in the circumstances, was phone his host in New Orleans with a personal explanation. He promised to do so, but did not, and on the night of the reading, with 800 tickets sold, there were frantic calls from New Orleans.

For Brinnin, who always tended to become flustered when placed in tricky situations, this was a major crisis, somewhat on a par with Truman's decision to drop the atomic bomb or Kennedy's stand-off with Khrushchev. Brinnin exaggerated the Tulane incident in *Dylan Thomas in America*, and this was another factor in the falsity of his portrayal of the poet. Whenever he had a commitment, either at the BBC or with Strand Films, Thomas usually kept to his deadlines and was punctual. To miss only one reading in over 150 was an extraordinary physical feat, especially when one recalls that Brinnin was inexperienced in planning such a schedule and seldom allowed sufficient travelling and relaxing time between appearances. The crux of the Tulane incident was that while Dylan's personal behaviour was tolerated by Brinnin, he became distressed on the one occasion when he thought it might reflect upon his own academic standing.

The nature of Dylan's illness in Chicago in late April 1952 was never made clear. It may have been just another hangover, but it is odd that although Thomas phoned Brinnin on 24 April to cancel Tulane, he still managed to fulfil an engagement at Northwestern University, Evanston, Illinois, that same evening and at Marquette University, Milwaukee, the following night. Whatever was wrong with his health did not cause him to cancel either reading. After their return to New York, Dylan began his final stretch of readings in and around Manhattan, with one or two in New England and another in Washington DC. He was initially too ill to attend a reception and book-signing at the Gotham Book Mart, but pulled himself together at the last minute.

Despite their dispute over Tulane, Dylan went on to Storrs, Connecticut, to read at the university where Brinnin taught creative writing classes. He arrived late by plane and was unsteady at first. As he warmed to the audience, 'His strong Welsh accent and the lilting cadences of his voice as it fell, then rose to a thunderous pitch was mesmerising'.[10] The auditorium was hot and without air conditioning. Dressed in a heavy tweed jacket, Dylan sweated profusely. By the end of the evening, he was exhausted.

A week later, at Dartmouth College in New Hampshire, he had to be helped on stage and 'planted' at the podium. Again, he seemed exhausted; there was no suggestion of drunkenness. At his final reading at the Kaufmann Auditorium, his voice sounded 'heavy with fatigue' and he slurred his words when reading from Sean O'Casey's autobiography.[11]

On their last night in New York, with all his earnings spent, Caitlin found more unopened love letters in Dylan's suitcase. They sailed home the following day, 16 May 1952, as penniless as they had arrived, unhappy, exhausted and not knowing which way to turn – and yet Dylan Thomas was now one of the best-known writers in the Western world.

9

Flattery, Idleness and Infidelity

Optimism was in the air that summer when the Thomases returned home to Wales. It was a wonderful moment for a writer to have broken through in Britain and America. Books were selling in vast numbers. Television was taking hold in every home. Wartime controls on food and clothing were being scrapped by Britain's new Conservative government, led by Winston Churchill, and with the war hero General Eisenhower poised for victory in the US presidential elections, the Atlantic alliance held strong and true.

This feeling of optimism was everywhere. Records were being broken in cricket and athletics. The largest house-building programme in Britain's history was under way, and for the only time this century crime fell dramatically. With the coronation of Queen Elizabeth just a few months away, leader writers penned dramatic editorials on the dawn of a new Elizabethan age. In a climate like this, faced with so many opportunities, Dylan Thomas was poised for the kind of international recognition usually reserved for film stars. No other poet had achieved such acclaim since the dawning of the Media Age.

Money started pouring into the family home with commissions from the BBC, requests for his writings from American magazines, his publisher urging him to finalise his *Collected Poems* (which were produced in both a signed, limited edition bound in leather and a trade edition for Britain and the United States), and the legendary film director Michael Powell asking him to write a cinema script on the adventures of Ulysses ... and yet none of it seemed to make any difference to the misery of the Thomases' lives, with Caitlin still complaining bitterly of their poverty, and Dylan choosing not to tell her how much he earned.

Always a nervous man, frightened of spiders and mice and running home in the dark for fear of bats and vampires, Thomas seemed to translate these inner anxieties into every layer of his being. He was permanently troubled. As his earnings soared, he worried endlessly over the National Insurance stamps he should have paid and because the Inland Revenue were seeking to tax him upon the £1,907 profit they believed he earned from his first US tour. Plagued by other debts, all of which he had the earnings to meet, he lived in constant fear of the postman delivering another writ or the bailiff threatening to strip The Boat House.

These imaginary crises triggered off the usual stream of begging letters to old friends and new patrons, but some were now reluctant to pour good money down the Thomas drain and others privately distressed by their improvidence. Among them was Brinnin, who ceased believing in their tales of poverty when he learned that Dylan's income 'had for a number of years been twice or three times the size of mine. On far less than this amount, families larger than this lived in Wales or England not merely with security but in luxury.'

Dylan continued to claim he did not have enough money to give Caitlin a weekly allowance or meet her household bills, but friends noticed that when he travelled to London, often for no more than lunch with an editor or a meeting at the BBC, he would arrive in expensive tweed suits and smoking the best cigars, and frequently did not bother to return home for several days. Somehow the marriage survived – but Caitlin continued to take casual lovers in his absence, and when she decided to have another abortion in January 1953 it was by no means certain the child was his. And yet there remained a tenderness between them, too, poignantly expressed in the dedication of his *Collected Poems*.

'I do remember the day Dylan brought home his *Collected Poems* for the first time,' she said.[1] 'I saw that he had dedicated what was, in effect, his life's work to me. That pleased me very much. He didn't tell me he was going to do it so it came as a great surprise.'

✠   ✠   ✠

The *Collected Poems* were published on 10 November 1952, five weeks before his father died. Thomas would have received advance copies several weeks earlier, and one can imagine the pride in old Jack's eyes as he held the book in his hands. Towards the end, his sight was poor. Some days his mind wandered, but there were frequent periods of lucidity when father and son were able to talk normally. Jack would have shared Dylan's pleasure in the fine reviews. He died on 16 December 1952, emaciated and in considerable pain, although he managed to survive to the age of 76. Nancy died exactly four months later in Bombay, only 46 and suffering from liver cancer.

These deaths, especially his father's, left Dylan with a deep sense of loneliness and depression. He told Caitlin with a quiet reverence that he would have been nothing as a poet if his father had not read to him and taught him everything he knew.

During this last period of his father's life, Dylan suffered at least four or five bouts of bronchitis which he misdiagnosed as pleurisy. His gout also flared up regularly, although this did not prevent him limping along with his walking stick from The Boat House to Brown's Hotel, always calling in to see his mother, who would stand at the front window peering from behind curtains to see if he fell over as he left the pub. From the letters, one learns that his gout was initially confined to a big toe and later affected his elbow.

The complaints of pleurisy, or chronic pulmonary infections or inflammation, are consistent with his history of asthma or smoking. This was not a new development but an old, nagging problem. Bronchitis was not life-threatening so long as it did not develop into a more serious infection or fulminant pneumonia. However, the biographer Ferris suggests that other new symptoms became apparent during 1952–53 – symptoms that Dylan does not mention in his letters, but which were ominous and heralded a subtle but definite change in his medical condition. These were blackouts and impotence, both of which are common in diabetics. Fitzgibbon indicates that the blackouts began in the summer of 1953, but they can be dated earlier than this. One night, Dylan 'fell like a stone as he stood by the mantelpiece of the bar in Brown's Hotel', was 'unconscious for two minutes', revived and 'ordered another drink as if nothing unusual had happened'.[2] Margaret Taylor and Florence Thomas both saw him suffering 'breathlessness' at about the same time. When Dylan walked from The Boat House to Pelican, Florence said he was 'so exhausted he could not speak'. Florence also reports a rumour that Dylan was suffering from 'sexual impotence'.

Breathlessness, blackouts and impotence could have been due to a wide spectrum of diseases, but a central tenet in science known as Occam's Razor maintains that the simplest explanation of phenomena is usually correct. A sick patient will present a doctor with a variety of symptoms. The doctor does not look for different diseases to explain each one, but ranks them in order of importance. Most look for a pattern of organ involvement which fits all or most of the patient's complaints.

In Dylan's case, breathlessness was easily explained by his history of asthma and bronchitis aggravated by incessant smoking. Most patients with bronchitis, inflammation of the airways, usually develop emphysema along the way, which destroys lung tissue and leads to a condition known as COPD (chronic obstructive pulmonary disease), which limits airflow in and out of the lungs. COPD often remains unidentified for years until the patient feels short of breath, especially on exertion. If the patient continues smoking and avoids treatment, this can lead to pneumonia. As we learned from his horrified reaction to the Swansea doctor's advice, there was little hope of Dylan giving up smoking or looking after himself properly, so his breathlessness would have continued as he stumbled around on his walking stick, starved of oxygen.

The onset of impotence, however, cannot be explained by this deterioration in his lungs. In general, impotence may result from diabetes, alcoholism, vitamin B12 deficiency or syphilis. Each was a reasonable possibility in Dylan's case and a doctor would have considered them one by one. Dylan had had 'the clap' before the war, but, as we have said, this was more probably gonorrhoea, for he never exhibited syphilitic skin sores on his face or trunk, hair loss, paralysis or recurrent genital ulcers. Alcohol and B12 deficiency were more likely explanations.

By 1953 he had been drinking for over 20 years, but it is rare for alcoholics to suffer impotence as a first symptom of involvement of their peripheral nerves without previous complaints of loss of memory or lack of feeling in their fingers or toes. A B12 deficiency was a strong possibility with Dylan's long history of poor eating habits and substitution of beer for food. One classic symptom of B12 deficiency is anaemia, which Dylan suffered from as a child and which was also discovered on his admission to St Vincent's Hospital in 1953. Another symptom is clumsiness in walking due to degeneration of parts of the spinal cord which usually transmit information about limb position. Dylan was not described as clumsy at all during this period, but later in New York he would fall and break bones and this, coupled with his history of anaemia, strongly suggests he suffered from chronic, lifelong B12 deficiency, essentially due to malnutrition. It was another irony that at the height of his fame, Dylan Thomas was literally starving himself to death while his friends stood by and cheered him on.

To the clinical observer, where there is one symptom there are usually others of which the patient may not be aware. Impotence was just another clue that something was wrong with Dylan's health. Blackouts suggested a new development, but were they? He was known to fall into such deep sleeps that no one could rouse him, and it seems likely that these 'blackouts' were simply an old symptom manifesting itself in a different way.

Overall, these 'new problems' are further proof that his non-insulin-dependent diabetes was now affecting his nervous system, causing impotence and blackouts. The central nervous system consists of the brain and spinal cord with the peripheral nerves considered a separate but connected system. The nervous system is the most crucial in the body because it directs and integrates the ability to circulate blood, digest food and reproduce. Control over the nervous system is only partly conscious and voluntary. When we want to go for a walk, we simply stand up and go – and while we walk, our heartbeat, breathing, blood flow and metabolism continue uninterrupted because of their automatic control by a parallel nervous system known as the autonomic nervous system, or ANS. This not only controls all the basic functions of living but also our will to live and survive, the fight or flight syndrome experienced in the face of fear.

Classically, diabetics complain of numbness or tingling in their feet when peripheral nerves are affected. Eventually, many develop foot sores and ulcers because of this lack of feeling. While these classic symptoms had been known for years in Dylan's day, involvement of the ANS as a result of diabetes was considered rare. However, today neurologists recognise that over 50 per cent of men who suffer diabetes for five years will also suffer impotence through diabetic involvement of the ANS. This condition has been given the name diabetic autonomic neuropathy (DAN) and includes a wide range of other symptoms depending upon which organs are affected. Among diabetic men, the most common symptom is impotence. Erectile dysfunction may be the first indication, or it may parallel others. Low blood pressure is also a hallmark of DAN. If the blood pressure drops far enough and deprives the brain of the blood it needs, blackouts will occur, as they did in Dylan's case.

The onset of impotence and blackouts indicates that Dylan's diabetes was reaching a new but not irretrievable stage. There were also other symptoms that were being repeatedly ignored.

After readings in America, whether in summer or winter, Dylan was always breaking into profuse, clothes-soaking sweats, especially around his face. Abnormal sweating and heat intolerance are additional symptoms of DAN. Dylan's history of gastric problems, often attributed to alcoholic gastritis, probably involved another element of DAN, gastric atonia. Degeneration of the nerves to the stomach could have contributed to Dylan's habit of retching, stomach cramps and refusal to eat food. The symptoms of excessive thirst, uncontrolled urination, weight loss and gain, depression, debility and exhaustion had been evident since 1933. Over a 20-year period, Dylan had manifested over a dozen different symptoms of diabetes.

Dylan's health was now so bad – though no one knew why – that neither his wife nor his mother wanted him to return to America for a third tour in 1953. Caitlin refused to go there again herself and accused him of wanting 'flattery, idleness and infidelity' when he insisted it was for 'appreciation, dramatic work and friends.[3] In the end, Dylan agreed to limit his third tour to six weeks, with its highlight being the première of his new play for voices, *Under Milk Wood*.

✻ ✻ ✻

The relationship between Thomas and Brinnin was now deteriorating. There were several reasons for this. Thomas felt aggrieved at having so little to show financially after the first two tours, blaming this on Brinnin's failure (as he saw it) to make sufficient provision for his travelling costs and out-of-pocket expenditure. Laundry was a constant problem and he continually ran out of shirts. In his own peculiar way (Dylan had a lifelong reputation for petty theft), he solved it by raiding his hosts' wardrobes when colleges put him up for the night. Nevertheless, he still managed to convince himself he would have returned home to Laugharne with enough money to solve his current problems if only Brinnin had been more businesslike.

That was not the way Brinnin saw it. He considered Thomas wholly irresponsible, and despised what he thought to be moral corruption in his character. Brinnin still believed Dylan Thomas a great poet, and the *Collected Poems* were published in the United States in March 1953 to extraordinary acclaim, but he was now beginning to think that Thomas's creative powers were failing. 'The fact remains that when Dylan Thomas came to the attention of Americans as a major poet, he was creatively past his prime,' Brinnin argued in *Dylan Thomas in America*.[4] This was no 'fact', merely an opinion, but in dressing up his argument with a mass of tittle-tattle, not all of it accurate and most of it written in complete ignorance of Thomas's true state of health, Brinnin established a theory that was later taken up by Fitzgibbon and Ferris, and accepted without further analysis by newspaper columnists. None knew the whole story – that Dylan Thomas was a very sick man who was not looking after himself properly, and was failing to get the medical attention he needed. This tragedy was compounded by his wife and closest friends being all too willing to blame demon drink rather than call in a doctor.

We would argue that Brinnin, Fitzgibbon and Ferris were all mistaken in their analysis. This was not a poet past his prime but a sick man, trapped within a desperate marriage, subject to constant depression, but forever wrestling with new challenges, rising to nearly every occasion as a public performer during his American tours, maintaining a punishing work schedule and realising that every new poem, play or short story had to reach the highest levels of public expectation. His output during the last phase of his life – *Under Milk Wood*, the short essay on *Laugharne*, the short story *The Outing*, the poems *Over Sir John's hill*, the *In Country Heaven* sequence, *Lament* and *Do not go gentle into that good night* – attained these peaks, and he was managing to combine it with constant work for the BBC, frequent public readings in Britain as well as America and development work on long-term projects like *Two Streets* and *Ulysses*, despite a home life for which he was largely to blame but which was misery nonetheless.

* * *

Travelling on board the SS *United States*, Thomas arrived in New York on 21 April 1953 for his third American tour. He appeared 'clear-eyed, hale, sober',[5] complaining only that the other passengers were boring. After checking in at the Chelsea Hotel, Dylan set out with Brinnin on a pub crawl that lasted all day and well into the night, admitting *Under Milk Wood* was still not finished.

Brinnin was dismayed. Posters were already up, announcing the première for 14 May, and ticket sales were well under way. His assistant, Liz Reitell, had recruited amateur actors to each read several roles, and now here was Thomas admitting some scenes needed fleshing out and there was no ending. As Dylan's first day back in New York wound from one bar to the next, they found themselves in the bar of the Algonquin Hotel, drinking with Howard Moss of *The New Yorker.* Brinnin phoned Reitell, who joined them from the Poetry Center. By then, Dylan was already in his cups and suffering from lack of sleep, and their first impressions of each other were not good; he had failed to answer her letters to Laugharne asking for advice on the stage directions, and now here he was saying the play was not ready, just as she was making arrangements for the first night. 'He thought, "She's one of those cold American girls." I thought, "Why all the fuss over this fool?"' recalled Reitell.[6]

Leaving Thomas on his own for four days, Brinnin returned to Boston, signalling yet again that he felt less and less responsibility for Dylan's personal affairs. During the first two tours, Brinnin booked the engagements and planned the schedule. Now, everything was being left to Reitell. It was a serious error of judgement on Brinnin's part.

While she may have been able to cope with all the usual enquiries, letters and phone calls that flow through a small administrative office, Reitell was totally unequipped to handle the new roles thrust upon her – handling arrangements for Thomas's personal appearances, helping him finish *Under Milk Wood*, directing its first public performances and acting, in effect, as Thomas's personal nurse, cook and housemaid.

✻　✻　✻

Liz Reitell had been on the fringe of New York's Bohemian literary/arts scene for years. Born and brought up in the city, she was five years younger than Dylan, an only child of well-off parents who felt unable to control her. In a desperate attempt to provide her with the discipline that was beyond them, they sent her to four private boarding schools, but each new beginning always ended messily, with them being asked to take her away because she was headstrong and bad tempered, refused to obey teachers and insisted on smoking.

Like many troubled rebels, she decided to become an artist, enrolling in 1937 at another private institution, Bennington College, in the rolling green mountains of Vermont, where she graduated in 1941 with a degree in dance and theatrical costume design. Her life was marked by a succession of failed marriages and frequent changes of direction. This pattern was established early. In 1941, she married Adolph Green, a songwriter and performer. They divorced within two years because of differences over money and professional jealousies. In 1943, she joined the Women's Army Corps and became a lieutenant, helping to arrange Armed Forces entertainment and meeting her second husband, Clement Staboletski, an engineer. They briefly lived in San Francisco, but the marriage lasted little more than a year before Reitell decided to head back to New York and then travel on to Europe, planning to become a painter and set designer.

None of her plans ever came to much. She would pick up odd jobs here and there, sometimes in theatrical design, but gradually sank into depression and alcohol as she began to realise she did not have the creative spark essential in any art form. By the time she met Dylan, the troubled girl was already a troubled adult with a tortured life ahead of her that would end in two more failed marriages, failed relationships, illness and dementia.

Nevertheless, Reitell soon began pressuring Thomas into finishing *Under Milk Wood*, bombarding him with phone calls after he travelled down to Boston to deliver a reading at the University (25 April), staying at Brinnin's home. For the first time in any of his American tours, Dylan knuckled down to work and began writing extra material for *Under Milk Wood* between engagements at Bennington (27), Syracuse (28) and Williamstown (1 May).

By 3 May, Thomas felt sufficiently confident in his rapidly changing manuscript to deliver a one-man reading of *Under Milk Wood* at the Fogg Museum at Harvard University. Encouraged by the enthusiastic response, he travelled south to Washington, Virginia, North Carolina and Pennsylvania, still revising the playscript and completing 14 readings in 18 days. His health seemed relatively stable, but at the end of a performance Thomas was usually exhausted, quiet, passive and barely interested in a drink. After a meal, he often revived, and he was able to eat a steak one night before a performance in New York, but there were frequent reports of him suffering profound physical fatigue.

These vague but persistent descriptions painted a picture of a classic diabetic. While his collapses were not quite diabetic crises, Dylan's constant lack of energy was far from normal in a man who was only 38 years old. It indicated continuing abnormal swings in his blood sugar levels caused by varying and fluctuating insulin levels. Diabetics who have learned to properly regulate their food intake and thus their blood sugar levels are indistinguishable at work or at home from people without diabetes.

Whenever Dylan's sugar soared out of control from too much drinking or smoking, lack of proper sleep or food, or exertion – just the stress of a public performance – he would use up his minimal amount of functioning sugar. When his sugar level dropped low enough, he collapsed. For the first three weeks of this tour, he may not have been overtly ill, but he still exhibited symptoms of the disease.

When Dylan returned to Boston after visiting Philadelphia, Brinnin was surprised to find Pearl Kazin waiting for him. Since their last meeting in London in September 1950, Pearl had married, divorced and lived in Mexico – and now the ever-prim Brinnin was bewildered to learn she and Dylan met again in New York and spent the night together in Cambridge. However, that seemed to be no more than a one-night stand for, within days, Thomas was claiming to be in love with Liz Reitell.

As the date of the *Under Milk Wood* première approached, Thomas became more and more involved with the rehearsals, still working every day on the script. One day, Rollie McKenna met him with Liz in a bar near the Poetry Center, his speech slurred as 'he alternated between wild gestures and a tearful blubbering'.[7] When they moved on to the Kaufmann, he vomited and passed out. No doctor was called. Once the rehearsal began, 'Liz shook Dylan awake' and persuaded him to take part. This episode occurred on either 8 or 9 May, before Thomas visited Philadelphia on 9 May – and its significance lies in the fact that all this happened shortly after his first visit to Dr Milton Feltenstein, when he was injected with a shot of cortisone. This was meant to ease his gout.

✳   ✳   ✳

Liz Reitell's affair with Thomas started a few days later, after the première, but already she was trying to persuade him to cut back on his drinking and lead a more orderly life. Her first move was to introduce him to Feltenstein, who treated her for severe depression, colic, infections and alcoholism. As he had always worked wonders for her, Reitell was certain Feltenstein could do the same for Thomas.

Dr Milton Darwin Feltenstein was in his late forties with a lucrative private practice centred on his surgery at 44 Grammercy Park, a chic area of New York. He graduated from the College of Physicians and Surgeons at Columbia University in 1931 and became board certified in internal medicine after his residency.

Despite Brinnin's many assertions to the contrary, Feltenstein was not and never had been an attending or staff physician at St Vincent's Hospital, but did have admitting privileges at Beth Israel Hospital on East 16th Street. As we shall see later, this is an important point. To underline it, we would point out that Feltenstein was Jewish and St Vincent's was a Catholic charity hospital run by nuns, with Cardinal Spellman as one of their major patrons. Beth Israel was where many of New York's Jewish physicians practised and was well known for its discreet treatment of well-paying patients with alcohol and, more recently, drug problems.

Feltenstein's practice initially concentrated on general internal medicine, especially patients with heart, lung and gastrointestinal problems. For those patients with chronic diseases a cure was impossible, limiting Feltenstein's capacity to earn much from them, so he began taking on more and more patients with straightforward psychiatric problems, including depression and chronic alcoholism, to supplement his income and expand his patient pool. Many could be treated at home or by visits to his surgery. Often all they required was a shot of cortisone, a change in diet and some pills to sober them up or help them through a tough period. He was, in effect, a 'pill doctor' – and because he was dealing with patients who could recover quickly if they took themselves in hand, his reputation grew among New York's artistic community.

Unfortunately, Dylan Thomas was a genuinely sick man who needed something more than a quick fix, which was all he got. From that first visit, he was treated as a celebrity patient. Dylan did not need an appointment. His medical history was not established and there was no physical examination. The interview lasted minutes, with Dylan making no mention of diabetes and saying only that he had had asthma as a child, had occasional bouts of bronchitis and suffered from gout. Feltenstein gave him the shot of cortisone and said he should have two shots a week whenever his toe was painful. When Dylan complained of fatigue and exhaustion, Feltenstein also prescribed benzedrine to get him going during the day and help him when he had to travel or perform. Feltenstein was aware of Dylan's reputation as a serious drinker, but this was not discussed in any detail, because he did not know Dylan well enough to bring up such a sensitive subject. Later, he admitted making a serious error in not carrying out a routine examination, taking blood or urine samples or making arrangements for a chest X-ray.

Rollie McKenna met Thomas just a few hours after his injection. By then, with his toe less painful, he would have been grateful for the relief. No one was unduly worried when he collapsed because this had happened so often before, but this time it was the cortisone that was making him ill. It is now well known that cortisone raises the level of glucose released into the blood while also inhibiting the ability of insulin to regulate glucose levels. Use of cortisone in diabetics has to be carefully monitored. If their glucose level rises too high or sinks too low, they will crash into diabetic shock. Because the insulin is not working as it should, their bodies are unable to make use of high levels of glucose. In other words, they starve in a sea of plenty. This is exactly what happened on this occasion – and without knowing of his diabetes, Thomas's behaviour would have been inexplicable to McKenna or Reitell, or to Feltenstein.

✻　✻　✻

As 14 May drew near, Thomas worked frantically to finish the script. He spent the day itself at McKenna's apartment on 88th Street, writing as fast as he could, with two typists preparing the script. As each new section was finished, the pages were rushed across to the Kaufmann where the actors were rehearsing. The strain was exhausting, and at one point Dylan suddenly stopped, saying he was too tired to continue, but he rallied again and carried on, with the last pages being handed to the cast as they took their places on stage, sitting on high-stools.

The audience did not know what to expect. They sat in total silence as Thomas himself performed the role of First Voice, softly setting the scene for the play. As its gentle rhythms began to flow, one or two chuckles were heard, then ripples and peals of laughter, as the audience began to realise this was a comic masterpiece, a study of his home town decked in bawdy detail. There was a moment of silence as the play ended and the stage lights faded, and then an explosion of applause with 15 curtain calls and Dylan taking the final bow, tears and sweat streaming down his face. There would be other finer, smoother, better-mounted productions than this, but never one so exciting for Dylan Thomas, tasting success both raw and sweet.

That night affected his life in many ways. Whatever doubts he may have had about his ability to meet the new demands for his work were dispelled; to this day, it is the royalties from *Under Milk Wood* that provide much of the income for his estate. But there was also another, more personal, dimension. For the first time he collaborated closely with a woman other than Caitlin. Throughout their marriage, he often turned to her or his father, reading poems as they progressed, testing their reaction to subtle changes in words or emphasis, and this was an intimate part of their relationship that Caitlin treasured – but now there was Reitell, who helped him get the script ready on time, mulling over every detail, finding the cast and choosing the lighting so that the written page adapted fluently to the public stage.

Almost inevitably, Dylan and Liz fell in love, but they managed to keep it secret. Caitlin did not hear about it until after his death. It was just the kind of relationship she feared most. Caitlin could just about live with the thought of him having 'a drunken fuck'. After all, she had quite a few herself, but she dreaded him preferring the company of what she called 'those blue-stocking women', well-educated career women who were able to hold their own socially, which she was not. That was what troubled her most about Dylan's affair with Pearl Kazin, but this was worse; Liz Reitell now became not only Dylan's literary assistant and stage producer, but lover, mother and keeper. It was these last two roles that she would have the most difficulty fulfilling, and her failure eventually cost Dylan his life.

✳   ✳   ✳

The couple had almost a week to consolidate their new relationship. When he arrived in Boston to stay with Brinnin after a reading at Amherst on 20 May, Dylan talked openly of Liz with obvious happiness. Clearly she was already having a good effect, for he seemed happy and healthy and was no longer drinking. What Dylan did not say was that he was also under the care of Dr Feltenstein, who was giving him the twice-weekly injections of cortisone which, by lessening the pain in his toe, made him feel better and lifted his spirits.

Curiously, Thomas did mention his twice-weekly shots to Igor Stravinsky, whom he met in Boston on 22 May to discuss their working together on a new opera. Stravinsky was in Boston attending the première of his first such collaboration, *The Rake's Progress*, for which the libretto was written by W.H. Auden and Chester Kallman. Stravinsky thought the production a complete disaster, and when the audience began shouting his name during the curtain calls, he was outside in an alley behind the theatre, throwing up. Afterwards, he retired to his sick bed at the Sheraton Hotel and it was there that Thomas saw him. They took an immediate liking to each other, with Dylan nervously chain-smoking and complaining about his gout. Stravinsky recalled Dylan's exact words when he described the pain: 'But I prefer the gout to the cure; I'm not going to let a doctor shove a bayonet into me twice a week.' [8]

Stravinsky's memory was extraordinarily clear, and he described Thomas's appearance in clinical detail, saying he was short and fat with a face bloated and red, glazed eyes and a red nose, which Stravinsky thought was probably due to drinking. They drank whisky together and Dylan said he was worried about his wife and needed to hurry back to Wales 'or it would be too late'.

That same afternoon, Brinnin returned from teaching at the University of Connecticut at Storrs to find Dylan in ebullient spirits. He was excited by the immediate acclaim for *Under Milk Wood* and now here was the world's most famous living composer asking him to work in a new medium. Once again, fame and fortune lay just across the horizon and Dylan was sure his days of financial crisis were over.

This is another of those occasions where Brinnin's version of events differs crucially from those of an eye-witness. Brinnin had the details of the collaboration correct but never mentioned the sudden change in Dylan's appearance or the fact that he was getting regular shots of cortisone that were causing him some discomfort. Why did Stravinsky remember Dylan's complaint about gout when Brinnin did not? And why, for that matter, was Feltenstein's name not mentioned?

Thomas was so thrilled by meeting Stravinsky that he immediately wrote to Caitlin – the only substantial letter home from his third tour – and told her of his good news, promising to take her to stay at Stravinsky's home in Hollywood, which was being extended to accommodate them. All their travel would be first class and 'there'll be plenty of money', he said, the whole family then being able to go to Majorca the following winter.

Although the letter seemed loving enough, it was written for another reason, too. Thomas was letting her know he was staying on for a few more days in New York and would not be back in London before 3 June. Of course, there was no mention of Reitell or Feltenstein – and he also failed to say that despite the success of *Under Milk Wood* and his 20 readings, he would once again be returning home with almost no money.

✻   ✻   ✻

Thomas returned to New York from Boston for a final poetry reading and a performance of *Under Milk Wood* at the Kaufmann. On 26 May, he fell downstairs while leaving a dinner party with Reitell, on their way to see Arthur Miller's new play, *The Crucible*. Not realising Dylan had broken his arm, they took their seats at the theatre, only to be asked to leave when he began complaining about the pain during the performance. Liz decided they should consult a doctor, and they went to Feltenstein's surgery, where he set Dylan's left arm and wrist in a cast. The gout was also flaring up again, so Feltenstein gave Dylan a shot of cortisone and then a shot of morphine to relieve the pain.

Despite his now-fragile condition, Brinnin and Reitell both pressed Thomas to continue with his reading two nights later at the Kaufmann; after all, it was *their* reading, too. No doctor was consulted about the suitability of such a stressful event for so sick a man. He gave a 'beautiful performance', according to Brinnin, with his arm and cast in a black sling, but afterwards collapsed. Once again, no doctor was called to help him and no one took him to hospital. 'His face went chalk-white . . . Liz and I took him back to the Chelsea and put him to bed,' says Brinnin, who continued the story the next day as if he were present, which he was not.

Based on information relayed to him by Reitell, Brinnin insists that Thomas again saw Feltenstein, who 'found occasion to talk seriously with him about the general state of his health'.[9] All doctors have these kind of conversations with patients who are thought to be drinking too much. Dylan was told to cut back on alcohol and smoking, eat properly, take vitamins and sleep regularly – the same kind of advice he had been given since 1933. No explanation was offered for his latest collapse.

✻   ✻   ✻

Feltenstein later admitted privately that once he began treating Dylan for gout, gastritis, asthma and fatigue, he never considered any other diagnosis possible. Not until Dylan lay in a coma five months later in St Vincent's Hospital did Feltenstein begin to suspect he might have made a terrible diagnostic mistake, missing an occult disease such as diabetes as a complicating factor in Thomas's bouts of illness. Had Dylan Thomas been a more forthcoming patient Feltenstein might have uncovered the problem, but there was no way that he would challenge the integrity of his celebrity patient after being given free tickets for the première of *Under Milk Wood* and being told that here was the man who was the world's finest living poet.

10

The Summer of Their Ruin

Dylan Thomas returned from his third American tour physically shattered, with his arm in a sling, his wrist broken and his clothes soiled and crumpled. The day before he left New York, Dylan made a recording of his poems for Caedmon Records, the company formed by Barbara Holdridge and Marianne Mantell that has released his work on LP, cassette and CD for the last 40 years. 'His features were bloated, there was a cut over his eye, and his suit was smeared with what looked like vomit,' says Holdridge, who was alarmed by the way he stumbled through the recording, uttering a string of profanities that she was able to edit out. She still recalls the occasion well, and remembers wondering who was looking after him and why he was not in hospital.[1]

Even his closest friends assumed Dylan was drinking too much, not realising his speech became slurred after only one or two drinks. No one knew how ill he was. As always, he gave little away, but now he had much, much more to hide.

The plane touched down at Heathrow on 3 June, the day after the coronation of the Queen, and, instead of going straight to Margaret Taylor's house to join Caitlin, Dylan slipped down to the Oval to watch an afternoon's cricket.

His relationship with Caitlin was now more difficult than ever. She resented his success, frequently threatened to leave him, and yet remained wholly dependent upon him, not only pleading poverty but alternating between fearful headbanging rages and pathetic bursts of self-pity, accompanied by tearful pleading that *he* should not walk out on her and the children. A strange kind of jealousy seemed to be the main problem. Caitlin hated being left alone in Laugharne, and talked miserably of 'this filthy bog'. Ever since she discovered his letters from Pearl, she wondered where his infidelity might end, but there was also another, deeper, far more insidious side to her jealousy; she envied all the attention he was getting and, as if to prove that she was as good as he was, took to correcting his use of words or phrasing whenever they happened to be out together.

'That's not the way you say it,' she would snap if he was reciting a poem, choosing just the right moment to throw him off his stroke.

'I should bloody know – I wrote it,' he would snarl, triggering off another round of jeers and accusations – and yet, for all their constant squabbling and frequent bursts of violent anger, as with the husband and wife at war in *Who's Afraid of Virginia Woolf?*, Dylan was forever swearing his devotion and undying love. Even on that third American tour, when he was sleeping with Liz Reitell, Thomas would write:

> Caitlin my love three thousand miles away darling Cat you are so near. And your beautiful letter tore all the time and distance away and I was with you again, again in our bed with the beating seaweather.[2]

Letters like that would stream on for hundreds of words, and make joyous reading for everyone but Mrs Caitlin Thomas, who would open their envelopes with a sneer half-formed, muttering, 'Lies, lies, lies – more bloody lies. Of course, he's good with words. That's his gift. But it's always lies.'

Moral coward that he was, Dylan avoided these confrontations if he could. And on the day of his return to London, with the streets strewn with torn bunting and old newspapers and 'miles of cock-deep orange peel, nibbled sandwiches, broken bottles, discarded vests, vomit and condoms'[3] in the wake of the coronation, Thomas made his way across town to Margaret Taylor's home, where a party to celebrate the coronation was running into its second and third day. Everyone made a fuss of him, but he did not seem pleased to be back and, instead, complained that sitting in the sun at the Oval had given him sunstroke, 'and now I think it's turning into pleurisy'. This was an absurd claim and no one took any notice, least of all Caitlin, who carried on dancing and drinking until Margaret's tap ran dry and they caught the train to Wales.

'Poor Dylan,' wrote Caitlin.[4] 'When he got back to Laugharne he was exhausted. I blame myself for that. I made him stay on at the party all that time: he was dying to get home and have a complete rest, but I insisted on staying. I

The interior of Dylan's workshed, much as it was when he left it in October 1953
— and preserved thus in his memory

John Malcolm Brinnin at his home in Key West, Florida, 1996

The Kaufmann Auditorium in New York, where Dylan Thomas gave the readings that consolidated his reputation in the United States

Plaque in memory of Dylan Thomas at the Chelsea Hotel, West 23rd Street, New York

The Chelsea Hotel, where Dylan was given the fatal injection of morphine

The White Horse Tavern, Hudson Street, Dylan's favourite bar in New York

Peter and Florence Grippe, Orient
Point, New York, 1996

Peter Grippe's bust of
Dylan Thomas, circa 1952

St Vincent's Hospital, New York, where Dylan Thomas died

Dylan Thomas's personal physician in 1953: Dr Milton Darwin Feltenstein, as he was in 1931. He had Caitlin sent to a mental institution in a strait-jacket when she became extremely distressed at the bedside of her dying husband

Dr Joseph G. Chusid, Neurology
Attending Physician, St Vincent's
Hospital, New York, circa 1938

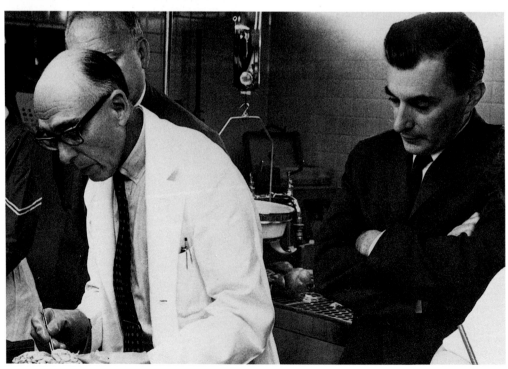

Dr William de Gutierrez-Mahoney, Chief of Neurosurgery and Neurology (left), and
Dr George Pappas at the weekly neuropathology brain-cutting session at St Vincent's
Hospital, circa 1955

Dave Slivka, the New York
sculptor who was a friend to
both Dylan and Caitlin

The bust of Dylan Thomas that
was made from his death mask by
Dave Slivka and Ibram Lassaw in
November 1953. It is now at the
Young Men's and Young Women's
Hebrew Association Poetry
Center in New York

A simple wooden cross marks the grave in St Martin's churchyard, Laugharne, where Dylan was buried in November 1953. Caitlin was buried with him in August 1994

wanted to have some fun. I'd been stuck in Laugharne for so long that I didn't want to see it ever again.'

She could see Dylan was suffering from 'an immense fatigue'. He barely talked to her at Margaret Taylor's party or on the journey home, and when they walked back into The Boat House she could sense he was neither happy to be back nor pleased to see the children. 'He didn't really become his old self again, though he still didn't think of going to a doctor,' she said.

✳ ✳ ✳

Dylan was now holding so much back from his wife that she did not know of his twice-weekly injections from Dr Feltenstein, how much money he was earning, who was commissioning his work, of the role fulfilled by Liz Reitell, or of his plans to return to New York in less than four months. This was more than just being secretive; he was now planning his life without her – and taking care not to provoke questions.

He may not have gone to see Dr Hughes in St Clears, but Dylan Thomas was certainly taking medical advice. He cut back on his drinking after consulting Feltenstein and sent away for a newspaper diet sheet.[5] However, he did not look well, with his arm still in a sling and the cut over his eye, and was probably still taking medications prescribed by Feltenstein. That summer, his blackouts became more frequent and lasted longer, and he also suffered headaches, especially at night, which only went away during the day after eating, with neither he nor Caitlin noticing the connection.

✳ ✳ ✳

In spite of his fragile health and usual money worries (caused by overspending rather than lack of earnings), Thomas managed to work exceptionally well. As a writer, his work was in high demand on both sides of the Atlantic – but it was as a performer and celebrity that he now earned the bulk of his income. He was luckier than most authors in one respect: his work could be sold over and over again.

When he read his own work on radio (and just once that summer on television), he was paid separate fees, firstly as performer, and secondly as the author. He also received fees and royalties if he recorded new material for Caedmon, earned extra fees when his radio work was published in both British and American magazines, and picked up nice little sums of cash on the side by selling rough drafts of each new piece of work to collectors. This helped make

129

him one of the highest-paid writers of his generation, but it was all a mystery to Caitlin, who had no idea where his money came from or where it went.

As demand for his work grew, he found himself with a backlog of projects in which he had lost interest – and a constant stream of new requests from BBC producers offering commissions, publishers wanting him to write books, magazines seeking articles or book reviews, and journalists hoping to interview him at home.

Instead of organising himself efficiently (if, indeed, he knew how to), Thomas allowed some projects to wither on the vine. *The American Diary* was never written and he was threatened with legal action by Allan Wingate. Similarly, he agreed a contract with the Oxford University Press to write a children's book, *Welsh Fairy Tales*, that also failed to come to fruition. And while he continued to work for the BBC in Wales, concern was expressed at higher levels of the BBC management in London that Mr Dylan Thomas was several years behind schedule with delivery of the script of *Under Milk Wood*, and had also failed to deliver a radio adaptation of the seventeenth-century play *The Plain Dealer* by William Wycherley and a television treatment of Ibsen's *Peer Gynt*, for which he had been partly paid in advance.

Several explanations have been suggested for Thomas's failure to finish these works on time. Most widely touted, notably by Ferris, was the theory that his powers were failing, but it seems more likely that the real problem was that he was taking on more work than he could handle now that his untreated diabetes was having a debilitating effect upon his general health. There is, in fact, compelling evidence that his creative powers were in good shape – but his health was not.

✿　✿　✿

Dylan Thomas was now a writer with an international reputation to protect, and for the first time in his life he consulted a solicitor. Having never owned a house or a car, or taken out any form of insurance, Thomas had not needed to seek legal advice before. All matters relating to his literary contracts were dealt with by his agent, David Higham (whom Thomas nicknamed 'Lavatory Brush' because of his wiry hair). The only occasions on which he ever felt the full majesty of the law was when a creditor served him with a writ – and he knew enough about those situations to realise that the time had come to find the money quickly, by hook or by crook, to remain two steps ahead of the bailiffs.

However, his status was now changing. During his third American tour, the US magazine *Time* described his lifestyle graphically:

> When he settles down to guzzle beer, which is most of the time, his incredible yarns tumble over each other in a wild Welsh dithyramb in which truth and fact become hopelessly smothered in boozy invention. He borrows with no thought of returning what is lent, seldom shows up on time, is a trial to his friends and a worry to his family.[6]

This was largely true, but for one key point. Whenever he was working, whether in his workshed, for the BBC, or undertaking an American lecture tour, Dylan Thomas was more punctilious than one might suppose. He might be late in keeping to deadlines for delivering manuscripts in which he had lost interest, but he was nearly always punctual in his public engagements and was immediately anxious lest this story might damage his reputation.

Instead of consulting one of the London firms that specialise in libel law, Thomas asked Daniel Jones if he knew a lawyer and Jones mentioned the name of Stuart Thomas, who was no relation but also attended Swansea Grammar School and went on to qualify as a solicitor, joining his father's firm, D.O. Thomas and Co. of Walter Road, Swansea. In considering this carefully (and all that follows later in this book), it is important to remember that Swansea was a relatively small town, far from London, and within its legal community the now-defunct practice of D.O. Thomas and Co was a small firm with little influence.

'Stuart always used to say he was a childhood friend of Dylan's, but this wasn't true,' Caitlin insisted. 'He was a friend of Dan's at school and Dylan didn't remember him at all. We never met him once socially in all the years we were married.'

As Stuart Thomas knew nothing whatever about the American laws of libel, the writ was served on *Time* at their London office. Had Dylan lived, the case would have come to court in Britain – but the editors of *Time* in New York decided to gather evidence to defend the action and hired a private detective, who tailed Dylan around New York when he returned in October for his fourth tour.[7]

✲ ✲ ✲

Dylan Thomas understood better than anyone that writing poetry 'wouldn't keep a goldfinch alive',[8] but also knew that it was for this that he would be remembered. 'I know I'm good,' he told Vernon Watkins when they met in Laugharne that July. 'I think I have written a lot of good poetry, but I don't think I've written great poetry. I think Mozart was both good and great.'[9] But it never came easily; there was 'no work in the world harder than making a poem', and it had taken him three weeks to get the first line right for *In the White Giant's Thigh*:

Through throats where many rivers meet, the curlews cry

and 160 pages of manuscript to complete his *Prologue* for the *Collected Poems*.[10]

Faced with so many demands upon him, Thomas put aside the *Elegy* he was writing in memory of his father and spent much of the summer of 1953 on projects that brought an immediate reward. There were offers coming in from all directions, and now the British press were beginning to give him the kind of attention he had been receiving in the United States for the past three years. The leading popular literary magazine of the day, *John O'London's Weekly*, devoted the whole of its front page and another page within to a biographical feature on him written by Mimi Josephson, 'Poet in The Boat House', illustrated with photographs of Dylan at his desk, The Boat House and Caitlin with Aeronwy and Colm.

Josephson went down to Laugharne for the interview, and found him 'dressed in an old tweed jacket, open-necked shirt, grey flannels and a pair of plimsolls; his usual attire for almost every occasion' with 'a passion for science fiction . . . engrossed in a paper-backed volume with a luridly coloured picture of spacemen on the cover'.

After running through the highlights of his career, which were not as familiar then as they are now, Josephson said he was revising *Under Milk Wood*, describing it as 'not exactly a verse play, although there is some verse in it. You'd better say it's prose with blood pressure.' He was also finishing the novel *Adventures in the Skin Trade* and planning to begin work shortly on another play for voices, *Two Streets*, 'which will include the love story of two people who live within a few blocks of each other, but don't meet until the end of the play'.[11]

In addition to these original, long-term projects, Thomas was also developing his ideas for the Stravinsky libretto,

The opera will describe the holiness of Earth which has been devastated leaving alive only one old man and his children. Visitors from another planet come to take the children away; and the old man, who alone remembers the beauty and mystery of Earth, tries to describe them to the visitors who were too young to know these things.[12]

and working on the structure of his film script for Michael Powell, the story of Ulysses, based upon Homer's *Odyssey*.

During July, he spent a week in Llangollen, North Wales, with Caitlin and Aeronwy and an old friend, Aneirin Talfan Davies, who worked at the BBC and commissioned him to write and read a radio talk on the International Eisteddfod. This gave Davies the opportunity to study Thomas at work: 'The week was spent in apparently aimless meanderings through the crowded streets of the town, occasional half-hours in the Eisteddfod marquee, and many hours standing at the bars of the far from few pubs in the town. Now and then, while standing at the bar, Thomas would tear open an empty cigarette carton, take out a stub of pencil from his pocket, and behind the shelter of a friendly pint he would scribble a few words, sometimes a single word, and deposit it in the depths of his capacious coat pocket. By the end of the week he had a harvest of these scribbled phrases. There was a moment of panic in the car on the way home when he thought he had lost these notes. His jottings were afterwards copied out onto a sheet of paper, and then the task of writing began. He spent the whole of Sunday and most of Monday at this work, and arrived at the studio about an hour before the broadcast with his talk carefully written out in his boyish hand.'[13]

That summer he also wrote one of his most popular short stories, *The Outing*, which he read live on BBC Television on 10 August (this was published in *The Listener* in Britain and by *Harper's Bazaar* in the United States). He also wrote the radio talks 'A Visit to America' and 'Laugharne', recording them for the BBC Wales Home Service before leaving for New York in October.

✵   ✵   ✵

Dylan was firming up his plans for a fourth American tour within days of returning home to The Boat House, centring them around two more performances of *Under Milk Wood* at the Poetry Center in October, his visit to Stravinsky and an international literary conference in Pittsburgh, where he was due to appear with some of the world's leading writers, among them Thomas Mann, Arthur Miller, Albert Camus, Ernest Hemingway, E.M. Forster, Thornton Wilder, William Faulkner and T.S. Eliot. 'With those boys' names, there must be money,' he said.[14]

Faced with temptations on this scale he had, as Caitlin put it in a letter to Oscar Williams and Gene Derwood, 'as good as given up writing for the actor's ranting boom and lisping mimicry' – and who could doubt that he lay in bed at night, wondering which way to turn, and whether or not to put one life behind him and start another. In truth, the marriage was dead – and Caitlin did not realise that he was now on the point of earning such huge sums of money that he could abandon them all if he wanted to and start a new life in the United States.

This new financial security was being offered by an agent and promoter in New York, Felix Gerstman, who said he would guarantee Thomas a minimum of $1,000 a week for future US lecture tours. This would have been enough to put his finances on a secure footing while he finished the novel, plays and film scripts already in the pipeline.

✳   ✳   ✳

Caitlin knew something was troubling him. Dylan tossed and turned in his bed at night, often lying awake in the darkness with the moonlight shining in through the window, but he would not tell her what was on his mind. She had no idea of the scale of his infidelity, but her suspicions were aroused. Caitlin did not know his affair with Pearl Kazin was over and no one, least of all Brinnin, told her that Dylan was now in love with Liz Reitell, using a London club as his postbox. She was helping him plan his itinerary in New York and sharing his medical secrets. To this day, Rose Slivka blames Brinnin for undermining the Thomases' marriage by implicitly encouraging the affair.

✳   ✳   ✳

Brinnin visited Laugharne again early in September 1953. *Under Milk Wood* was due to be published in the leading American women's magazine *Mademoiselle* and its editor, Cyrilly Abels, commissioned Brinnin to write a biographical feature on its author. He was accompanied by Rollie McKenna, who was going to take photographs to illustrate the feature.

It was now ten weeks since Dylan had returned home from his third American tour. He had recovered from the broken arm and wrist. The third cast was removed by Dr Hughes some time in July or early August, but Dylan still looked ill and bloated and there was a deep cut over his right eye, freshly scabbed, the result of a fall as he was walking home to The Boat House from Brown's Hotel.

The tension between him and Caitlin was now constant. A few days earlier, Thomas told Dan Jones, 'Last week I hit Caitlin with a plate of beetroot, and I'm still bleeding.'[15] Their misery was also observed by Gwen and Vernon

Watkins, who visited The Boat House and watched them screaming and shouting at each other over the right way to pronounce the word 'tear'.[16]

To the embarrassment of their friends, 'They screamed their own versions of the word back and forth, until Dylan, his face contorted, bawled, "But, for Christ's sake, the bloody word is *there* – I wrote it!" and seemed about to attack Caitlin. Aeronwy ran away and Colm began to scream; and both combatants were sullen and resentful, not speaking to each other for some time after that.'[17]

This was how their American visitors found them, too, poised on the edge of rage, with Dylan angry, morose and quiet, and Caitlin looking tough, thin, beautiful and alive, a cigarette permanently clenched between her lips. They soon noticed that Dylan behaved differently at home in West Wales, only drinking beer when he called in for a lunchtime game of cards at Brown's Hotel and not touching a drop the day he visited Llangain, Llanybri and Llansteffan to be photographed with his mother, visiting the church, chapels and cottages he had known since childhood. Dylan was much more wary in Caitlin's presence. Already, she was blaming Brinnin, and all Americans, for the tensions in their marriage.

The experience two years earlier, when Margaret Taylor intercepted the letters from Pearl Kazin addressed to the Savage Club, taught her how devious Dylan could be in keeping in touch with women. Now she knew, Caitlin was always suspicious. Instinct told her Brinnin was hiding something. But what? And who else besides Kazin? Brinnin refused to say, sidestepping all questions about Kazin, making no mention of Reitell's role in staging *Under Milk Wood*, but spending sufficient time alone with Dylan for Caitlin to wonder what the two men were discussing out of earshot. 'Typical bloody men,' was her response, believing that women always had a raw deal.

The depth of these tensions does not come through clearly in *Dylan Thomas in America*. Brinnin plays down some aspects of Dylan's health. Did he realise how much he was open to criticism for facilitating a fourth US tour so soon after the last? Did he knowingly withhold all that we have now established about Dylan's condition during the third tour? What persuaded him to encourage Thomas's affair with Reitell while also acting as a family friend to Caitlin? Had he not noticed a pattern emerging in Dylan's illnesses? Such questions come readily to mind when one rereads the Brinnin narrative, not because they are answered – but because Brinnin seems to anticipate them being asked.

Initially, Brinnin creates the impression he only went down to Laugharne as a friend who happened to be on holiday in Europe and did all he could to persuade Thomas to settle back into his writing routine and forget all about another American lecture tour for the next four or five years. This does not ring true. Brinnin knew that Dylan had been making plans for the fourth tour since early June; he knew all about the Stravinsky libretto and the offer from Felix Gerstman, and he could not have been unaware that the next performances of *Under Milk Wood* were taking place at the Poetry Center, since he was still its director.

Brinnin is careful not to go into any of this too deeply, and one can understand why. He was now caught between husband and wife, with Dylan hoping to raise enough money in New York to finance his visit to Stravinsky and Caitlin bitterly opposed to him going to the United States again so soon, and deeply suspicious of Brinnin's motives. 'I had the feeling that Dylan wanted to convince her that we were not engaged in any sort of complicity that might exclude or displease her,' said Brinnin, surely realising that this was precisely what he was doing.

Overall it was an unhappy visit for the Americans. Brinnin acquired the material for his essay accompanying publication of *Under Milk Wood* in *Mademoiselle* and McKenna took the photographs, but they both left Laugharne in no doubt that Caitlin resented their influence upon her husband – and yet was powerless to prevent him returning to New York.

McKenna's photographs of the family capture the mood. Only Caitlin or the children smile, but they all appear thoughtful, restrained and removed, posing together for group shots with no gestures of affection, no holding hands, no arms around shoulders, but a palpable feeling of sadness and alienation.

✳   ✳   ✳

Brinnin returned to New York and tried to make reservations for Dylan and Caitlin to travel by liner, but all the tickets were sold. He cabled Dylan to say he could fly over by plane to deliver his first readings at the Kaufmann on 24 and 25 October, with Caitlin travelling on the first available boat. That was fine for Dylan, but Caitlin felt brushed aside again and decided not to go. Intentionally or not, Brinnin drove another wedge between them. He never explained why he could not book flights for them both.

✳   ✳   ✳

And so the stage was set for Dylan Thomas's fourth visit to New York. Florence was against it because she thought he was ill. Caitlin was in a state of continual anger, knowing she was being elbowed aside – and the couple left Laugharne for the last time on 9 October 1953, with Dylan returning three times to the door of Pelican to kiss his mother goodbye.

11

And Then — the Final Casting of the Dice

Wearing one of his heavy tweed suits with a woollen scarf wrapped tightly around his neck, Dylan Thomas stepped off the plane at Idlewild Airport, complaining about the heat and thirsting for a drink. Liz Reitell was waiting for him but refused to accompany him to the airport bar which was being picketed during a trade union dispute. Socialist though he professed to be, Thomas would have cheerfully crossed the picket line in search of another pick-me-up, but Reitell was made of sterner stuff.

'No,' she said. 'We can't do *that!*'

'All right,' said Thomas, 'but only for you and the Rights of Man.'

As they left the airport for the taxi-ride into Greenwich Village, he told her of his miserable days in London waiting for the muddle over the plane tickets to be sorted out, with Caitlin constantly complaining about her lot. 'It was the worst week of my entire life,' said Thomas, as he went on to give a comic account of the journey.

Roaring drunk after visiting the home of his ancestors, an Irish-American priest joined the plane when it stopped at Shannon to pick up passengers and became so noisily offensive that the airline steward closed the bar. According to Brinnin, whose account was based on what Thomas told Reitell, 'without liquor he soon had an attack of delirium tremens, and finally had to be bound and shut in the men's room. He was kept prisoner there until, at Gander (Newfoundland), he was taken off the plane in the care of a physician.'

This is the first time in his narrative that Brinnin uses the words 'delirium tremens', and it is important to note that either he or Dylan (or both) misapplied them. It would have been clinically impossible for the priest to have had delirium tremens so soon after being roaring drunk. The human body does not work in that way, and all the story probably amounts to is that the priest became such a nuisance that he was strapped in one of the strait-jackets planes carry in case something like this happens in order to protect the aircraft and the other passengers.

Brinnin suggests Thomas was shaken by what he had seen, but it is much more likely that with his droll sense of humour Thomas was turning the anecdote into black comedy, which was how he had been entertaining his drinking buddies since his teens. For this story, as for much else in *Dylan Thomas in America*, Brinnin's only source was Liz Reitell, whose memory of events changed with each new telling. We have been able to establish where she went wrong in her account of Thomas's last days in New York, but have been unable to challenge her ourselves as she is now living in a residential home in Montana, suffering from dementia.

✶   ✶   ✶

After taking the taxi into Greenwich Village, Thomas booked into the Chelsea Hotel only to find that because he was several days late in arrival, the management had given his room to someone else. Instead of a large, spacious room overlooking 23rd Street, he found himself tucked away in a tiny room at the back of the building. This upset him enormously, and he kept saying so throughout the evening as they walked down to Seventh Avenue for a drink at the Silver Rail and then booked into a Spanish restaurant for supper.

'He was in a sober and serious mood,' says Brinnin, recounting how at the end of a long day, having travelled against the clock, Thomas joined the cast he had worked with four months earlier to rehearse his revised version of *Under Milk Wood*. This went well and he and Reitell repaired to the White Horse, where they talked until 2 a.m. before returning to the Chelsea.

The following morning, the couple were walking through Greenwich Village when Dylan spotted a poster for the new Tony Curtis film *Houdini*, based on the life of the famous escapologist, magician and star of silent movies.

'He's always fascinated me,' said Thomas, talking about the dangers and skills of attempting stunts that could only end in death if something went wrong, and drawing a parallel with one of his current projects, probably a reference to the underlying idea of *Adventures in the Skin Trade*. 'This is really the story of an escape artist,' he said.

'Autobiographical?' asked Reitell.

'You know me too well,' said Thomas, whose unfinished novel described his misadventures when moving to London for the first time.

That afternoon, after drinking alone at Julius's, Thomas said he felt unwell. This was no more than what we would now call jet lag, for by travelling against the clock and then staying up all the previous day in New York, he had gone 40 hours without proper sleep before finally crashing down some time around 2.30 a.m. 'I think I'd better go back to the hotel and rest,' he said, and Liz accompanied him, sitting by him through the afternoon and early evening before going out to a delicatessen to buy their supper.

Thomas slept well that night (21 October), right through until late the following morning, when he appeared much healthier. There was another rehearsal of *Under Milk Wood* during the afternoon and that evening the couple caught a taxi down to Sixth Avenue for an 'enormous dinner' at Herdt's. He was talking animatedly, saying what a relief it was to be in New York after that terrible week in London. It is clear from Brinnin's account that Reitell did not spend the night with him and did not see Thomas again until they met for lunch at a seafood restaurant on the Friday (23 October).

Something happened to him on the night of 22 October, unknown to either Brinnin or Reitell – for she arrived at the restaurant to find him distressed and angry, refusing to eat the food that was ordered. Later that afternoon various friends either turned up or were invited to his room at the Chelsea, where he soon became very drunk. When Reitell phoned him, his speech was slurred and she immediately rushed over from the Poetry Center and broke up the party.

Why had he been unable to face food at lunchtime? And why did drink affect him so quickly? Could it be, as we suspect, that this secretive man slipped off on his own on the Thursday evening in search of company and ended up taking something that affected both his palate and his ability to absorb alcohol? Knowing as we do that Thomas had experimented with opium in Persia, made strange references to drug-taking to Gwen and Vernon Watkins and readily took both barbiturates and sleeping pills, it seems likely that there were now drugs in his bloodstream. He probably drifted down that night into Greenwich Village. But what drugs was he offered? And where did he get them?

✻ ✻ ✻

After a few hours' rest, Thomas was sober enough to make some last-minute revisions to the script of *Under Milk Wood*, having found many minor errors in the duplicated typescript that Cleverdon's secretary had prepared at the BBC, and that evening went to another rehearsal at the Poetry Center. Suddenly, without touching a single drink, he collapsed, suffering from hot and cold flushes, falling into a deep and instant sleep.[1] On waking, he was persuaded to eat and given brandy before staggering out on stage for the last 20 minutes of rehearsal, when he collapsed again, this time with nausea and vomiting.

One friend who was there that night was the architect Herb Hannum, who later became Reitell's third husband. 'I can't do anything more,' Thomas told Hannum. 'I'm too tired to do anything. I can't eat, I can't drink – I'm even too tired to sleep . . . I've seen the gates of hell tonight. Oh, but I do want to go on – for another ten years, anyway. But not as a bloody invalid. I'm too sick too much of the time.' After sleeping for a few minutes, Thomas opened his eyes and said, 'Tonight in my home town the men have their arms around one another, and they are singing.' He clearly knew it was Friday, the day men received their pay packets and went down to Brown's Hotel, the Cross House or the Corporation Arms to play darts, have a few drinks and end the evening singing like angels.

Reitell and Hannum took Thomas back to the Chelsea, and she stayed with him through much of the night, not going back to her apartment until he was fast asleep. The next morning, Hannum and Thomas went to the Chelsea Chop House for breakfast.

'How long have you been this way?' asked Hannum.

'Never this sick,' said Thomas. 'Never this much before. After last night and now this morning, I've come to the melancholy conclusion that my health is totally gone. I can't drink at all. I always could, before . . . but now most of the time I can't even swallow beer without being sick. I tell myself that if I'd only lay off whisky and stick to beer I'd be all right . . . but I never do.'

The conversation, reported by Brinnin who was not present, shows Thomas in a maudlin state of mind, sorry for himself, appealing for sympathy, not always making sense, saying he sometimes drank 'in a mad hurry' when there was no reason to hurry at all and had felt 'as sick as death' on the plane from London.

'I know I've had a lot of things wrong with my body lately, especially the past year or so. Since I was 35 I've felt myself getting harder to heal. I've been warned by doctors . . . but I could never really believe them . . . or maybe I did believe it, but couldn't accept it.'

✫   ✫   ✫

From Brinnin's account, it is clear that Thomas should have seen a doctor on the night of Friday 23 October. It would have been better to have taken him to hospital. Instead, his friends at the Poetry Center administered brandy, took him back to the Chelsea and began worrying about his condition on the morning of Saturday 24 October.

Not being medically trained, they did not know that his collapses from fatigue and exhaustion, the mood swings which accompanied them, and the scene in the seafood restaurant followed by him suddenly appearing drunk after just a few drinks were all indicative of great swings in his metabolism and vacillations in his sugar levels. As before, they assumed it was all due to alcohol, and when they persuaded him to go back to Dr Feltenstein on that Friday, this was his assumption, too – because that was what they told him.

In fact, one can establish from many sources – not least Brinnin's own account – that Thomas had been drinking far less since his third tour, but his mood swings ranged from depression to rage and were accompanied by complaints that he could not eat, drink or sleep. All these symptoms indicate his blood sugar levels were out of control because so little insulin was being supplied by his pancreas. Whenever he collapsed and started vomiting, this was a classic prodrome of a diabetic crisis which at any time might push the patient into a diabetic coma.

✵   ✵   ✵

By now Dylan Thomas was not only a celebrity patient under Dr Feltenstein's care, but one whom the doctor thought he wholly understood. Instead of taking blood and urine tests or having him admitted to hospital for observation, Feltenstein gave him a shot of cortisone and (as he had done during the third tour, although this is not recorded by Brinnin) a prescription for benzedrine.

Feltenstein still thought he was treating Thomas for gout, gastritis and alcoholism and, basically, blamed alcohol for all Thomas's problems. His use of benzedrine and cortisone was a serious medical mistake based on confusing the symptoms of diabetes with those of alcoholism.

Having used cortisone and benzedrine with so many other patients, Feltenstein unwittingly assumed the role of a 'Dr Feelgood', prescribing 'quickfix' drugs without taking proper precautions. With those patients who were simply alcoholic, such solutions often worked, but they had a catastrophic effect upon Dylan Thomas. His blood sugar bounced up and down on a daily, sometimes hourly, basis. Reitell says he was buoyant after cortisone shots, and this was a common reaction. Cortisone temporarily drove the blood sugar up by stimulating the liver to release its limited supply of glucose. That did a diabetic like Thomas no good at all, because he needed the blood sugar for energy but was incapable of making use of it because cortisone also depressed his insulin.

Benzedrine was another wonder drug in the early '50s, having been developed in Nazi Germany during the Second World War. Many high-ranking officials, including Hitler, Goering and Goebbels, became benzedrine addicts, or 'speed freaks', and the drug was also widely prescribed for soldiers and airmen during prolonged battle conditions. After the war, benzedrine was taken to the United States. Exactly like cortisone, benzedrine created a hypermetabolic state in the body where all organ systems operated far beyond their normal levels. Fantastic amounts of energy became available and great physical feats were possible because of this hypermetabolism. Benzedrine enabled those who took it to stay awake for days on end, with a heightened sense of their environment. However, when the drug wore off, even a normal body crashed with exhausted levels of sugar and insulin. This was the precipice upon which Dylan Thomas stood on Saturday 24 October, when he was given the injection and the prescription for benzedrine.

✲ ✲ ✲

That Saturday afternoon, Brinnin travelled down from Boston and arrived at the Kaufmann to find Thomas attending the final rehearsal of *Under Milk Wood*, which was being performed for the first time in its revised form that evening. As the lights came on, Brinnin was horrified by Thomas's appearance. 'His face was lime-white, his lips loose and twisted, his eyes dulled, gelid and sunk in his head,' said Brinnin, adding, with a touch of hyperbole, 'He showed the countenance of a man who has been appalled by something beyond comprehension.'[2] Not so. What was really happening was that Thomas's body was failing to cope with cortisone or benzedrine (or probably both) flowing through his bloodstream at the same time.

Throughout that night's performance, Thomas continued to look unnaturally pale, and when he went on to a party at Rollie McKenna's apartment, he declined every offer of drinks. When asked why he was being so abstemious, Thomas said, as if a new joke had come to mind, 'It's just that I've seen the gates of hell, that's all' – which suggests that he, too, was blaming drink, rather than the drugs he had taken, for his condition. The party continued into the early hours of the morning, and as the effect of the drugs wore off, Thomas became chattily cheerful and began amusing them all with funny stories.

The following day, Sunday 25 October, Thomas was in sparkling form when he appeared in a matinée performance of *Under Milk Wood*, although by then his relationship with Brinnin was becoming strained. Thomas wanted to earn more money than Brinnin could provide and was on the point of signing his long-term contract with Felix Gerstman. Brinnin could feel himself being elbowed aside and Reitell, still Brinnin's assistant, was torn in her loyalties.

After the matinée, Thomas and Reitell went to a party at Sutton Place where, according to Brinnin, a friend procured Thomas 'a handsome refugee countess' – and 'after gulping down one tumbler of Irish whiskey after another . . . [he] became boisterous and brawling, and shortly disappeared for hours with her into the upper regions of her large town house'.[3] This is a strange story that has never been independently verified. The name of 'the countess' has also not been disclosed. Brinnin maintains that it brought Thomas's affair with Reitell to a sudden and painful end.

By this point in his narrative, Brinnin was becoming tearful. He was losing his seat on the celebrity chariot. There would be no future role for him and he was trying to convince himself that Dylan was as distressed as he was – which was unlikely, for Thomas was not a sentimental man when it came to making money or preserving relationships. There is one acutely embarrassing page[4] in which Brinnin describes himself weeping and Thomas trying to comfort him, putting his 'strong arms about me' – and it is only by searching through the text that one discovers this was the last time John Malcolm Brinnin met Dylan Thomas.

✳   ✳   ✳

Despite hinting that Thomas spent several hours in a bedroom with 'the countess', it also becomes clear from the Brinnin narrative that Reitell and Thomas were barely together when the Sutton Place party ended. They caught a taxi back to Greenwich Village, dropping Brinnin at Grand Central Station so he could catch a late train to Boston.

'Would you like to come to the White Horse?' asked Thomas, but she declined, asking to be dropped off at her own apartment.

'I used to have a friend who lived near here,' said Thomas petulantly.

'You still do,' said Reitell, as Thomas was driven off, determined to end the night with a few drinks in his favourite bar. According to Brinnin, a friend there 'loaned' Thomas a woman for the night – but that too is not independently verified.

✲   ✲   ✲

With their affair apparently at an end, Reitell's role reverted to that of nurse and semi-secretary. She had no contact with Thomas until midway through the following afternoon, Monday 26 October, when he phoned from the Algonquin bar, where he was already drunk, saying he missed her 'terribly'. She joined him there and found him talking gibberish to a Dutchman, telling stories about his war exploits (of which he had none), with fantasies about blood, death, burning and mutilation. A waiter tried to calm him down and when Reitell held his hand, Thomas began sobbing. As they left the hotel, he 'spoke four-letter words loudly with complete disregard for who might hear them' and pulled faces at passers-by, before steering her into a cinema on 42nd Street where he happily sat through a double-bill, a western and a thriller, for the next three or four hours.

Later, they went to another bar in Greenwich Village, Goody's, where Thomas told her, 'I'm really afraid I'm going mad. There's something terribly wrong with my mind. Perhaps it's sex, perhaps I'm not normal – perhaps the analysts could find out.'

Something was markedly different about Thomas's behaviour throughout the day. At times he seemed to stumble, and his outbursts were disjointed. The thought that he should have seen a doctor does not seem to have crossed Reitell's mind, for she accompanied him to the White Horse Tavern some time after midnight, where he was 'too distressed and ill to stay for more than a few minutes', and then left him at the Chelsea, promising to phone in the morning.

Ravings, bizarre behaviour, confusion, mood swings, despair and a stumbling gait were not the ways Thomas behaved when drunk. Usually (and this has been verified from many sources) he would become boisterous, telling stories and sometimes picking fights (which he invariably lost), and then, if he really had drunk more than he could handle, Thomas tended to sink into silence, turning morose while the fun continued without him.

On this occasion, his reaction to drink was out of character, which leads us to suppose that his blood sugar levels were now fluctuating so widely that his brain as well as his cerebellum was being affected by his diabetes. Diabetic cerebellar degeneration; periods of low blood pressure, diabetic peripheral nerve degeneration and vitamin B12 deficiency could all have affected his gait and the ability to walk smoothly.

Ironically, this was one of the few days on this fourth tour when his alcoholic intake was high. Mostly he was far more abstemious, often going without drink at all for many hours at a time, indicating that he thought cutting back would help him. The fact that he was getting sicker suggests that the course of cortisone and benzedrine that had begun on 23 October was pushing his diabetes into more and more danger.

✵ ✵ ✵

The next day was Tuesday 27 October – his 39th birthday. Always a curiously superstitious man, Thomas attached great significance to birthdays, writing one of his most famous works, *Poem in October*, to mark his '30th year to heaven', and *Poem on his Birthday* to celebrate his return to Laugharne and moving into The Boat House during his 'driftwood 35th wind turned age'.

Now here he was, alone at the Chelsea, 3,000 miles away from home, as conscious as ever that for the last 20 years he had been telling anyone who would listen that he would 'never make 40'. There is no evidence that he was suicidal, but Dylan Thomas was undoubtedly depressed. There had been that 'worst week' of his life in London and Caitlin's constant threats to leave him, and even as he sat in his hotel room there was a letter from her on its way, saying not just that the marriage was over, but that she did not know whether to kill herself or 'go on the streets':

> . . . nothing will ever make me go near you again. I knew you were abysmally weak, drunken, unfaithful, and a congenital liar, but it has taken me longer to realise that on top of each one of these unpardonable vices, you are a plain, stingy, meany as well . . . After this dose of concentrated humiliating ignominy, I am, once and for all, finished . . .
>
> There is, without exception, no wife in the whole of creation treated like I am, and at last it's over, for better or for worse. And no more slop talk, let's at least cut that out – you may be good at it, but it stinks to high heaven, turn it on one of your new adulators, it always goes down. Whatever you do or say, however foul, always goes down, fuck you.[5]

Without seeing the letter, Thomas must have known what was on her mind. Caitlin would not have written like that without reaching the end of her tether during that final week in London. And now here he was, mentally anguished and undoubtedly ill, but taking no one into his confidence. Had he told Reitell when they met for breakfast, or Howard Moss whom he met for a birthday drink at the White Horse Tavern, how unwell he must have felt, they could have taken him to hospital; it was not too late.

Instead, Thomas struggled to attend a party that evening organised by Dave and Rose Slivka to mark the occasion, said he felt sick and was driven back to the Chelsea, accompanied by Reitell. There, so Brinnin tells us, he fell upon his bed, crying, 'What a filthy, undignified creature I am' – which is a little too close for comfort to Charles Laughton's dialogue in *The Hunchback of Notre Dame*. This is another problem with Brinnin's reportage. On several occasions such as this, he reports an incident deadpan without realising how often Thomas, with his extraordinary knowledge of films and literature and sense of black comedy, amused himself by playing games with words.

✲ ✲ ✲

On Wednesday 28 October, Thomas had two engagements which he fulfilled cheerfully and well – reading his poetry to the City College of New York and then going on to participate in a symposium on film art, organised by the arts group Cinema 16, with the celebrated playwright Arthur Miller and the avant-garde filmmaker Maya Deren. He drank intermittently during the day, but there was no bizarre behaviour, raving, mood swings or difficulty walking. There was, however, a distinct coolness between him and Reitell. Arthur Miller has told us that Thomas was treating her with indifference while Reitell laughed inappropriately, trying unsuccessfully to impress people with her importance to him. He seemed sad and introspective, while she was a shadow in the background.[6]

The next day, Thursday 29 October, Brinnin claims that Thomas met 'the countess' for lunch and 'dallied through most of the afternoon with her in her town house', before accompanying Reitell to dinner with Cyrilly Abels and her husband Jerome Weinstein. The other guests were the writer Santha Rama Rau and her husband. On this occasion, too, Thomas was clearly in good spirits, for he and Rau entertained them all with ghost stories.

Reitell went off to work at the Poetry Center in the morning (Friday 30 October), having arranged to join Thomas for dinner at the home of Ruthven Todd, the poet, where he spent much of the evening engaged in a long literary discussion. Afterwards, Reitell and Hannum joined him at the White Horse Tavern for the last drink or two of the day. By then it was 2 or 3 a.m., the time he usually wound up there. There was nothing untoward in his demeanour, having drunk nothing but beer all evening, and they all said good night quite happily.

On the Saturday morning (31 October), Thomas arranged to take Reitell and another woman for a 'pleasant, even merry' lunch at Luchow's restaurant in Manhattan, before moving on for a few drinks at Costello's on Third Avenue and dinner with Harvey Breit. No one saw him any the worse for wear and he cheerfully arranged to meet Reitell and her friend back at Costello's at 11 p.m. – but failed to turn up.

The next morning, he phoned Reitell complaining of 'a real horror' of a hangover, saying that all he could remember was taking a dislike to a woman and throwing her out of a taxi, which sounds improbable. Brinnin had no idea what had happened to Thomas that night, and the evening would have remained as much a mystery as the night of 22 October but for the fact that *Time* magazine was employing a private detective to tail Thomas around New York, gathering evidence to defend themselves against his libel action.

At 9 p.m. that evening, the detective found Thomas at the White Horse Tavern, not with Harvey Breit but with Dave Slivka, the American writer David Lougee and two other companions. Thomas was already drunk and the detective noted him rapidly working through glasses of lager, whisky and beer. As the evening wore on, the party adjourned to Toppers restaurant on Seventh Avenue, where Thomas began regaling them all with his repertoire of sexual stories – of the night he lost his virginity in the back of a lorry, of the dose of 'the clap' he caught in London (and managed to keep secret from his mother), and so on. Eventually, his tone became more maudlin (as it usually did), and at 2.30 a.m. the detective observed him taking benzedrine. This explains why he had such a 'real horror' of a hangover – but how much benzedrine had he taken? And how often did he wash benzedrine down with alcohol to give himself a lift at the end of a tiring day?

✻   ✻   ✻

Food was what Thomas needed. His eating had been erratic since he had arrived in New York on 19 October, and although there are various references to him going out to dinner, these invariably sound like buffets where the main attraction was drink – and more often than not whisky, which did him no good at all. Most days his pick-me-up would be raw eggs and beer (as it was on the morning of Sunday 1 November), but this was not an adequate food supply and there is no evidence of him eating a full meal since his dinner at Herdt's restaurant ten days earlier.

Throughout much of that Sunday Thomas sat at his usual table at the White Horse Tavern, drinking with friends made on his previous tours, and in the evening he moved on to yet another party, this time in Central Park West, where Brinnin reports he was 'drunk, unstrung [and] messy in behaviour', pursuing a young dancer around the room until they fell awkwardly, leaving the girl in need of medical care for concussion. Whether Thomas was as drunk as Brinnin suggests is unclear, for later that evening, some time after midnight, Howard Moss invited several of the guests back to his apartment where they talked and listened to music.

Reitell was still with him, and made much of the fact that Thomas said, 'I just saw a mouse. Did you see it?' This had been another of his party jokes for the past 20 years, one of his excuses for crawling across the floor and trying to see if the mouse had run up a woman's leg. This was another situation where Brinnin, who was still in Boston, missed the whole point of the story. 'Dylan was obviously so distraught that Liz said yes, she had seen it, and he seemed relieved,' Brinnin reported.[7]

It seems more likely that Thomas was trying to keep the party's spirits up, for he readily agreed to give a spontaneous reading, not only of his own works but also those of Yeats and Auden, lasting over an hour. The party did not break up until 5 a.m. and he returned to the Chelsea with his eyeball hurting after scratching it on a thorn when he walked out onto the terrace of Moss's apartment to get some fresh air.

The next morning (Monday 2 November), Thomas was suffering from so great a hangover 'that he was unable to leave his bed'. This begs the question: had he again taken benzedrine to give himself the energy to recite poetry for an hour in the middle of the night and stay up drinking until 5 a.m.? It would be surprising if he had not, for we know he had the pills, and the evidence of the *Time* detective confirms that Thomas had done just that only 24 hours earlier.

✳   ✳   ✳

Monday 2 November was 'a long and painful day for Dylan Thomas and Reitell nursed him through it, trying hard to persuade him not to leave the Chelsea that evening to attend the unveiling of a statue of the Scottish philanthropist Sir Thomas Lipton at the Wildenstein Gallery. Thomas was determined to go, but did not know what to wear. His pace had been so hectic during the past two weeks that he had not been able to organise his laundry. All his socks and shirts were dirty and his suits were soiled, probably with vomit.

A friend took him to a bargain clothes store in Greenwich Village, where Thomas acquired an ill-fitting, baggy suit. He managed to find a shirt that was almost wearable in the laundry basket, and arrived at the distinctly upmarket

Wildenstein Gallery to see his sculptor friend Frank Dobson's latest work dressed like a refugee and wearing no socks. Once the ceremony was over, he and Reitell moved on with the publicist Ben Sonnenberg to the equally opulent Colony restaurant, with Thomas not the slightest bit concerned by his appearance. There, he had a brief conversation with the Nobel Prize-winning author William Faulkner before ending the day at Costello's.

Once again very little food passed his lips, and when they went back to the Chelsea at midnight, armed with a bag of delicacies from a delicatessen, all Thomas could manage was a bowl of soup.

✳   ✳   ✳

Tuesday 3 November was presidential election day in the United States, always an occasion for parties and celebrations, and Reitell was anxious that Thomas should not start drinking too soon and miss the night's excitement. There was little fear of that, certainly in the morning and early afternoon, for his new American lecture agent Felix Gerstman was due at the Chelsea with the contract guaranteeing him $1,000 a week. At last, his financial future looked secure. There would always be fees and royalties and advances from publishers or film companies against delivery of commissioned manuscripts, but now all this was underpinned by a guaranteed income for his US tours.

Thomas studied the contract, checked the wording of clauses, signed it and exchanged small talk before Gerstman's departure, and then lay back on his bed to rest. According to Brinnin, who was still in Boston, Thomas 'seemed exhausted, preoccupied and morbidly depressed' – but not enough to deter him from spending the evening with Santha Rama Rau, her husband and their small son, and the theatre producer Cheryl Crawford. He drank very little before going on with Liz Reitell to meet Frank Dobson at his hotel.

The previous night, he and Dobson had arranged to see the play *Take a Giant Step*, but now Thomas felt too exhausted and withdrew apologetically, returning with Reitell to the Chelsea Hotel, where he immediately fell asleep. She sat by the bed while he tossed and turned, speaking fretfully between bouts of sleep about the misery of his existence, his youngest son Colm ('I can't bear the thought that I'm not going to see him again') and Caitlin ('You have no idea how beautiful she is. There is an illumination about her . . . she shines.'). Thomas enjoyed wallowing, and one cannot tell from the Brinnin/Reitell description whether this was yet another appeal for sympathy or a genuine cry for help.

'You don't have to die,' said Reitell, assuming the role of Mother Confessor for which she was, unfortunately, ill cast.

This agonised conversation continued until 2 a.m. when Thomas suddenly arose from his bed, saying, 'I've got to have a drink. I've got to go out and have a drink. I'll come back in half an hour . . .' She begged him not to go and an argument broke out between them, causing Reitell to burst into tears and refuse to go with him. She sat waiting until approximately 3.30 a.m. when Thomas walked back into the room, announcing with bravura the now-famous words: 'I've had 18 straight whiskies. I think that's a record.' According to Brinnin, he then sank to his knees, reached out his arms and fell into her lap, saying, 'I love you . . . but I'm alone,' before falling fast asleep.

✼   ✼   ✼

Whether or not he really did drink 18 straight whiskies is a moot point. It seems unlikely, for Ruthven Todd later retraced Thomas's steps and discounted the claim, while an eye-witness who saw Thomas that night at the White Horse Tavern, the artist John CuRoi, gave a totally different explanation:

> I had taken a table near the window of the back room for my wife and self on the way home from another activity. Dylan was seated at a table with a few academic types, one of whom was an Asian; one of whom looked like a tart. Dylan's eyes were unfocused, he swayed in his chair. His colour was horrifying. The man seemed a monster puppet. His condition was clearly a source of amusement and contempt to his companions. The 'tart' progressively dipped thin cigars in one of the eight highballs before him and slid them into his mouth. She finished with three in his mouth. I thought, now all that's needed is a red robe, a crown of thorns and the final casting of dice.[8]

From this description, especially the reference to his eyes being unfocused and the 'horrifying' colour of his skin, it seems more than probable that when Thomas arose from his bed and went out into the night, he took more benzedrine, just as he had on other nights, hoping that this would give him the usual lift – which it might have done had there not been so much else in his system.

The next morning he complained of suffocating, and tried to pick himself up with two beers after walking to the White Horse Tavern. Whether or not he also drank raw eggs is not recorded, but when he returned to the Chelsea, Reitell insisted on calling Feltenstein, who came to the apartment. After being told by Reitell of the 18 straight whiskies, Brinnin reports that Feltenstein 'gave him

151

medications that would relieve his suffering'. Brinnin does not say what they were, but we have established that Feltenstein later admitted injecting Thomas with morphine and cortisone, having been given additional (and false) information by Reitell that Thomas suffered from delirium tremens.

The starting dose for treating delirium tremens was one-eighth to one-sixteenth of a grain of morphine, the equivalent of four to eight milligrammes, according to Dr Lehrman. This was used to sedate the patient, while the cortisone was supposed to improve his spirits after rest.

The first injections were given around midday on Wednesday 4 November. Thomas slept throughout much of that afternoon, waking with 'another severe attack of nausea and vomiting'.[9] Reitell again phoned Feltenstein, who returned to the Chelsea between 5 p.m. and 7 p.m. and gave Thomas second injections of both morphine and cortisone.

With Thomas now fading in and out of consciousness, Reitell and Feltenstein harangued him about his over-drinking, not eating enough food and getting insufficient sleep. Telling him he had 'to begin immediately on a regime of medical attention', Feltenstein prescribed a diet and Reitell went out to buy some food for supper. When she returned, Thomas seemed no better so, at her request, Feltenstein went back to the Chelsea between 8 p.m. and 10 p.m.

This time, Reitell again insisted that Thomas was suffering from delirium tremens and was 'seeing not animals . . . abstractions, triangles, squares and circles'.[10] With Thomas begging to be 'put out', and believing his earlier injections of morphine had not quite done the trick, Feltenstein prepared a third injection, this time increasing the dosage to half a grain. This was the equivalent of over 30 milligrammes and was enough not only to send Thomas to sleep but to put him into an irreversible coma by totally suppressing his brainstem's ability to control his breathing.

Jack Heliker, the painter, called at the apartment and sat with Reitell while Thomas drifted in and out of consciousness. When Reitell said she knew someone who saw white mice and roses when suffering from delirium tremens, Thomas asked playfully, 'Roses plural, or Rose's roses with an apostrophe?' – which indicates his mind was still lively even as the morphine was beginning to take effect upon his nervous system.

Moments later, his hand stiffened and his face turned blue. For the fourth time in 12 hours Reitell phoned Feltenstein, who rushed over from Grammercy Park to find his patient no longer breathing. An ambulance was called.

✻   ✻   ✻

Even if he had drunk six or seven whiskies rather than 18, as Ruthven Todd concluded, such an amount of alcohol would have metabolised within four to six hours. Modern textbooks of pharmacology attest to the scientific basis for the body's ability to metabolise 30 millilitres or one ounce of whisky in an hour. Thomas's body would have been free of alcohol long before Feltenstein's injections and the ease with which he played with the pun on 'Rose's roses' shows he was not in the violently disturbed, uncontrollable state of a man with delirium tremens.

It can be said with certainty that Dylan Thomas did not die of 'an acute alcoholic intoxication of the brain' or, as it was also described at the time, 'an acute insult to the brain'. Nor was he suffering from delirium tremens, which only begins between 48 and 72 hours after the last drink. With DTs there is always mental confusion, and hallucinations occur, not of abstract, geometric shapes, but of bugs or animals such as snakes crawling up the walls or up the patient's body. The patient may also think he sees family or friends who are not there and tries to converse with them, sometimes picturing himself somewhere else, such as a country store known in childhood. As he becomes more and more agitated, there is often fever and the heart beats faster, accompanied by profuse, uncontrolled sweating. 'The patient picks at the bedclothes or stares wildly about and intermittently shouts at or tries to fend off hallucinated people.'[11]

No such symptoms were exhibited by Dylan Thomas, yet Feltenstein stepped up the morphine injections, largely on the word of Reitell — and for the rest of his life he refused to discuss an error that could have been avoided if only he had insisted upon taking blood and urine samples when he first met his patient. To another patient, Howard Moss, Feltenstein admitted giving Thomas morphine because he was 'in pain', and the fact that this last dose was half a grain can be verified. Forty-four years later, the fact remains clearly stated in the Admissions Record at St Vincent's Hospital.

12

Back from the Brink of Death

D
r William McVeigh, a second-year medicine resident from New York University, was on call in the emergency room at St Vincent's Hospital on the night of 4 November 1953. The emergency room was on the ground floor of the hospital, located between 11th and 12th Streets in West Village. The Wednesday night was quiet. There were two admissions: an old man with a suspected heart attack and an elderly woman suffering from dehydration after falling down in her apartment and breaking her arm.

Unlike some New York University residents who did not enjoy working at the charity hospital, McVeigh and his colleague Dr Jerry Turnball (a pseudonym) liked the late-night atmosphere at St Vincent's, where there was less supervision. They were able to work like fully experienced doctors, and McVeigh and Turnball often found themselves together on the same night-shift.

At approximately 1 a.m., Turnball answered the phone and spoke to Feltenstein, who was anxious for an ambulance to be sent immediately to the Chelsea Hotel. It pulled up at the emergency room entrance shortly before 2 a.m. and McVeigh and Turnball wondered why the driver had taken so long. 'They insisted on coming with me,' the driver told McVeigh, nodding towards Feltenstein, Reitell and Heliker.

A nurse managed to persuade Reitell and Heliker to leave the emergency room while Feltenstein stood behind the two young doctors, telling them this was Dylan Thomas, a famous poet who had suddenly collapsed into a coma in his room at the Chelsea Hotel. No one told McVeigh and Turnball that Thomas had already been unconscious for possibly as long as an hour. This delay alone caused such hypoxic damage to his brain through a complete lack of oxygen that Thomas was entering an irreversible state of cerebral oedema, or swelling of the brain, although they were not to know that immediately.

When asked for details of Thomas's medical history, Feltenstein said he was unsure of his exact age and that he had fallen into a coma having been sick after a bout of heavy drinking. Questioned in more detail by Turnball, Feltenstein said he injected Thomas with half a grain of morphine some time before midnight when the patient complained of severe stomach pains, vomiting and delirium tremens.[1]

The desperate urgency of Thomas's condition prevented McVeigh and Turnball from enquiring further, and they did not realise at that stage that stomach pains and vomiting were not symptoms of delirium tremens. They noted that Thomas was draped in a yellow raincoat, an obese middle-aged man with curly hair who was not breathing. He was dry and clammy with blue lips and a splotchy, red and white, bloated face. For the moment, the cause of his coma was less important than establishing whether or not he was still alive. On checking his neck, wrist and groin, they found a weak but steady pulse. Removing the raincoat, they loosened Thomas's clothing. One doctor listened to the faint heartbeat with his stethoscope while the other straightened the patient's head and neck and checked the mouth in case there was anything blocking the windpipe; there was not. However, they noted that the pupils of Thomas's eyes were small, not dilated, which indicated the presence of narcotics. Thomas's tongue was pulled from his mouth while an elderly Navy medic who worked at St Vincent's as an anaesthesia nurse attached a metal tube to brown rubber pressure tubing from an oxygen tank, which he turned up to its highest setting.

The medic inserted the rigid tube into Thomas's nose, pinched the open nostril closed and told one of the doctors to close Thomas's mouth, while still keeping the tongue held out. After a few seconds they opened his nose and mouth, repeating this technique of artificial respiration for almost 15 minutes. There was still no spontaneous breathing – and no one in the examination room, apart from Feltenstein, yet knew that Thomas had not been breathing for at least an hour.

Thomas's pulse was now weak and thready. The Navy medic, who had served on a Navy hospital ship during the Korean War, had handled more patients with asphyxia than anyone else in the room, sometimes treating airmen shot down in flames and sailors pulled from the sea. He pulled Thomas's arms sharply above his head and then put them back upon his chest, repeating the movement many times. When this did not restart his breathing, the medic told the doctors to compress Thomas's thorax on both sides of the lower ribcage, and then release it – and when this also failed, they resumed lifting the arms above his head. For what seemed like an hour, they tried pumping Thomas's chest back into life until, eventually, a nurse heard shallow, weak breaths. The oxygen tube was attached to a new supply tank and turned down from maximum. Thomas was still in a coma, but at least he was breathing.

While the nurses kept up their observations, the doctors tried to establish why Thomas had gone into a coma in the first place. Feltenstein insisted that alcohol was the cause and morphine the appropriate treatment. The doctors did not challenge this and neither did they question his right to be present in St Vincent's Hospital. As often happens with celebrity patients, the rules were broken. This would become a serious problem in Thomas's case.

* * *

The obesity of Thomas's body made the doctors' work difficult, which is one of the reasons why they can remember so clearly what happened that night. His legs and arms were thick and flabby and it was not easy finding a suitable vein from which to take blood samples for laboratory analysis. There were similar problems attaching a saline and sugar drip, which they would never have used had anyone known of Thomas's diabetes.

Once the intravenous drip was connected and they could see that Thomas was breathing on his own, McVeigh and Turnball rolled Thomas gently onto his side to perform a lumbar puncture, so that they could obtain cerebrospinal fluid (CSF) for laboratory analysis. This was as important as taking the blood sample in trying to find out what had caused the coma. The CSF bathed the brain and spinal cord, and if it was anything but crystal clear, it might provide an indication of brain haemorrhage or infection.

McVeigh and Turnball had performed lumbar punctures before, but never upon anyone as fat. They bowed Thomas's back and drew his knees up into a foetal position, preparing the area of his lower lumbar vertebrae with alcohol and iodine before injecting cocaine just below the surface of the skin to anaesthetise the area. McVeigh took a ten-centimetre needle from the sterile tray and inserted it low in the lumbar spine. He tried several sticks but could not find the dura, the tough, fibrous membrane that surrounds the nervous system above the CSF. Turnball then took over, and after his third attempt, CSF fluid as clear as gin flowed into the needle. Fluid was drained into test tubes for centrifuging and a single drop placed between glass microscope slides for staining.

Relieved that Thomas was still breathing, after his lumbar puncture had taken longer than expected, they turned him on his back. He was covered in sweat and his hair was matted to his head. This was a good sign, showing that his sympathetic nervous system was still able to respond with an outpouring of adrenalin. They realised that even in his coma, Thomas had felt the lumbar puncture, although no one had seen him move.

With him now having been pulled back literally from the brink of death, the nurses at last removed Thomas's clothes and replaced them with a hospital gown. An oxygen mask was placed over his face, which was still splotchy, but they noted that his lips were no longer blue, indicating that some of the peripheral perfusion of oxygen in his body had been restored. It would be several hours before the results of the blood and CSF tests came back from the laboratory. Meanwhile, Thomas was kept in the emergency room and McVeigh and Turnball urged Feltenstein to find out whatever he could about Thomas's medical history.

✲ ✲ ✲

While this drama was unfolding, Reitell and Heliker remained in the waiting-room. No one came through to speak to them until after 2.30 a.m., when a sister said, 'It's looking bad, very bad. He's still in a coma and the doctors are having trouble getting him breathing again.'

Reitell awoke Brinnin at his home in Boston and told him that Dylan was near death in St Vincent's Hospital and that there were fears he might have had a brain haemorrhage. Brinnin caught a plane from Boston, arriving at the hospital to find Reitell being comforted by Ruthven Todd. The results of the CSF test had now come back from the laboratory, showing no sign of a cerebral haemorrhage but 'some evidence that Dylan had sustained a diabetic shock'.

Suddenly, the doors of the emergency room swung open at the far end of the corridor in which they were sitting and Dylan was wheeled past them on a trolley, stretched out beneath sheets, his face covered by an oxygen mask, his hair still wet, on his way to St Joseph's East Ward, a public wing run by the neurology service for non-operative patients. Brinnin, Reitell and Todd were joined by Feltenstein, who asked whether they had ever heard Thomas talk of any trauma, such as a fall, or if he had mentioned diabetes.

'When we first met in 1950, Dylan told me he believed he had cirrhosis of the liver, but he's never mentioned diabetes – and I haven't heard him talk about cirrhosis again, apart from that one time,' said Brinnin, who had long dismissed Thomas's complaints of ill health as no more than a childlike search for attention and sympathy.

'No, I can't remember him saying he'd fallen,' said Reitell.

By late morning on Thursday 5 November, the possibility of diabetic shock was no longer being considered and Feltenstein continued to insist, solely on the basis of the '18 straight whiskies', that acute alcoholic poisoning was the cause of Thomas's coma. Forty-three years later, when we interviewed him again, Brinnin admitted there was a fundamental discrepancy in his account. 'Yes, yes – I can see it now. If Dylan was diabetic, that explains much that we couldn't understand at the time. All these years, we've been waiting for an explanation and I think you've come up with it,' he said.

* * *

By the evening of Thursday 5 November, a crowd of spectators had gathered at St Vincent's Hospital, sometimes obstructing the corridor outside the room in which Thomas was lying. Through the glass window that ran the length of his ward, they could see him lying in bed, still wearing an oxygen mask, with the saline drip maintaining a food supply. Sometimes faces would be pressed against the glass, as strangers, wandering in off the street and claiming to be 'friends', demanded to know how he was and whether or not he might recover consciousness. Sometimes there were as many as 200 people in the crowd and, when asked by the nurses to leave Thomas's bedside while they washed him or dealt with his medication, Reitell would take up a seat at the far end of the corridor, sitting hunched and dressed in black.

The confusion in the crowd was paralleled among the doctors, for no one was in charge of the patient. Feltenstein, who had no right to be there, continued to argue that this was a case of acute alcoholic poisoning. Believing he was acting with authority, McVeigh and Turnball went along with that, but they became disturbed when they realised no one seemed to be following up the possibility that Thomas was suffering from diabetic shock.

Initially Feltenstein claimed that with his treatment, Thomas's metabolism would soon return to its proper balance. However, when there was still no sign of improvement in Thomas's condition he tried to contact a brain specialist, Dr Leo Davidoff, chief of neurosurgery at the Beth Israel Hospital. Davidoff was out of town and not expected back for another 24 hours, so Feltenstein approached Dr William de Gutierrez-Mahoney, chief of neurosurgery and neurology at St Vincent's and, like Davidoff, a former pupil of Dr Harvey Cushing, father of American neurosurgery.

With everyone still in ignorance about Thomas's true condition, Brinnin decided someone ought to speak to Caitlin. He did not phone her himself, even though he knew the telephone number at The Boat House and had made several calls there to Dylan. Saying 'I don't think I should give Caitlin bad news over the phone in case there's a poor connection', he asked James Laughlin, Thomas's American publisher, to convey the message. Laughlin phoned Thomas's British agent, David Higham, and it was he who sent the telegram that was delivered to Caitlin as she sat in the Laugharne school hall, saying Dylan was 'hospitalised' at St Vincent's. No details of his condition were given. There was no advice on how to make her way to New York, and no offer of help, but she decided that if Dylan was ill enough to be in hospital she ought to fly to his side, not knowing whether he had read her letter, or whether this might have precipitated whatever had happened.

✳ ✳ ✳

McVeigh and Turnball returned to St Joseph's East Ward late in the evening of Thursday 5 November. They had both had a full day. McVeigh had seen to his ward patients during the day and Turnball had been on duty in the operating theatre on the eighth floor of the Spellman Building.

Naturally curious as to what might have happened to Dylan Thomas during the day, they checked the laboratory tests and were surprised by the results. They knew there had been no blood in the CSF because the fluid had been clear and tests on the microscope slides had revealed no trace of meningitis from bacterial infection. However, what the tests did show was that the sugar level in Thomas's blood, urine and spinal fluid were all sky high, roughly five times the norm in the case of the blood. The tests showed a level of over 500 milligrammes against a norm of between 100 and 120 milligrammes. In their 18 months at the hospital, they had never seen anything quite like this. It was proof that Dylan Thomas was in a state of diabetic shock.

When they went to see what was being done to help him on St Joseph's East, McVeigh and Turnball were astonished to find that Thomas was still being given dextrose through the saline drip, and no insulin treatment had started. While they were standing by Thomas's bed, Feltenstein returned.

'This patient is in diabetic shock,' said McVeigh, with Turnball's agreement.

'No, he's not,' argued Feltenstein, annoyed that two young doctors should question his judgement.

'He is – look,' they said, showing Feltenstein the laboratory tests.

'That's nonsense. They've made a mistake in the laboratory. This is a clear-cut case of alcoholic poisoning,' Feltenstein insisted, adding that Thomas had no history of diabetes and that there were neither ketones, a product of incomplete metabolism of fat that is usually found in the blood of uncontrolled diabetics, nor any sign of acidosis.

McVeigh and Turnball held their ground in what turned into an angry confrontation, pointing out that there were known cases in which patients had severely increased glucose, or hyperglycaemia, and went into diabetic coma without the classic signs of ketones and acidosis.

'That's a very new theory and it's unproven,' said Feltenstein angrily. 'It could only happen in the rarest circumstances . . . this is a classic case of alcoholic abuse – and he's my patient,' he said with a glare, forbidding them to make any change in Thomas's treatment.

McVeigh and Turnball were stunned by Feltenstein's intransigence in the face of what, to them, was clear evidence that he was wrong. They later heard that Feltenstein also forbade any other doctors to become involved in the case, and they were forcibly warned that if any of Thomas's friends asked how he was, all they were allowed to say was 'He's still in a coma'. All other information had to come from Feltenstein.

'If you try to obstruct me, I shall report you to the hospital authorities for interfering with my patient,' said Feltenstein, again asserting an authority that he did not possess (although they were not to know that).

McVeigh and Turnball finished their work and left the hospital on Thursday 5 November in an unhappy frame of mind. They believed Thomas's life was being put at risk unnecessarily and agreed that over the next few hours they would both consult their medical reference books to see what more they could learn about hyperglycaemic coma, and then seek the advice of Dr George Pappas, chief resident of neurosurgery, who worked directly with Dr William de Gutierrez-Mahoney (known in the hospital as 'Will Mahoney').

✳   ✳   ✳

While McVeigh and Turnball were wondering what to do, Caitlin was mulling over the telegram. When it had first arrived, she had looked at it briefly and put it in her pocket. Later that night, alone at The Boat House, she thought to herself, 'There must be something really the matter for him to be in hospital – I'd better go.' Many years later, she described a strange sense of foreboding and said she vomited. On the Friday, she travelled to London and spent the night with friends, dining out at Wheeler's restaurant in Soho, roaring tight and screaming with frenzied laughter. No one told her Dylan was dying; she wondered only whether he had received her letter.

✵　✵　✵

Turnball returned to St Vincent's on Friday 6 November after reading his textbooks, made sure Feltenstein had left the hospital and went up to St Joseph's East on the third floor. The waiting-room was now packed with visitors after a brief announcement in *The New York Times* that Dylan Thomas was sick in St Vincent's, suffering from an 'insult to the brain'. McVeigh joined him shortly afterwards. They had both timed their arrival for the period when nurses changed shift and it was temporarily quiet on the ward.

Making sure no one could see them, they turned Thomas on his side to perform a second lumbar puncture. The CSF pressure was even higher than before. They filled two test tubes and checked the final pressure with the manometer, which indicated that the pressure was now back within its normal range. There was still no trace of blood or cloudiness; the fluid was clear.

Thomas's breathing became more shallow while he was on his side, but soon resumed its normal pattern when they gently rolled him on to his back. They cleaned his skin with iodine and alcohol before puncturing a vein to take a blood sample, and then obtained a urine sample.

What they had done by taking second samples without the approval of the doctor in charge was contrary both to the rules of St Vincent's and accepted medical practice, but they felt compelled to intervene, believing that Thomas's life was now in peril. The samples were sent off for laboratory analysis in the name of another patient, who was also in St Joseph's East, recovering from a bout of meningitis. To protect themselves, McVeigh and Turnball agreed that if anyone discovered what they had done before the results came through, they would say they had tested Thomas's body by mistake.

Just before noon the results came back, confirming their worst expectations. The glucose level in Thomas's CSF, blood and urine were now even higher than the day before because of all the dextrose that slipped into his system through the saline drip. His bloodstream and kidneys were unable to handle the load and glucose was spilling into his urine. They knew that unless urgent action was taken to reverse the sugar levels, Thomas would die.

McVeigh and Turnball immediately went to see Pappas, catching him between operations, and said, 'You must get Dr Mahoney to have a look at Dylan Thomas as soon as you can . . .'

Phoning through to Mahoney's office, Pappas discovered he was out of the hospital and would not be returning until later in the day; his secretary said that Feltenstein was also asking to see Mahoney urgently about the same case. 'We think he's making a mistake,' said McVeigh, explaining that Feltenstein was treating Thomas for alcoholic poisoning when there was now clear evidence he was suffering from diabetic shock.

Pappas ran a busy clinical service and spent most of every day in the operating theatre. There were constant demands upon his time. His next operation was a large brain tumour, but he listened carefully to the two young doctors, impressed that they should be willing to put their careers at risk by challenging a patient's treatment. Forty years later, their conviction that what they were doing was right stood out clearly in his memory. 'I'll never forget that moment,' he said. 'They were clearly worried by what had happened and they wanted to save the patient's life . . .'

⚹ ⚹ ⚹

The visitors in the corridor maintained an all-night vigil through 5–6 November, knowing nothing of the conflict between the doctors and Feltenstein. Brinnin, Reitell and Dylan's friends the critic David Lougee and the poet John Berryman were in the crowd, and at 4 a.m. Sister Consilio came out to speak to them, saying, 'There's no change in the patient's condition . . . I think you all need to go home and get some rest.'

Unknown to Brinnin, the hospital authorities were becoming disturbed by the ever-changing crowd of sightseers milling around the waiting-room and outside Thomas's ward. They were interfering with the smooth running of the hospital, obstructing nurses and asking questions for which there were no answers. Eventually, admission was restricted to those with blue passes, which were issued to Brinnin, Reitell, Berryman and a few others.

When Brinnin and Reitell returned the next morning, they were again told there had been no change in Thomas's condition, but this was not strictly true. Brinnin noticed, 'The oxygen was still on Dylan's face, his eyes, spasmodically turning, fluttering, were open, but their unseeing gaze only confirmed his unfathomable sleep.'[2] This detailed description of Thomas's eyes indicates he was having seizures, a dreaded development in hyperglycaemic shock. They were caused not only by high glucose levels but by increased intracranial pressure. This was what McVeigh and Turnball had observed that morning when the CSF flowed out under high pressure. It meant Thomas was now suffering from cerebral oedema, a swelling of the brain cells directly caused by the hypoxic injury when he was left without breathing for at least an hour, and maybe two, after Feltenstein's last dose of morphine.

☆　☆　☆

Mahoney returned to St Vincent's on the afternoon of Friday 6 November. Feltenstein was waiting for him and they walked over to St Joseph's East, conferring for about an hour at Thomas's bedside. 'This is a straightforward case of acute alcoholic intoxication,' said Feltenstein, explaining that Thomas was a notoriously heavy drinker whom he had met six months earlier when Thomas had come to his surgery seeking treatment for gout and asthma.

'Other than alcoholism, there is nothing of significance in his medical history. The day of his coma, he drank 18 whiskies in less than an hour and a half and began suffering hallucinations, indicating the onset of DTs. I gave him mild sedation at his hotel, but he became more and more unwell and then lapsed into a coma . . . There is no history of head trauma or anything else significant. He stopped breathing for a while, but we brought him to the emergency room where he was revived . . . He has been fed intravenously and has also been given a blood transfusion.'

Feltenstein did not inform Mahoney of his repeated use of cortisone or the half a grain dose of morphine, and made no mention of the laboratory tests suggesting Thomas was suffering from diabetic shock. Faced with inadequate information, Mahoney examined Thomas and agreed with Feltenstein's presentation of the case, diagnosis and treatment.

After the examination, Mahoney and Feltenstein walked through to the waiting-room, where they talked to Brinnin and Reitell. 'I agree with Dr Feltenstein's analysis of alcoholic poisoning of the brain tissue and brain cells,' said Mahoney. 'This is not a case in which we can operate . . . We have tried to check on the patient's history by phoning Britain, but all they can tell us is that he has a history of alcohol abuse and, more recently, blackouts . . . There is not much more we can do, other than to wait and see whether his body recovers on its own.'

☆　☆　☆

There was some delay, maybe an hour or two, before McVeigh and Turnball were able to see Pappas again. His brain tumour operation had to be performed a different way when Pappas discovered the tumour was based in the frontal lobes and malignant. Realising the patient would be dead within six months whatever he did, Pappas reduced the size of the tumour (an operation called 'debulking'), leaving the patient able to speak, and then closed the patient's head.

As soon as Pappas emerged from the operating theatre, McVeigh and Turnball asked him whether he had yet spoken to Mahoney. Pappas explained what had happened with the tumour, and walked over with them to St Joseph's East. An oxygen mask lay across Thomas's face. His eyes were twitching up and down into his head, indicating seizures. Dextrose was still being supplied intravenously; he was receiving no insulin.

'I'd better check how my patient is doing in the recovery room,' said Pappas, leaving them a few moments while McVeigh and Turnball questioned the nurses on duty about Thomas's treatment. As they were talking, Feltenstein appeared and confronted Turnball angrily.

'I've told you not to interfere with my patient,' said Feltenstein.

'You're giving him the wrong treatment – he's diabetic,' said Turnball, holding out the laboratory tests.

Now raging, Feltenstein wrenched the medical chart from Turnball's hands, tore the contents apart, scattering them on the floor, and then began berating McVeigh and Turnball, threatening to report them to the management and wreck their careers. With his words falling about their ears, McVeigh and Turnball picked up the torn hospital chart and went off to find Mahoney, who was in his office in the department of neurosurgery and neurology, finishing a phone call. Normally, Mahoney never spoke to journalists, but there had been so many requests for information that he was asked to make an official statement on behalf of the hospital. It was from this telephone conversation that the legend grew that Dylan Thomas died of 'an acute alcoholic insult to the brain'.

Putting down the phone, Mahoney asked them what they wanted. Initially, he was reluctant to intervene, but when they produced Thomas's torn medical chart and described how Feltenstein ripped it from their hands, Mahoney listened carefully. They told him what had happened on the night of Thomas's admission to the emergency room and since.

'Dr Feltenstein may be right about hyperglycaemic coma. It's a rare condition and we still don't know much about it,' said Mahoney, who began to look anxious when they told him of the cortisone and morphine injections, the final half a grain of morphine and the laboratory tests indicating diabetic shock.

'I think we'll need to take another lumbar puncture and also blood and urine tests to see who's right,' said Mahoney.

McVeigh then admitted a second series of tests had, indeed, been taken, and these showed Thomas was now in an even deeper state of shock.

'Were there ketones present in the urine?' asked Mahoney.

'No, not in either set of tests,' said McVeigh.

'How about acidosis?'

'Present, but only mildly – probably due to asphyxia.'

'Sodium levels?'

'Slightly elevated, perhaps due to dehydration or early renal failure.'

Mahoney continued to question them closely and when Turnball told him Feltenstein admitted administering the half a grain of morphine in Thomas's hotel room, Mahoney fell silent. He realised as well as they did that while the overdose may have precipitated the initial coma, Thomas was now suffering the effects of hyperglycaemic shock and damage to the brain. It was too late to save him, but this could have been prevented.

His silence continued for many seconds. To McVeigh and Turnball it seemed like minutes, for they knew they had broken the hospital's rules and were now wondering whether Mahoney agreed with their analysis or would invoke disciplinary charges against them. 'We thought our careers were over,' said Turnball who, not surprisingly, remembered every moment with clarity.

As the seconds passed, they realised Mahoney was almost incoherent with rage. Feltenstein had lied to him and withheld medical facts, causing Mahoney to give the press false information that Thomas was suffering from 'an acute alcoholic insult to the brain'.

Eventually, speaking in a low, forceful voice, Mahoney said, 'Do not speak to anyone else about this case . . . I will handle everything from now on . . . Feltenstein is off the case, and I will speak to him personally about his conduct.'

Mahoney then called the chief of neurology, Dr Joseph Chusid, asked him to take personal charge of the case and arranged for Thomas's dextrose supply to be turned off and insulin provided. Mahoney kept Thomas's torn laboratory tests and had them reassembled. The nurses on St Joseph's East Ward were told to take no further instructions from Feltenstein.

✳ ✳ ✳

As head of the neurology and neurosurgery departments at St Vincent's, Mahoney was an eminent man within his profession but with few close friends. There was always a barrier around his personal life that emphasised his distinction and distance from others. Few knew of his background.

Mahoney was born in 1904 at Silao, Mexico, nearly 6,000 feet up in the mountains, 14 miles south of Gurrajuato, a railway junction with a livestock trading centre established in 1537. His father was an Irish engineer, his mother Mexican, and they brought him up speaking several languages, including English, Spanish, French and German. After his father died of tuberculosis, Mahoney was raised by an uncle in Ohio and graduated as the valedictorian of his high school class before attending college at Holy Cross and graduating in medicine at Harvard Medical School in 1929. He trained in neurosurgery with Dr Harvey Cushing, the foremost brain surgeon of his day, and after being awarded a Travelling Fellowship by Harvard in 1932 worked with Foerster and Krayenbuhl, two of the most renowned neurosurgeons in Europe.

After the Second World War, Cardinal Spellman of New York and Sister Bernard launched an ambitious programme to make St Vincent's one of the finest hospitals in the world and Mahoney was appointed the first chief of neurosurgery and neurology in 1945. He was offered the post for two reasons. He was a Catholic and had worked for Dr Cushing.

Within St Vincent's he became a legendary figure, affecting a slight British accent, dressing in a dapper fashion and ordering all his clothes tailor-made from London. He was a perfectionist and a strict disciplinarian, feared to some degree because he would dismiss any staff who failed his expectations.

'There were many things that puzzled me about this case,' he told Pappas. 'Dylan Thomas did not have any neurological problems and I doubt whether he was truly alcoholic . . . we could have tried surgery to remove part of the cranium (the bony vault that protects the brain) to relieve the pressure, but that had been tried in the past in cases of cerebral oedema and the patients still died.'

The only person in Britain whom Mahoney is known to have contacted was not Dylan Thomas's own physician, Dr Hughes of St Clears, but Dr Daniel Jones, who was not a doctor of medicine but a composer of music. It was almost certainly Jones who mentioned Thomas's recent blackouts. 'It always perplexed me that Thomas's friends knew so little about him,' Mahoney told Pappas. 'But the phone call did explain something. Jones mentioned, "Of course, we knew about Mr Thomas's diabetes." I did not understand what he meant by that, but now that I've seen all the medical facts, the case was clear.'

✳   ✳   ✳

When Feltenstein returned to St Vincent's that evening, he was directed to Mahoney's office. No record was kept of their conversation, but Mahoney made clear his anger to Pappas and later Turnball. Feltenstein also described what happened to Dr Joseph Lehrman, and we have based this part of our reconstruction upon their recollections.

From the moment he entered Mahoney's office, Feltenstein was defensive and Mahoney stayed silent while his visitor spoke. 'This patient has been lying to me ever since I took him on,' said Feltenstein, claiming he only agreed to see Thomas in the first place as a favour to Reitell. 'He's been an impossible patient.'

Mahoney listened quietly while Feltenstein recounted his meetings with Thomas in May and again since his arrival in New York on 19 October. 'He kept promising to give up drinking and eat regular meals,' said Feltenstein, before recounting what happened on 3 November.

'Did you give him half a grain of morphine?' asked Mahoney.

'Yes, to ease his pain and because he was suffering from DTs after drinking an enormous quantity of whisky . . . I was only trying to help him.'

'Have you ever given a patient that much morphine before?' Mahoney queried.

'Yes, when I've had to — and without any problems,' Feltenstein replied. 'This would not have corrected his metabolic problems, but who could recover easily from that much whisky?'

Mahoney let Feltenstein say his piece, and then calmly stated: 'Mr Dylan Thomas is now under the care of the neurology service of St Vincent's Hospital . . . You may come to the hospital, visit the patient and talk to his friends, but you are forbidden to give any medical instructions, touch the patient or refer to his medical chart . . . We are more experienced in dealing with patients in coma than you are, Dr Feltenstein, and so long as Mr Thomas remains here he will be treated only by our own staff. Have I made myself clear?'

The atmosphere was now icily formal as Mahoney continued, saying he had established that Feltenstein had no authority to admit patients to St Vincent's and was acting *ultra vires* in issuing instructions to hospital staff. 'Alcohol may have been a factor in this case,' he said, 'but the primary causes of the patient's condition were your overdose of morphine and his incipient diabetes. I have seen other cases of hyperglycaemic shock and coma where the patient has survived, but because of what has happened I do not believe this patient will pull through . . . finally, I want to emphasise again that you are forbidden to make any comment on the patient's condition.'

Feltenstein left Mahoney's office chastened and refused to discuss the case of Dylan Thomas with any journalist or biographer right up until he died in 1974. He did, however, have the conversation with Dr Joseph Lehrman to which we have referred, in which he spoke of his distress that Thomas died as a result of his failure to conduct diagnostic tests and his consequent failure to prescribe appropriate treatment. 'I think Feltenstein's problem was that he was in awe of Dylan Thomas from the moment they met, and he allowed that to distort his judgement,' Mahoney told Pappas.

Mahoney and Feltenstein never spoke to each other again.

✲   ✲   ✲

Later during the night of 6 November, a tracheotomy was performed because Thomas was having difficulty breathing. A breathing tube was inserted in his throat and another tube ran from his nose down to his stomach, suctioning off the gastric contents to avoid them being ingested by the lungs, which would be a disaster for a comatose patient.

The fact that the tracheotomy was performed so long after Thomas's admission was a curious oversight that puzzled the hospital staff who looked after him when they were interviewed 40 years later. They all agreed it should have been done earlier, although intubation was not as commonly practised in 1953 as it is today. The technique was introduced by the famous Scottish brain surgeon Sir William Macewen[3] in Glasgow in the 1870s, and was routinely used for surgical cases in the 1950s. However, this was always done in the operating theatre by staff trained in the tricky technique of inserting a breathing tube into the trachea via the mouth. Very few other staff knew how to do it.

There is a possibility that Thomas's life could have been saved had the tracheotomy been performed immediately when he arrived at St Vincent's, but his brain may have been too damaged by the delay in getting him to hospital for him to have made a full recovery. However, it was undoubtedly necessary when performed because his cerebral oedema, the swelling of the brain cells and tissues, was pressing his brain tighter against the main breathing centre in the brainstem and had still not reached its peak, which occurs two or three days after a brain injury. This is something all neurosurgeons dread, even today, because there is little they can do to intervene. It was this brain swelling that ultimately caused Thomas's death, but the tracheotomy kept him alive long enough for Caitlin to complete her journey from Laugharne.

13

The Death of the Poet

Caitlin could never remember what happened between receiving the telegram in Laugharne and her arrival in New York. Those 48 hours of her life were a total blank. She could not recall where her children were, although Aeronwy had recently started at a boarding school in Hertfordshire, Llewelyn was still at Magdalen College School, Oxford, and Colm, only four years old and the apple of his father's eye, stayed happily at home with Dolly Long, where there were plenty of other children to play with.

Someone must have driven Caitlin to Carmarthen station, given her the money for the fare to London, met her at Paddington, put her up for the night, arranged the plane ticket and seen her off at Heathrow, but whoever these helpers were remained a total mystery to her. Caitlin had no recollection of the Friday night at Wheeler's restaurant, where she was seen laughing, drinking and joking.

In fact, the events were easy enough to piece together. She stayed with Harry and Cordelia Locke in Hammersmith, Margaret Taylor did what she could to help, and Bill and Helen McAlpine, two of the Thomases' staunchest friends, came to her aid financially, booking the seat to New York and hosting the supper at Wheeler's when it was discovered that no plane seats were available until the Saturday evening. They met her again at lunchtime on the Saturday when she still had time to kill before booking in at Heathrow for an early-evening departure. Caitlin herself could remember none of it, only that she drank free airline whisky more or less continually from the time the plane left London until it landed at Idlewild Airport at 8 a.m. on the Sunday morning. In those days, the journey took 12 hours.

Dave and Rose Slivka were waiting on the tarmac with a station-wagon as she stepped off the plane, cheeks pinkened by the morning air, her hair shining. Caitlin seemed happy and cheerful as she kissed them both, but then noticed an escort of police motorcycles gathered around the vehicle. They were there at the request of Donald Maclean who, being told of Dylan's deterioration, wanted to be sure Caitlin would reach St Vincent's before he died. Her mood quickly changed.

'Suddenly it hit me – they wouldn't be there without a reason. For the first time, I realised this must be serious,' she said, many years later, remembering the moment precisely and recalling in detail how the station-wagon zoomed through the streets of New York to a chorus of motorcycle sirens, with her slumped in the back seat, wondering what on earth had happened.

It can only be conjecture, because Caitlin spent those missing 48 hours lost within her memory, but it seems likely that right until the moment on the tarmac she thought she was heading to Dylan's bedside for a tearful reunion, a mutual swearing of love and forgiveness, after all the bitterness of their last week together in London and the pain that caused her to send that final letter.

When they arrived at St Vincent's, Caitlin was guided through a rear entrance to avoid the crowd that gathered when it was heard she was on her way. She now seemed quiet and still within herself as she was taken up to the third floor, where she joined the queue outside St Joseph's East Ward until it was realised this was Dylan's wife. Little was said as she was shown through to the bedside where Dylan lay beneath an oxygen tent, the mask across his lower face, insulin flowing through the drip, rubber tubes protruding from his nose and the hole at the base of his neck.

'Why didn't you let me know what had happened?' she said. Brinnin did not answer, and still could not explain his silence 43 years later, saying only 'Everyone was upset' and 'I just didn't think of it'.[1]

As she turned away from the bedside for a moment, Caitlin saw dozens of faces pressed against the windows to the corridor. She shuddered. They were all strangers, waiting to see what would happen next, 'and I had no idea how I was expected to behave . . . No one had prepared me for this'.[2] She bent forwards, slid her hand beneath the oxygen tent and touched Dylan's hand, speaking softly to him. His body seemed to move and she comforted herself in later years with the thought that Dylan knew she was there, but neurologically this was unlikely and in her heart she knew he was as good as dead. She vividly described what she saw:

Dylan basely humiliated with the disgusting things he dreaded most; not one organ in his body working in its own right, without mechanical assistance: intravenal feedings, tubes attached blatantly to each vulnerable shy orifice; the head encased in a transparent tent, pumping oxygen into him; the eyes turned up, bulging, unseeing; the breath roaring like a winded horse pounding up a slope; and no Dylan there, no contact. Only the limp hands lying separate, speaking to me. And everybody knowing it was hopeless and all over; that this was a farcical prolongation of what had already gone. [3]

Caitlin now knew after seeing with her own eyes what everyone else in New York had known for days by listening to the radio or reading their newspapers: there was no way Dylan Thomas could recover from this coma. Understandably, Caitlin did not know what to do. She tried to roll a cigarette but could not control her hands, and still the faces watched her through the glass partition.

Leaving the bedside after only 15 minutes, Caitlin saw Reitell standing with Brinnin further down the corridor. They were not introduced, although later, a few weeks after the funeral, Caitlin wrote to Rollie McKenna asking her to help clear 'a few gnawing bafflements'. Among them were 'what was the acute thing that the doctors said happened to Dylan a day or so before he collapsed?' and 'how much had Elizabeth Reitell to do with it all?'. She added that she felt Brinnin had been unfair to her, treating her like 'a maniacal, marauding animal, which is true up to a point, but not entirely. Unfortunately, there is the seeing eye left. He wrote me a very sweet letter, but he is too sweet altogether ... The trouble is I love, respect and believe John, but want to kill him.' [4]

✻ ✻ ✻

The Slivkas took Caitlin back to their apartment. Brinnin spent that Sunday afternoon phoning friends, telling them there was no hope for Dylan now and it was just a matter of time, and seeking donations to a Dylan Thomas Memorial Fund to pay hospital and funeral expenses and provide support for Caitlin and the children.

Late on the Sunday afternoon, he returned to St Vincent's where Reitell was still maintaining her vigil. Both were there when Caitlin returned with Rose Slivka. They were dressed in black, with Caitlin drunker than ever, carrying bottles of whisky. This time there was no self-restraint. 'Is the bloody man dead yet?' Caitlin demanded, before hurling herself at Brinnin, kicking hard and trying to strangle him while Rose shouted, 'Go for the jugular, baby!' Brinnin wriggled free and escaped into the ward where Dylan was lying.

Peace was restored temporarily when Caitlin followed him, producing a packet of cigarettes. She tried to light one, but the matches kept snapping in her hand. 'No smoking,' said a nurse, trying to steer her away from the oxygen tent. Suddenly Caitlin started screaming, grabbed an overhead curtain rail and began to swing, kicking her feet in all directions before throwing herself across Dylan, wrenching away the tent, tubing and drip, and trying to press her body against his. Nurses tried to pull her away. She kicked and bit them, hurling plant pots until a statue of the Virgin Mary and a crucifix caught her eye. They were attached to the wall above her. Caitlin smashed them into pieces, cursing the God that was taking Dylan from her.

With nurses and doctors holding her down, Caitlin was injected with a sedative and strapped into a strait-jacket. Her mood immediately changed and she began whimpering. A doctor was called from the emergency room.

✳   ✳   ✳

Even before Caitlin returned, there were signs that Thomas's body was beginning to surrender its physiological will to survive. McVeigh and Turnball were on duty that weekend and continued to visit the ward. Use of insulin helped reverse Thomas's hyperglycaemia but it was difficult to control his level of glucose because his body had been starved of insulin for so many years. His intravenous fluids were also a problem. On admission, he was severely dehydrated by morphine and the effects of vomiting, but the hospital staff, under Dr Chusid, were afraid that if they overhydrated him they would pump up his blood pressure, further increasing the pressure on his brain. That could only have one outcome: even more rapid death.

So, while Caitlin neared the end of her journey, there was continuous activity at Thomas's bedside, monitoring his breathing, glucose and sodium levels and fluid volume. The neurology staff had not been told of the dispute between Feltenstein and the two young doctors, or of the intervention by Pappas and Mahoney. Even Chusid himself was given only the information he needed to know.

✳   ✳   ✳

It is still hard to believe that Caitlin could have been allowed to travel from Laugharne to London, spend over 24 hours in London and then 12 hours flying to New York without anyone telling her for three entire days that Dylan was dying. The Thomases had a telephone installed at The Boat House. Their number, Laugharne 68, was well known within their circle. They were intelligent people with sophisticated friends. Margaret Taylor was the wife of an Oxford don with an international reputation; McAlpine worked for the British Council; Locke was a music-hall star of considerable renown, a singer, comedian and comic actor who frequently topped the bill in variety shows. As a writer, Thomas himself was a national figure, with a leading literary agent representing him and established companies publishing his work. Admittedly, Caitlin travelled to London late on a Friday when offices were closing for the weekend. She flew to New York on a Saturday and was airbound for 12 hours. Even so, why did no one prepare her for the shock she received as she stepped off the plane? In particular, why did Brinnin, the man who arranged all four tours and was quick to claim credit for their success, fail to let Caitlin know what was happening?

✻   ✻   ✻

Mahoney was not in the hospital when Caitlin arrived on Sunday 8 November. He was attending Mass with his family and thus did not hear of the disturbance in St Joseph's East Ward. The duty doctor in the emergency room asked Brinnin and Reitell if they would authorise Caitlin's admission to Bellevue Hospital, the New York state mental institution. They were reluctant to do so and sought the advice of Feltenstein who, in turn, consulted Dr Adolph Zeckel, who was in private psychiatric practice on East 75th Street.

Zeckel, who trained in Groningen, Holland, and moved to the US before the Second World War, agreed that Caitlin was suffering from 'extreme hysteria' and should be sent to the private sanatorium, River Crest, if her friends were reluctant to sign the papers for Bellevue. A private ambulance was called and Feltenstein personally paid the $25 charge.[5]

In *Dylan Thomas in America*, Brinnin suggests Caitlin was by then calm and composed, but that was not how she remembered what happened and neither does it accord with the recollections of the staff at St Vincent's. On Feltenstein's authority, she was removed in the strait-jacket. On arrival at River Crest, a sprawling institution that accommodated patients with nervous and mental disorders, covering 12 acres and surrounded by high walls, she was stripped of her clothes, given a flimsy white cotton gown and put back in the strait-jacket, with the ties so tightly pulled that she could barely breathe. She was left all night in a locked room, dehydrated after drinking so much whisky, desperately crying for water. 'I was not as grateful as I should have been,' she wrote caustically in *Leftover Life to Kill*, 'and went so far as to grudge the high payment of my enforced "posh" establishment. I wondered who was so altruistic, or so desirous of having me out of the way, as to be responsible for it.'[6]

When Mahoney returned to St Vincent's on the Monday morning, there was a message awaiting him. One of the weekend duty doctors wanted to talk to him about the commitment of Mrs Dylan Thomas to River Crest. The two men spoke on the phone and Mahoney was flabbergasted when he realised that neither he nor Chusid had been notified of Caitlin's arrival.[7] The doctor told Mahoney how some of Dylan's friends had disrupted the hospital by drinking and fighting as if they had been in some local bar, and he was outraged when he learned that Feltenstein had been instrumental in sending Mrs Thomas to River Crest.

Mahoney immediately tried to phone Caitlin at River Crest, but the staff there refused to put him through and he was referred to her 'doctor', Zeckel. The staff said Caitlin would not be released for several days and certainly not before Zeckel gave his approval.

Unable to contact Zeckel at his office, Mahoney called Dr Layman Harrison the physician-in-charge at River Crest, and Dr Martin Pollin, the clinical director, telling them Dylan Thomas was dying at St Vincent's and his wife had been carried off in a strait-jacket, not only against her will but on the authority of two doctors, Feltenstein and Zeckel, who had no authority to act in any capacity at the hospital. He did not specifically threaten legal action, but he did say his complaint would be conveyed to the New York State medical authorities in such a way that River Crest would suffer repercussions if Mrs Thomas was not immediately released.

'I saw Dr Mahoney that morning and he was in a foul mood,' said Pappas, who had worked with him in the operating theatre, dissecting a peripheral nerve tumour. Mahoney stayed with Pappas while the surgery was completed, and then said in a hushed voice, 'I've never known a case like this . . . These people act as if they don't have to live by the same rules as the rest of us.' In a rare flash of anger, Mahoney added, 'With the kind of friends he's got, I'm surprised Thomas hasn't been done in sooner . . .'

✳   ✳   ✳

By the time Harrison tracked down Feltenstein that Monday morning, Feltenstein was already beginning to doubt his wisdom in committing Caitlin to River Crest. Since Feltenstein's signature came first on the committal papers, responsibility for her care fell upon his shoulders. Zeckel was called in by Feltenstein, not the other way round.

Harrison visited Caitlin himself after Mahoney's phone call and found her dehydrated and tired but completely lucid. He ordered that her strait-jacket be removed immediately. As far as Harrison could determine, Caitlin had been drunk at St Vincent's and had suffered an extreme, but not abnormal, grief reaction. She had no known history of mental disease or hospital treatment other than in maternity, and he agreed with Mahoney that she had clearly been committed against her will. 'If Zeckel doesn't sign the release papers, we'll ask two doctors here to do it,' he told Mahoney.

✳   ✳   ✳

Freed of her strait-jacket and able to walk around, Caitlin ventured out into the gardens of River Crest, sombre and withdrawn, reluctant to talk to anyone. She felt acutely alone, and was unaware of Mahoney's intervention.

Without her knowing it, there was to be one more medical twist in the story. Ruthven Todd discovered that at Bellevue Hospital there was a specialist in severe cases of alcoholism, Dr James Smith, and with the permission of Mahoney and Chusid, and with McVeigh urging him to act quickly, Todd sought Smith's opinion, knowing that Mahoney already believed that Thomas's condition was hopeless.

Smith made a few minor recommendations about fluid and electrolyte management, but admitted these would not be enough to affect the probable outcome.[8] Reitell told Gittins in 1985 of her own conversation with Smith and said she was beginning to have doubts about alcoholism being the true cause of Dylan's death. She claimed Smith argued alcoholism was a problem in people of Gaelic blood, but he later told Feltenstein and Mahoney that he had said nothing of the kind. 'It had long been my opinion that alcoholism ran in families, but there also had to be character defects which allowed alcohol to take over someone's life,' said Smith.

✳   ✳   ✳

Although the hospital authorities were now limiting access to St Joseph's East Ward, they tried to do so with discretion. Anyone who seemed a genuine friend was allowed through, and Mahoney and Chusid were sorry they had not been contacted on the Sunday. 'We would have found a room for Mrs Thomas in the hospital,' said Mahoney. 'There was no reason to send her away like that. If sedation was necessary, we could have given it. Had it been a matter of seeking outside psychiatric advice, that would have been no problem, either . . . Hospitals are used to coping with grief.'

Thomas was now in his fourth day of coma, with Brinnin and Reitell continuing to maintain a vigil at his bedside. According to McVeigh, they did not seem to understand the gravity of his condition and kept trying to communicate with Thomas. Reitell told Gittins this was 'an experiment' to see if they could rouse Dylan by talking to him. They believed he was trying to communicate with them by the changes in his breathing patterns and muscle twitches in his extremities.[9]

This was another misunderstanding of the medical facts. Relatives and friends are frequently encouraged to sit with patients by doctors who know this will do nothing to assist the patient, but may help his friends and family prepare for the inevitable. McVeigh and Turnball told Mahoney what was going on at Thomas's bedside, and he came down to the ward to speak to Brinnin and Reitell, warning them Thomas 'might die at any time and it would be better if he did . . . If he does manage to survive, he will need constant care and medical attention for the rest of his life, probably in an institution. Everything that can be done has been done, and it would be merciful if he simply died.'

✲　✲　✲

Two of the other visitors were the sculptor Peter Grippe and his wife Florence, friends of George Reavey who had known Thomas in London before the war. Reavey introduced them to Thomas during his first tour and they all met again in 1952 when he was accompanied by Caitlin, and spent some good times together. Hearing Dylan was dying, it seemed right to say farewell.

'When we arrived at the hospital, we saw Brinnin and then noticed a woman in black sitting in the waiting-room and occasionally walking through to Dylan's bedside,' said Florence Grippe. 'We asked who she was, and someone whispered, "That's Dylan's girlfriend." We were amazed by her proprietary air, acting like Dylan's widow before he was even dead, and wondered what on earth was going on.

'Where was Caitlin? Were they trying to keep her away? Why were they making all the decisions about Dylan's care? Did Caitlin know anything at all about it? Had anyone told her Dylan was close to death? When was she arriving?

'We found the whole situation quite astonishing. George told us he had already heard rumours about Feltenstein giving Dylan morphine, barbiturates and benzedrine, and he blamed Brinnin and Reitell for everything that happened.'

Similarly, Rose Slivka also angrily denounced Brinnin when he spoke to her. 'It was all his fault,' she said. 'He never looked after them properly.'

✳   ✳   ✳

Soon after midday on Monday 9 November, Nurse Margaret McIntyre began giving Thomas his daily bath. Brinnin and Reitell temporarily left the hospital, leaving John Berryman alone at the bedside. Nurse McIntyre washed the front of his body and was about to turn him over when Thomas gasped. All morning there had been long pauses in his breathing and she waited for a breath, but this time there was no movement in his chest. She checked his pulse. Again, there was no feeling of life. Without a word, she glanced at Berryman. There was no need for either of them to speak.

Dylan Thomas was dead.

Over at River Crest, Caitlin was now calm and self-possessed, trying to persuade a psychiatrist to sign her release certificate, 'because I have got to go and see Dylan'. He seemed unimpressed by her pleading and said coldly, 'I suppose you know your husband is dead.'

✳   ✳   ✳

John Berryman later described Dylan's death in a letter to Vernon Watkins. 'His body died utterly quiet,' he wrote, 'and he looked so tired that you might once more have burst into tears but your grief would have been general, for the whole catastrophe not for the moment . . . He did not have to die, as some other great poets have had to die, under the impression that what they had done was not worth doing. But this will not help you much. It doesn't help me.' [10]

✳   ✳   ✳

Shortly afterwards, McVeigh and Turnball both received messages asking them to go down to St Joseph's East Ward immediately. News of Thomas's death had quickly travelled far beyond the hospital, and already there were hundreds of people in a queue, waiting to pay their last respects.

McVeigh phoned Dr Bill Panke, a surgical resident from New York University attached to St Vincent's. They were classmates at the College of Medicine and had graduated together in 1951. 'Dylan Thomas has died and we're going to send the body down to the morgue for a postmortem,' said McVeigh.

Panke prepared the postmortem table and gathered together his instruments while the body was brought down by elevator. It was accompanied by Nurse McIntyre and a hospital attendant.

After the gown was removed, Panke was immediately struck by the grotesque appearance of Thomas's body. Despite his below-average height, his body was bloated beyond normal proportions by all the intravenous fluids that had been administered. His face was blotched red and white, his lips were a dusky shade of blue-grey, his eyes sunken in his head, the lids closed. Despite his swollen skin, the last facial impression was a kind of grimace with his teeth clenched tightly and his cheeks indented by the edges of his mouth. All the tubes were gone, but there was still a hole at the base of his neck where the tracheotomy site gaped like a second mouth, and there were other holes in his arms where the intravenous needles had been inserted and at the base of the spine where the lumbar punctures had been performed. Despite all this, the body still resembled that of a young man and this image impressed itself upon his memory.

Just as he was about to begin the postmortem, Panke received a telephone call instructing him not to go ahead. 'Do not alter the body in any way,' he was told, for the case was being turned over to the New York City Chief Medical Examiner's Office at the request of Mahoney, still troubled by all the confusion surrounding Thomas's admission to the hospital. This was an unusual decision in a case of this kind where the cause of death was known, but Mahoney was anxious lest there was some other factor that might have been missed and was acting within a long-standing guideline that the Medical Examiner had jurisdiction in 'all deaths that are caused by or contributed to by drug and/or chemical overdose or poisoning' and in situations where death may have been due to 'all forms of criminal violence or from an unlawful act or criminal neglect'.

✳   ✳   ✳

The dieners (mortuary attendants) arrived at St Vincent's during the evening of Monday 9 November to collect the body and take it to Bellevue Hospital where all New York City Medical Examiner postmortems were conducted. The dieners would have noted Thomas's body had not been prepared for autopsy in the usual way. Normally, cotton was stuffed in every orifice, the eyes were taped shut and a string was tied tightly around the end of the penis to prevent the escape of bodily fluids, but this had not been done.

Once the body arrived at the morgue, it was placed in a refrigerator like all the others awaiting autopsy, but by then several hours had elapsed. We have also established that details of Thomas's diabetes were sanitised from his medical records. This was an important omission. Had the pathologist known what to look for, he could have tested tissues from the kidneys to see whether there was a pathological clue to diabetes known as the Armani-Ebstein lesion – but without being given the hint, he would not have looked for such an unexpected change in the kidneys.

'I guess Dr Mahoney had a painful decision to take,' said Pappas. 'He knew what Feltenstein had done, but he also knew Dylan Thomas died unnecessarily in his hospital . . . and I suppose he had to decide whether or not to let the outside world know what had been going on. It was hard for him. He was proud of his hospital and no member of his own staff was in any way to blame.'

The one person who would have been given a straight answer if she had asked the right questions was Caitlin, but she was still at River Crest, awaiting the arrival of the Slivkas, who promised to look after her. 'I would like to go and see Dylan's body,' she said, but anxious to avoid causing her any further distress they advised against it and instead drove her to a bar in Manhattan, where Caitlin drank several whiskies. So far as we can ascertain, neither Caitlin nor Brinnin was told that Dylan's body had been taken to Bellevue for a formal autopsy.

✱   ✱   ✱

The autopsy was conducted by Dr Milton Helpern, New York City Deputy chief Medical Examiner and an Associate Professor of Forensic Medicine at New York University. A native of New York City, he had graduated from Cornell University Medical School and completed his residency at Bellevue. Apart from serving in the United States Air Force between 1943 and 1946, he had risen through the ranks in forensic pathology in New York and by 1953 was gaining a national reputation as one of the best pathologists of his generation.

All autopsies followed the same pattern, with the pathologist first opening the chest and abdomen. A Y-shaped incision was made, starting at each shoulder, allowing removal of the sternum, the breastbone that holds the ribs together. The single leg of the Y was then extended down the middle of the abdomen to the front of the pelvis, above the genitalia. Having first been observed *in situ*, the heart, lungs and entire contents of the abdomen were removed, a process known as evisceration. Each organ was then weighed and examined grossly by the naked eye before tissue samples were taken for microscopic-slide analysis.

Once this part of the process had been completed, the scalp was cut behind the hairline and folded back so that the top of the skull could be cut around like the band of a hat and removed, enabling Helpern to observe the brain *in situ* before taking it from the skull for gross and microscopic tissue examination.

Helpern's report concentrated upon the lungs, liver and brain. Of the lungs, he said, 'All lobes appear to be involved in the bronchopneumonic process,' adding that there was also evidence of emphysema, which one would expect from Thomas's history of asthma and smoking. The pneumonia was a direct result of him being in a coma for nearly five whole days. When death comes quickly in coma cases there is no time for the pneumonia to develop, but all patients who live more than two or three days in a coma will develop respiratory problems which then lead to full-blown lung infections.

Dylan's liver was described as having a 'consistency somewhat firmer than normal; fairly evident fatty infiltration'. This is interesting, because it reveals that despite his sister dying of liver cancer and his own drinking habits, his liver was not in a bad condition – and there was no evidence of cirrhosis. However, the amount of fatty infiltration of cirrhosis does not necessarily correlate with the amount of alcohol ingested in a lifetime.

Likewise, examination of his brain disclosed only 'pial oedema', a phrase that meant the cells and tissues were excessively swollen, causing the innermost layers of the three membranes that surround the brain to be swollen, too.

None of these findings of bronchopneumonia, fatty liver or cerebral oedema provided any proof whatsoever for the theory that Dylan Thomas died of 'alcoholic poisoning to his brain' or 'an acute insult to the brain'. These forensic findings could have resulted from other causes, and the only reason for alcohol being even mentioned in the postmortem report was because it was part of the medical history supplied by St Vincent's. There was nothing strange about this. It was standard practice in all cases referred to the Medical Examiner.

In the case of Dylan Thomas, Mahoney made sure there would be no controversy over his death:

> Patient brought into hospital in coma at 1.58 a.m. (5 November 1953). Remained in coma during hospital stay. History of heavy alcoholic intake. Received ½ grain of MS (morphine sulphate) shortly before admission . . . Impression on admission was acute alcoholic encephalopathy, for which patient was treated without response.

On a second notice, called 'The Telephone Notice of Death', there was another summary of Thomas's history: '(1) Heavy alcoholism (2) ½ grain morphine administered by a private doctor. Treated in hospital for toxic encephalopathy but diagnosis *unconfirmed*.'

✡ ✡ ✡

This phrase 'heavy alcoholic intake' was the only mention of alcohol in Dylan Thomas's medical records. It came directly from Reitell's account of what happened on 4 November, but *medically the diagnosis was unconfirmed*, leaving everyone free to disclaim responsibility.

All their tracks were covered. Dylan was dead, Caitlin was damaged beyond complaining . . . Mahoney was able to protect the reputation of St Vincent's, and in the process saved Feltenstein from public exposure and the risk of either criminal charges or a civil claim for damages. Reitell managed to project herself as the girlfriend who tried to save the dying poet, and John Malcolm Brinnin had all the material he needed for one final act of friendship, *Dylan Thomas in America*, with no one to correct him.

✡ ✡ ✡

On Tuesday 10 November the body was removed from the morgue at Bellevue to the midtown Manhattan clearing house, near Columbus Circle, where bodies were kept while arrangements were made for them to be collected by undertakers. Before Thomas's body was taken to a funeral parlour in the Bronx, where it remained for nearly a week, there was one more bizarre twist in the story.

Word reached the Slivkas, who lived at Washington Street in Greenwich Village, that the body was in the clearing house. By then Caitlin was staying at their apartment, phoning customs officials and Donald Maclean at the British Embassy in Washington, insisting Dylan 'must be taken home to Wales'. She was afraid that if he was buried or cremated in New York they would lose him forever, and maintained adamantly that 'he must go home so that we can give him a proper burial'. While she was fighting this battle, which she would never have won without Maclean's help, Ruthven Todd suggested to Dave Slivka, 'Someone ought to do a death mask of Dylan . . . We'll never forgive ourselves later if we don't get it done now while we have the chance.'

Knowing Caitlin might refuse permission and even be horrified at the thought of a death mask being made, Slivka sought the assistance of Donald

Maclean. Technically, as Caitlin had already discovered in trying to get permission to take the body home to Wales, the corpse was now the responsibility of the British Embassy and, without consulting her, Maclean said, 'Yes, I think that's a very good idea. People would wonder why we hadn't done it in years to come.'

And so, in one of the most extraordinary twists in the whole story, one of the leading Russian spies of the post-war era who was at that very time passing US nuclear secrets to the Soviets agreed that a plaster cast could be made of Dylan Thomas's head and torso. With very little time available, Slivka sought the help of the Egyptian sculptor Ibram Lassaw, who travelled with him by taxi up to Columbus Circle, carrying their tools and plaster of Paris. They were just in time. By a stroke of luck, a telephone call to Caitlin from the director of the Bronx funeral home was intercepted before they left the apartment.

'I'm looking for one of Mr Thomas's suits so that we can dress him properly in the coffin,' said the funeral director, who also wanted to know how he should embalm the body and was already at the clearing house.

'There'll be a suit at the Chelsea Hotel,' said Ruthven Todd, who volunteered to find a suitable tie at Walgreen's, a garish red which provoked the famous comment by Louis MacNeice on the day of the funeral: 'Dylan would never have been seen dead in a tie like that.'

'How do you want me to embalm the body?' asked the mortician. 'We can do a soft-embalm or a hard-embalm,' he explained, saying it all depended on how much formaldehyde was in the final solution.

'We were planning to make a plaster death mask,' said Slivka.

'Well, in that case it would be better if I did a soft-embalm. Otherwise, the skin might come off with the plaster mould,' said the mortician, and that was what was done.

Without consulting Caitlin, who was in no condition to make decisions, Slivka and Lassaw slipped down to the basement of the clearing house, knowing Caitlin was several floors above receiving visitors. 'The body is not fully prepared yet,' she was told, while Slivka and Lassaw, unknown to her, began work on the death mask. The large incisions in the chest and abdomen made at the autopsy were now sewn closed. Likewise, Dylan's scalp had been rolled back and expertly sewn so that no one would know a pathologist had removed his brain. The main problem facing Slivka and Lassaw was how to apply the plaster without Dylan's hair destroying the mould; they solved that by wetting his hair and smoothing it flat against his skull. 'I'll sort that out later, and recreate the hairstyle in my studio,' said Slivka.

The two sculptors used the stringmould technique in making the death mask, drawing nylon fishing line across Dylan's head and torso so that when the plaster set, the mould could be cut in five sections. The plaster was then mixed and applied to the head and torso. Once the plaster dried, the nylon wires were pulled, cutting the mould. The sections were then removed separately. They then cleaned his face and body, removing all trace of plaster, knowing that at any minute the mortician would return from the Chelsea with Thomas's suit.

None of this was made known to Caitlin. She was not told that a death mask had been made, even though she regarded Rose Slivka as her closest friend in the United States – and no one sought her permission to enter Thomas's room at the Chelsea and remove his suit.

Slivka used the plaster death mask to create several busts, using extra clay to fill out the head and missing portions of the original mask. Several bronze busts were eventually made. One ended up in Cardiff at the studios of the BBC; another went to the University of Southern Illinois, Slivka's teaching alma mater, and a third, naturally enough, went to the Poetry Center in New York. Strangely, each one was slightly different. The Poetry Center bust showed Dylan's last grimace, with an impression of agony that was missing in the others, where the cheeks and edges of the mouth are smoother. 'I did take some artistic liberties,' Slivka admitted, having deliberately removed all trace of the tracheotomy.

✳   ✳   ✳

Most of the participants in this strange drama came together one last time when a memorial service was held at St Luke's Episcopal church in New York on Friday 13 November. William Faulkner was there and so were e.e. cummings, Ruthven Todd and John Berryman. Caitlin sat through the service in the front row with Rollie McKenna. Liz Reitell stood at the back alone. That night, Caitlin left New York on board the SS *United States* with Dylan's coffin in the hold. She still knew no more about the causes of his death than when she arrived, and already the myth of 'The Alcoholic Poet' was replacing the facts of a tragedy.

14

Enter Dan, Stewbags and Lavatory Brush

It was what Caitlin wanted to do, and something she insisted the people of Wales would appreciate in generations to come: she had to bring the coffin back home to Laugharne, with the eviscerated corpse of her husband prepared for eternity with all the gruesome attention to detail of the American mortician's art. Nothing written by Evelyn Waugh could prepare the townspeople of Laugharne for this.

Caitlin possessed strong inner resources, but under emotional pressure she turned to whisky and started to dance. It may have been her Irish background or lack of conventional upbringing, but the deeper the pressure the wilder she danced. As the SS *United States* prepared to cross the Atlantic, she headed straight for the ship's bar, tanked herself up and began a whirling cancan that ended with the Captain having her strapped in a strait-jacket and confined to a lavatory.

There, as at River Crest, miserably aware of her loneliness, she promised to behave if the Captain would allow her to travel in the hold with the coffin. This was permitted, and she sat by the box, not in the least perturbed when the crew joined her, using its lid as a cardtable. 'Dylan would have liked that,' she said.

As the boat docked at Southampton, still bedecked with streamers and balloons after the Captain's Farewell Ball, she looked down at the quayside, and there stood Ebi Williams, who had driven up from Laugharne, picking up Dan Jones in Swansea. Perhaps it was an act of kindness, but with no one asking him to, Jones took charge of the funeral arrangements. He was there to see the coffin unloaded, he travelled back to West Wales in the hearse (a journey that turned into a pub crawl with Ebi, Caitlin, Dan and the dead Dylan ending up lost in the bowels of Somerset) and on the day of the funeral – in 'my self-appointed role of generalissimo'[1] – he turned Pelican into his headquarters, requiring the lesser ranks to 'report' to him there.

Before the day was over, Caitlin agreed to put her personal affairs in the care of Jones, his schoolfriend the solicitor John Stuart Hamilton Thomas (whom she later nicknamed 'Stewbags') and Dylan's literary agent David Higham (whom Dylan had long referred to as 'Lavatory Brush' because of his hairstyle). They may well have been trying to help a widow in distress, but that was not how she thought of it in later years.

✳ ✳ ✳

Why such a decision had to be made so quickly and on the day of the funeral remains a mystery, but this was a strange occasion. In England or Scotland, funerals of famous men are often a private, family affair, with a public memorial service held later where friends and colleagues join in tribute. This is not the custom in West Wales, where poets or dustmen receive no less respect in death than mayors or millionaires. All funerals follow a similar pattern, with no eulogies or special tributes, just hymns, prayers and the committal of mortal remains. 'We come into the world equal and we leave the world equal' is the way they look at it.

Inevitably, Welsh funerals are more intense. Tribute and grief are joined in one. Hundreds of mourners may turn up, sometimes thousands, and afterwards they adjourn to the pubs and the wake begins. Often these are wild affairs, lasting well into the night. Mourners may end up singing, fighting or making love, and no one is very surprised if they do.

His friends in Laugharne gave Dylan Thomas that kind of send-off. It was their way of honouring him, but the smart boyos of Swansea and besuited literary gents down from London looked on in horror as trays of drinks flew at the Brown's Hotel, faces were slapped, punches thrown and Caitlin started to dance another cancan. Reports travelled fast to Generalissimo Jones, who could barely believe his ears. Someone wanted to put a jar of pickled onions and a pint of beer on Dylan's grave. A lady 'was making herself available to all comers. A middle-aged roué, with a sports car and an unmistakable glint in his eye, had borne off the youngest of the visitors, a nymphet barely nubile . . . to the nearest Carmarthenshire meadow.'[2]

✳ ✳ ✳

Jones liked to portray himself as Dylan's closest friend. He claimed to have known him since earliest childhood, which was not strictly true, for Dylan dated their friendship precisely in his short story *The Fight*. This describes them scuffling in the playground at Swansea Grammar School and becoming firm friends thereafter. Dylan was three months short of his 15th birthday and Dan was two years older.

Daniel Jenkyn Jones, born in Pembroke on 7 December 1912, was that strangest of all characters, a natural polymath. He was tall and broadly built, a bulging figure of a man with a thick but cropped mop of hair and a distantly lost look behind his pebbled spectacles, but there seemed to be no intellectual discipline that he could not master. By the time he was 12, Jones had written seven novels and played both piano and violin; he later wrote 13 symphonies (which have all been performed on BBC Wales) and innumerable other classical scores, and read fluently in eight languages. During the war he was employed as a linguist at the Intelligence headquarters at Bletchley Park, cracking Japanese military codes. But, as sometimes happens with men of extraordinary intelligence, there was something lacking either creatively or in his approach to music and literature, for he failed to gain much recognition beyond Swansea. Perhaps he did not sell himself hard enough, unlike Dylan, who combined his gifts with the sheer commercial drive of a natural salesman.

It was a close friendship, but not a constant one. As teenagers they wrote poetry in alternating lines, produced their own magazine and engaged in precocious literary wordplay. They met occasionally during the war, with Jones turning up at Manresa Road and feeling 'a tinge of jealousy' because Dylan was often the centre of an admiring crowd and he was not,[3] but then there was a long gap with them neither meeting nor writing until their mid-to-late thirties. It was always a relationship with a juvenile undertone. 'Whenever they met they behaved like kids, bashing each other over the head with rolled-up newspapers and chasing around the garden, which always seemed odd to me,' said Caitlin, who found their jokes and storytelling a total bore.

✳ ✳ ✳

The funeral was held on 24 November. The coffin was left in the downstairs front room at Pelican with the lid removed so the townspeople and literary figures from afar could line up to pay their last respects, only to gasp with astonishment when they saw this unfamiliar work of body sculpture in its oddly immaculate suit, strangely spotted bow tie with a face pancaked with foundation, powder, rouge and bright red lipstick. As a small crowd gathered outside in the street for the procession down to the church, Dylan's Swansea friends and distant cousins made their way through to the back of the house where Granny Thomas presided chirpily over her kitchen, taking her third death in less than a year with surprising calm, dispensing endless cups of tea, sandwiches, scones and Welsh cakes as she welcomed them to her hearth.

Caitlin hovered on the edge of it all, reinforcing herself from a bottle of whisky she had hidden, determined to follow the body to the church. Jones stood by her in St Martin's as final prayers were said and gripped her firmly by the elbow as they led the congregation out to the churchyard, where mourners always gather *en masse* to witness the burial.

'I wanted to throw myself into the grave, like those Indian women on funeral pyres,' Caitlin recalled many years later, admitting that only the firm grasp of Generalissimo Jones prevented her from doing so. Thereafter, he returned to his headquarters and she repaired to the Brown's Hotel, throwing a box of chocolates at a man who thought them an appropriate gift for such an occasion and upending a tray bearing six pints of bitter over the mild-mannered and eternally loyal Swansea friend, artist Fred Janes, when he murmured, 'What a good thing it was Dylan managed to meet Ceri Richards before leaving for America.'

As the wake continued late into the afternoon, Caitlin withdrew from the bedlam with her sister Nicolette, walking in silence up Victoria Street towards The Cliff where, suddenly, without a word of warning, she tried to clamber over a waist-high wall to throw herself down on to the rocks below. As Nicolette grabbed her, Caitlin burst into tears. 'Let's go back to Castle House,' said Nicolette, knowing Richard and Frances had invited them to spend the night there if they wanted to.

There, in the second-floor bedroom where she had slept on her first visit to Laugharne nearly 20 years earlier, Caitlin's defences finally collapsed. Since receiving the telegram nearly three weeks before, she had maintained a frantic momentum, fuelled more by whisky than food, driving herself on, cursing and dancing, crossing the Atlantic with hope in her heart to endure a constant nightmare of hospitals, doctors and strait-jackets, with Dylan dying and the battle to bring him home, and never more than a few pounds in her pocket. Now it was all over, really over – with the grave filled, the mourners drinking and she alone in the world with three children, a house she did not own, debts of every kind and no means of providing herself with an income.

Perhaps it was this realisation, or maybe just a feeling of anti-climax as the day drew to a close, but bodily she collapsed, losing control of her bladder and bowels, and falling helplessly into pools of her own urine and faeces, part-sobbing, part-screaming with peals of hysterical laughter.

High Wind Hughes heard the noise and came running up the stairs, bursting in through the bedroom door and reacting with horror at what he saw. He began to shout and swear, which only made Caitlin's laughter more hysterical. 'Hughes was a pompous old stuffed shirt,' she recalled. 'A cold, unresponsive man with all that beard and bearing, the sort who dresses up for dinner in his own house and always insists on the best china and cutlery, whatever the food . . .'

✵ ✵ ✵

In the months after Dylan's death, the legend of 'The Destitute, Drunken Poet' took hold on the public imagination. Sympathy for Caitlin and the children ran deep, fuelled by press reports of her admittance to hospital and being left virtually penniless. Seldom has there been such a widespread response to the death of a poet.

This ranged from a stately anonymous obituary in *The Times* (written by Vernon Watkins), proclaiming,

> no poet of the English language has so hoodwinked and confuted his critics. None has ever worn more brilliantly the mask of anarchy to conceal the true face of tradition. There was nothing God ever made that Dylan Thomas, the revolutionary, wanted to alter . . . The most mistaken of his admirers were those who loved [his work] for its novelty. It was, even in its first phases, an ancient poetry, not rejecting antiquity for the present but seeking, with every device of language, the ancestry of the moment . . . [this was] a poet who was able to live Christianity in a public way, and whose work distilled it – a poet narrow and severe with himself and wide and forgiving in his affections. Innocence is always a paradox, and Dylan Thomas presents, in retrospect, the greatest paradox of our time.[4]

to a page-long tribute in what was then the world's most widely read newspaper, *The Daily Mirror*, whose columnist Cassandra (William O'Connor) hailed Thomas as 'The Genius of the Year':

> The flabby baby-face: the chubby and slightly seedy get-up: the uproarious nights in pubs: the monumental laziness: the raffishness: the suspicion that someone deeply devoted to the shadier side of dog racing had come into the room: the dazzling trail of debts – the Creator never wove such a deceiving coat and never cast such a strange mantle around such a favoured son.

Dylan Marlais Thomas, poet, roisterer and lover of mankind, had the divine flash within him. Not for him the bloodless world of slide-rules and isotopes; not for him the clinical detachment of frosty reason.

Thomas – fierce, fine and foolish Thomas – had hotter fires to stoke and brighter flames in which to consume himself.

Words were the jewellery that he scattered before him in cascades of sparkling brilliance. No poet in living memory hauled such lovely diamonds from the deep mines of vocabulary.[5]

In addition, his close friend the cricket commentator and poet John Arlott wrote in *The Spectator* that Thomas was:

the most original poet of the '30s and '40s. In a too-large tweed jacket or a seaman's jersey and flannel trousers, cigarette hanging from his lips, pint pot in front of him, perhaps he looked too much the Bohemian for some to believe him a genuine artist . . . he was, perhaps, most hurt of all when Wales did not understand the man who wrote with Wales at the heart of his imagination and understanding. He was himself a very generous and very Welsh Welshman.[6]

Equally remarkable was the sudden outpouring by fellow poets who felt compelled to commemorate their fallen comrade, with Louis MacNeice writing his *Canto in Memoriam Dylan Thomas*, which ran to 44 verses, and George Barker mercifully ending *At the Wake of Dylan Thomas* after 26. Other poems poured from the pens of Dannie Abse, Ronald Bottrall, John Malcolm Brinnin, Alex Comfort, Anthony Conran, Allen Curnow, Ken Etheridge, Gavin Ewart, Lloyd Frankenberg, C. Day Lewis, Jack Lindsay, Emanuel Litvinoff, Hugh MacDiarmid, Huw Menai, Thomas Merton, Leslie Norris, George Reavey, Kenneth Rexroth, Theodore Roethke, Vernon Scannell, Edith Sitwell, Stephen Spender, Ruthven Todd, Jose Garcia Williams and, of course, Vernon Watkins, who kept on writing poems about Dylan for the rest of his life.

Literally tens of thousands of words streamed from the world's writers, but many also dipped deep into their pockets and helped promote the various funds established in the United States and Britain to ensure Caitlin and the children did not have to spend the rest of their days in poverty, living on state hand-outs.

It was all well intentioned. In New York, an appeal was signed by W.H. Auden, Marianne Moore, Arthur Miller, e.e. cummings, Wallace Stevens and Tennessee Williams, while in London a separate fund was launched by T.S. Eliot, Dame Peggy Ashcroft, Sir Kenneth Clark, Walter de la Mare, Graham

Greene, Augustus John, Louis MacNeice, Edwin Muir, Goronwy Rees, Dame Edith Sitwell, Sir Osbert Sitwell, Vernon Watkins and Emlyn Williams. A third fund was established by the Lord Mayor of Swansea.

In addition to these appeals for donations, sponsored by so many eminent literary figures of the day, *The Sunday Times* staged *A Homage to Dylan Thomas* at the Globe Theatre, London, on 24 January 1954, with readings by Richard Burton, Emlyn Williams, Louis MacNeice and Huw Griffith and programme notes by Dame Edith Sitwell. The performance was recorded and released in LP form by Decca.

Three weeks later, on 14 February, the National Book League, the English Centre of PEN, the Apollo Society, the London Welsh Association and the Institute of Contemporary Arts presented a memorial recital at the Royal Festival Hall, London, in association with the Arts Council. This time, Emlyn Williams appeared with Dame Peggy Ashcroft, Christopher Hassall, Dame Sybil Thorndike, Sir Lewis Casson, Michael Hordern and Cecil Day Lewis.

When the widely acclaimed radio production of *Under Milk Wood*, starring Richard Burton and produced by Douglas Cleverdon, was released by Argo as a double LP, the whole cast donated their royalties to help Caitlin and the children, raising many thousands of pounds.

These laudable acts of charity were driven by the most poignant of images, handed down by Victorian writers, of the widow desperately trying to save her children from the workhouse. It provided a powerful parallel to the New York myth of 'The Poet's Final Binge'. And it was equally false.

✳   ✳   ✳

No one liked to admit it, least of all Dan, Stewbags and Lavatory Brush, but money was now cascading into the Dylan Thomas Estate. If the truth be known, Caitlin and her children had no need of charity – but no one chose to say so. Caitlin herself had no idea what she was worth, and if the world had known how she was living, barely a penny would have dropped into the Dylan Thomas poorbox.

✳   ✳   ✳

The Trust initiated in the hours following the funeral (some say agreement was reached in the churchyard well before the grave was filled in) soon came into being. One could understand the honourable intent of Dr Daniel Jones, anxious to protect the family of his dearest friend. One might also appreciate why David Higham, who had been Dylan's agent since before the war, preferred to channel all monies earned through a solicitor rather than deal directly with Caitlin, for there is a long literary history of poets' widows being exceptionally difficult to handle. But it is altogether much more difficult to comprehend why an obscure Swansea solicitor, who was barely known in the town he lived in and had few literary connections beyond a drinking friendship with a junior lecturer at the University College of Swansea by the name of Kingsley Amis, should quickly emerge as the key figure in the Trust's affairs.

Given that the total value of Dylan's worldly goods and possessions was said to be *de minimus*,[7] John Stuart Hamilton Thomas moved with remarkable speed. Six days after the funeral, he and Dan Jones drove over from Swansea and personally accompanied Caitlin to the Carmarthen District Probate Registry, where she reported that her husband had died and applied formally for letters of administration, i.e. legal authority to administer his estate.

Seven days later, on 7 December 1953, the District Registrar issued the document certifying that 'Caitlin Thomas of The Boat House' was 'the lawful widow and relict and the only person now entitled to the estate'.

Whether or not this certificate was issued to her or to someone acting on her behalf is a matter of some interest, for immediately after making the initial application Caitlin travelled up to London with a man she met at the funeral, planning to stay with the Lockes at 260 King Street, Hammersmith. On the evening of 1 December, she attacked a stranger in a pub and later tried to commit suicide, this time by throwing herself out of a third-storey window at the Lockes' apartment. A shop canopy broke her fall, possibly saving her life, but her collarbone was broken and she was taken to the West London Hospital.

The following day, she applied to be admitted to the Holloway Sanatorium, a mental clinic at Virginia Water, saying:

> I desire to enter your hospital as a voluntary patient understanding that I can leave at any time on giving three days' notice.[8]

Her application, signed with some difficulty because of her injuries, was accompanied by a letter from Dr A.S. Paterson, Physician-in-Charge of the Department of Psychiatry at the West London Hospital, reporting that Caitlin was 'intoxicated' when she fell and giving information about her background which had been provided by her sister, Nicolette:

> Patient has always been impulsive and difficult. She is apt to be suddenly violent. She quarrelled a great deal with her husband who was quick-tempered

... She has been drinking a half-bottle of whisky daily and much beer ... Patient is a chronic alcoholic at present. Not a typical melancholia. She may be violent. She may be a paranoid psychopath. Needs careful handling. Likely to be demanding, I'm afraid. Will insist on leaving before long.[9]

As expected, Caitlin soon demanded to be released, and she left the clinic on 7 December, against medical advice, with her discharge certificate noting her 'history of lifelong instability, characterised by bouts of aggressive behaviour and alcoholism'.

The significance of these medical details lies in the fact that here was a widow, plainly suffering great distress after the loss of her husband, and in no good state to make important decisions about her future – and yet even as she lay in the clinic, receiving dosages of paraldehyde, sodium amytal and vitamin B, Jones, Higham and Thomas were pressing ahead with their plans to create the Trust.

Their urgency is hard to explain, for in her application for probate, Caitlin testified upon oath, on Stuart Thomas's advice, that the value of her husband's estate amounted to no more than £100 'so far as at present can be ascertained' – and this was the figure reported in the press.[10]

✽　✽　✽

The Trust deed, of which we have a copy, was signed on 28 December 1953. Again, it seems rather strange that all the parties should have been so anxious to interrupt their Christmas and New Year holidays to agree how such a small estate should be administered. Without taking any independent advice, Caitlin agreed to assign the whole of her inheritance to the Trust: £100 in cash that was held by the Lloyds Bank branch at St Helens Road, Swansea, and 'all copyrights and interests in copyrights in respect of the literary works of the late husband of the Settlor, Dylan Marlais Thomas'. Caitlin agreed that the Trust's income should be divided with one half going to her and the other divided equally between Llewelyn, Aeronwy and Colm.

✽　✽　✽

From the beginning, the three Trustees saw themselves with different functions. Jones assumed the role of 'Literary Trustee' and Higham handled renewal of publishing contracts and sale of subsidiary rights, collecting any monies due and (after deducting the usual 10 per cent commission) remitting the balance to Thomas's office at 103 Walter Road, Swansea, where Thomas oversaw the Trust's day-to-day administration.

Initially these arrangements ran smoothly enough, although Jones tended to overplay his hand, insisting on writing the music for *Under Milk Wood*, attending rehearsals for the radio production and blocking any corrections to the script typed up by Cleverdon's secretary Elizabeth Fox, including those incorporated by Dylan himself in New York. When *Under Milk Wood* was published, Jones wrote a preface and made many changes in punctuation, sometimes altering the meaning of words or phrases without textual authority. Later, he edited a collection of Dylan's short stories, *A Prospect of the Sea*, and produced what he described as the definitive edition of *The Poems*, which included one poem Dylan did not write, many mistakes of analysis and several claims that one Daniel Jenkyn Jones inspired particular poems.

Stranger still, Jones wrote a personal memoir, *My Friend Dylan Thomas*, which made no mention of Caitlin's name whatsoever, and left the reader with the uncomfortable impression that its author thought Thomas uncommonly blessed to have had such a fine friend.

The motivations of John Stuart Hamilton Thomas are altogether harder to assess. Like his friend Amis, he was a jolly, convivial, hard-drinking man with extreme right-wing opinions on nearly every public issue. He disliked 'blacks', immigrants and trade unionists and, although married, enjoyed telling jokes belittling women.

Throughout the ups and downs of Amis's career, the rare acclaim for good novels and frequent abuse for bad, the years of writing potboilers and even poetry criticism for *The Daily Mirror*, the times he left one wife and was deserted by the next, Thomas remained his staunchest friend, united in misogyny. Whatever the state of Amis's love life or finances, he would leave London in August when the Garrick closed to spend the month at Thomas's bungalow in the Mumbles, where they would souse themselves in whisky every lunchtime, often remaining sozzled for the rest of the day.

The strange thing was that neither of them ever expressed the slightest respect for Dylan Thomas or his widow, with Amis (who eventually became a Trustee of the Dylan Thomas Estate) demonstrating his contempt for the Thomases in many book reviews, essays and newspaper articles, and portraying Dylan as a lecherous drunk in *That Uncertain Feeling*. In his *Memoirs* (1991), Amis described Dylan as 'an outstandingly unpleasant man' and 'a pernicious figure, one who has helped to get Wales and Welsh poetry a bad name and generally done lasting harm to both' and

Caitlin as having 'a personal disagreeableness all her own and a purer egotism, one that calls for others' attention not through wit or other quality, but just by being there . . .'

✻   ✻   ✻

For the time being, it suited Caitlin to have someone to turn to, and there can be no denying Jones and Thomas did what they could to help her in the months after Dylan's death. There was less need to involve Higham, for he was London based. She looked upon Jones and Thomas as personal friends. They visited each other's homes and dined and drank in harmony, with Llewelyn eventually marrying Stuart's stepdaughter, Rhiannon. In their relative innocence, the two old boys of Swansea Grammar School probably believed honour would be satisfied once Dylan's debts were paid and enough money flowing through to cover his children's school fees and a regular allowance to his widow. But it was never to be that easy.

Caitlin herself had no idea what money was raised by the different appeals and did not know for several years how much was handled by the Trustees, who thought this none of her business now that *they* were entrusted with her late husband's estate. She would have liked £1,300 to buy The Boat House when Margaret Taylor, now strapped for cash, offered it to her for a knockdown price. The Trustees, however, said she could not afford it, yet six months later bought it themselves at the same price so that Caitlin became their tenant.

This, in a nutshell, represented what happened to her within months of her husband's death; she became beholden to the Trustees, whom she had appointed by the deed dated 28 December 1953 to look after *her* inheritance. And not only did they acquire her home; Jones also went door to door in Laugharne telling the butcher, baker, grocer, milkman, chemist and pubkeepers that Mrs Caitlin Thomas was to be allowed no further credit.

Just what they thought they were playing at is hard to imagine, for Trustees of any estate usually confine themselves to protecting the assets vested in them and ensuring an equitable distribution of income. These Trustees refused to keep Caitlin informed about the estate's affairs, accumulated funds without her knowledge, drew extraordinary expenses (which will be mentioned later), sought to exercise some kind of control over her private life – and never spoke to the press, with the result that few people realised the growing scale of Dylan Thomas's posthumous achievement.

For 40 years thereafter, the Trustees could never understand why 'the widow' (as Stuart Thomas usually chose to describe her, seldom mentioning her by name) could rarely bring herself to say a good word about them.

✤ ✤ ✤

At the same time, Caitlin gave the Trustees every cause to doubt her sanity. Dan Jones resigned after two years, complaining the experience left him 'in as unstable a condition as many of the most hysterical around me'[11] and convinced Caitlin was clinically mad.[12] His opinions may have been affected by Caitlin's attempt to strangle his wife.[13]

The root cause of all the hostilities were those twin devils, money and sex. Whenever they sent her money, Caitlin always came back for more, dressing up her appeals with threats and curses, or wails of poverty. They might have been able to cope with that under normal circumstances, but her sexual adventures shocked them to the core.

Her first lover was the cameraman David Gardner, who had filmed Dylan reading *The Outing* on BBC Television in August 1953. Gardner came down for the funeral, travelled up to London with her a week later and was with Caitlin the night she threw herself from the Lockes' window. On her release from the clinic at Virginia Water, they became lovers. The relationship lasted two years, but there were usually other men in her life as well, including a travelling draper based in Laugharne, whose marriage she destroyed, and a ship's captain who spent much of each year away at sea. Neither he nor she expected the other to be faithful, and they would happily pick up the relationship when he returned.

Few were inclined to be censorious about these affairs, realising Caitlin had been through a hard time, but eventually she became indiscriminate, picking up teenagers at dances and taking men home from pubs. At the time a firm called Watson and Horrocks were laying down the pipes to bring Laugharne its first piped water supply, and somewhat to the annoyance of local people (who would have liked the work), the firm brought in a gang of Irish labourers to dig the trenches. In the early hours of one morning, Caitlin was observed in an alleyway off Victoria Street, being fucked (which is the only word one can use to describe the situation) by the Irish diggers, who were standing in a queue, each waiting to take his turn.[14]

No matter where she went, Caitlin seemed determined to shock. In London, she staged noisy scenes in theatres and restaurants and often turned violent with drink. On at least one occasion she was arrested for drunkenness in the street and kept overnight in police cells. In Laugharne, the town stared in silence on the day of the annual carnival when she dressed herself up in full

Moulin Rouge costume and danced a vigorous cancan from the church lych-gate to the Grist Square, a distance of roughly half a mile – for they could see she wore no knickers. No one could tell what was on her mind, or why her life now seemed to be absorbed by a daily process of self-abasement.

15

Searching for Explanations

Within days of her husband's funeral, Caitlin started to worry about the role of Liz Reitell. They had seen each other at St Vincent's, both dressed in black, and may have been introduced, yet initially Caitlin was so caught up in the drama of her transatlantic flight to Dylan's bedside and subsequent removal to River Crest that she did not stop to ask why another woman was sitting there, publicly mourning the poet before he was even dead. But as soon as she returned to Laugharne, Caitlin began asking questions.

Had Stuart Thomas been a better solicitor, or a more experienced lawyer with access to advice on the American legal system, she might have filed claims for damages against Dr Feltenstein or the hospital authorities, but as a widow on her own, beset by Dylan's debts and with hardly any money, she found herself wholly dependent upon the Trustees, who sent her £8 a week to live on and reacted with cold disapproval whenever she asked for more to buy clothes for the children or a few personal luxuries, even though they were soon handling many thousands of pounds. Wherever she looked, Caitlin faced a wall of silence. Even among those who had an inkling there was no one willing to explain what had happened, and she realised soon enough that Reitell and Brinnin were in cahoots. With Rose Slivka a personal friend of Liz Reitell, Rollie McKenna similarly close to Brinnin and the hospital authorities closing ranks to prevent a scandal (and thereby shielding Feltenstein), Caitlin had no authoritative sources of information in New York to go to.

Instinctively she turned to women for advice, being never wholly trustful of men. Caitlin began seeing far more of her mother and sister Brigid, eventually arranging for them both to receive allowances through the Trust as its income grew; her other sister Nicolette, Ivy Williams of Brown's Hotel, Helen McAlpine and Wyn Henderson all became part of what was, in effect, a sisterhood, a coming-together of long-standing friends to whom she could turn, knowing that none of them ever would (or did) betray her confidence.

From men, she wanted sexual comfort – and not much else. 'All men are bastards' became her pre-feminist cry, citing not only her father's wanton promiscuity, Dylan's infidelity and her molestation by Augustus John, but what for her was the equally vulgar behaviour of Dan, Stewbags and Lavatory Brush. For them, as in her last letter to Dylan, she reserved her ultimate words of abuse: they were plain stingy.

✻   ✻   ✻

In those early years of the Trust's affairs, Jones, Higham and Thomas (and later the broadcaster Wynford Vaughan-Thomas, another old boy of Swansea Grammar School who replaced Jones on 24 May 1955) probably believed in all sincerity that they were doing well by Dylan's memory in ensuring his debts were paid, his children expensively educated and Caitlin given a weekly allowance that was more than many people earned at the time.

Because of Dylan's beggarly, mendacious and disorderly way of life, they may well have convinced themselves that Caitlin was now better off than she had ever been. This was not true. The Thomas legend of poverty had long been a lie. As we have already pointed out, for at least his last six or seven years, Dylan had access to large sums of money every year. These might not fall within the usual classification of 'earnings', since only part of the money was handled by his agent, cheques were often cashed without passing through his bank account and he managed to conceal it all by pleading poverty to his friends and deceiving his wife; but not always. Sometimes, the Thomases were awash with cash – and then they dined and drank like nabobs, always choosing the best restaurants, splashing out at the top nightclubs and buying themselves expensive clothes.

Caitlin could not live like that on £8 a week and she now began bombarding the Trustees with requests for more, frequently using her allowance to buy shoes or cosmetics – and then accusing them of not giving her enough money to pay for food or medical bills. This erratic behaviour was exacerbated by constant drunkenness, a messy sex life and a desire to get away to London whenever she could, usually accompanied by women friends who would quietly melt away as soon as she became unstable.

One might have expected any normal bunch of men, finding themselves running a Trust in circumstances such as these, to find something more congenial to do with their time. But David Higham was left to look after the Trust's income and rarely had to deal with Caitlin personally; Wynford Vaughan-Thomas had a much more leisurely approach than Jones to the role of 'Literary Trustee', and was willing to leave Stuart Thomas to administer the Trust virtually singlehandedly. Inevitably, Thomas became the butt of all Caitlin's claims and accusations, but this did not seem to bother him and he gradually began to treat her with contempt.

Although convivial in male company and always loyal to Jones, Vaughan-Thomas and Amis, Stuart Thomas did not suffer fools gladly. He dealt with his firm's business efficiently every morning, often dictating single-paragraph letters that dealt with a matter at issue precisely and to the point, but anyone who had cause to deal with him knew better than to do so after lunch.

Heaven knows what drove him on, for Stuart Thomas had no literary interests and never expressed the slightest enthusiasm for Dylan Thomas's *oeuvres,* but as 'the widow' became more and more demanding, he dug in his heels, resisted her claims and hung on to the Trust's reins with remarkable tenacity.

Soon enough, there was justification for his stewardship. Income to the estate rapidly rose beyond £10,000 a year, and within four years (i.e. by the end of September 1957) reached a grand total of £47,234 16s 1d.[1] It could now be seen that the dead Dylan Thomas, just like the live one, was earning more than a government Minister or a High Court judge – and these monies did not include the cash that came flowing through as well from the various appeals and fund-raising events organised to relieve the 'distress' of the family.

✲ ✲ ✲

All this made little difference to the lifestyle of Caitlin Thomas. Whatever she had, she spent. Money was never saved, but for the first few months of her solitude Caitlin was relatively constrained. This was largely due to the support of her women friends, who made sure she was rarely left alone in The Boat House. Wyn Henderson stayed with her for weeks at a time, as did Nicolette, and initially Caitlin's affairs with men were almost decorous. She and Gardner, who lived in Bristol, exchanged flirtatious letters, and he frequently came down to Laugharne in his sports car to take her off around the country, which was something she had never been able to do with Dylan, who never drove anything more exciting than a bicycle; but always at the back of her mind lay the niggling thoughts that she could find no explanation for Dylan's death, or the way Brinnin, McKenna and Slivka managed to avoid giving her the answers she wanted about his relationship with Reitell.

As we have already mentioned, she wrote to McKenna asking for help in resolving what she termed 'these gnawing bafflements'. Eventually, she also wrote twice to Reitell, who promptly sought advice from Brinnin, but the real shock came when Caitlin learned that Brinnin was writing an account of Dylan's four visits to America just as she was beginning work on her own book, *Leftover Life to Kill*.

* * *

Long after their return to Britain, Caitlin looked upon the family holiday in Italy, and especially their weeks on Elba, as one of her happier times. Dylan did not enjoy the sun any more than he liked Italians, but she revelled in its warmth and the miners' earthiness in the small town of Rio Marina.

Once Llewelyn and Aeronwy had gone back to their boarding schools after the long summer holidays, Caitlin returned to the hotel – and the same room – that the Thomases had stayed in seven years before, accompanied only by Colm and with an allowance arranged by Stuart Thomas of £14 a week. And there she began to write. Day after day she sat at a table, scribbling furiously on loose sheets of paper, often writing for hours on end, while Colm attended an infant convent school. At night, they 'clung together, like the white-haired, shipwrecked ancient mariner and son; and this scrap of Dylan contact was both comforting and disturbing to me'.[2]

Soon the burly, possessive hotel owner Giovanni became Caitlin's lover, driving her around on his motorbike, but then she fell for Joseph, a strong-thighed 'beautiful boy'[3] of only 18, who worked ten-hour shifts down the local iron mine and looked after Colm in the late afternoons while she learned Italian with the wife of an Englishman who lived nearby.

To begin with, it was no more than an innocent friendship. Joseph would take her out in a boat with Colm and she found herself laughing at his 'comical terror at wetting his feet',[4] but then one day, impulsively, there was no stopping the 'heady, rushing' speed with which they made love, ignoring all the social constraints of age and motherhood that had previously made that seem impossible. 'This state of affairs was far from pleasing to me,' she wrote.[5] 'It brought back sensations I hoped never to suffer again: going weak at the knees, the stomach turning over, and dropping down, the heart thumping in the throat, a dizzy spinning of sickness, and an incurable impulse to bolt, at the sight of him . . . All the time hammering into my head were those pathetically insufficient years, making a silly farce of the situation . . . I experienced an inexplicable guilt at taking something that did not belong to me.'

And then there was the sense of ridicule, Giovanni's jealousy at being supplanted by a mere boy, and the women outside her window shouting 'prostituta, prostituta' as the hotel bill began to mount, and she found herself unable to raise any more money from Stuart Thomas, not because he was unhelpful but due to the strict currency controls that were then enforced upon travellers by the Bank of England.

✳   ✳   ✳

Caitlin returned to Laugharne and the arms of David Gardner with her unfinished manuscript. This was in April, shortly before she heard the disquieting news from Higham that Brinnin had finished writing *Dylan Thomas in America*. The book was due to be published in America in October, but a copy of the manuscript was sent over for her to read, not because the publishers wanted her approval but through a general anxiety (that was also shared by the London publishers) that the overall effect of the book might be libellous.

Brinnin was far too careful to lay himself open to civil proceedings. There was very little mention of drugs, although he must have known how foolishly Thomas washed them down with alcohol, and he was so circuitous in describing Thomas's sexual behaviour that he undoubtedly created the impression that Dylan was far more promiscuous than he really was. As we have already noted, many of the incidents that seemed to shock Brinnin to his virginal core were no more than flirtatious games of a kind Dylan played with cheerful vulgarity in the pubs of Swansea and London for the whole of his adult life. But one underlying message lay there, in uncompromising black and white: Dylan had clearly had two important affairs, the first with Pearl Kazin and the second with Liz Reitell.

Caitlin could cope, just about, with Brinnin's recollections of Pearl (whom he gave the name of 'Sarah'), for she and Margaret Taylor had managed to put an end to that affair by diverting the letters Thomas was receiving at his club in the late summer of 1950, but it was still a humiliation to know that the world would soon be reading all about her husband's preference for another woman. Even more distressing to Caitlin, however, was the realisation that Dylan was in love with someone else at the time he died.

She could read between the lines: Brinnin might be dressing up his narrative with a degree of *double entendre*, but the fact that Reitell was in Dylan's room at the Chelsea Hotel and he collapsed in her arms was a total body blow. Caitlin might have poured her heart out in that final letter, saying the marriage was all over, but she still considered that this was private between them. In fact, she did not tell anyone about the letter for over 30 years, until suddenly she burst into tears while talking to Tremlett at her home in Catania – and there can be little doubt she flew to New York on 7 November 1953 hoping for a tearful reunion at Dylan's bedside.

Whether or not it was at Caitlin's request we do not know, but one vital phrase was deleted from Brinnin's manuscript between its delivery to the American publishers Atlantic, Little Brown and the printing of the actual book. This phrase appears on page 224 of Brinnin's original manuscript, which can now be found among his papers at the University of Delaware. This page describes the moments before Dylan walked out of the Chelsea for the last time, saying, 'I've got to have a drink.' He was in tears, talking of the misery of his existence and how much he loved his youngest child, Colm. 'Poor little bugger, he doesn't deserve this,' said Dylan. Reitell asked him what he meant and Thomas continued, 'He doesn't deserve me wanting to die. I truly want to die . . .' He then started talking about Caitlin's beauty, with the famous words, 'You've no idea how beautiful she is. There is an illumination about her. She shines' – and then followed the words that Brinnin missed out: '*But we can't live together.*'

And there you have it, as clear as clear can be – the corroboration that Dylan realised as much as she did that the marriage was dead. They might still love each other – and we believe they did, in their own unusual way – but there had been so much misery, violence and mistrust since Caitlin saw Pearl's letters protruding from his pocket and Margaret Taylor came down to Laugharne with her words of confirmation, that they could no longer live together under the same roof. He knew it. She knew it. But for the rest of her life, Caitlin battled daily with the knowledge that her one true love, as she continued to call him, had been bodily torn from her just at the moment she was expecting a reconciliation.

We believe Caitlin was deeply traumatised. Had she been part of a more cohesive family, had her children been old enough to help her, she might have benefited from psychiatric treatment. Instead, Caitlin began behaving in the ways we described at the end of the last chapter. Her desperate need for love became a constant search for sexual satisfaction. She picked up young men and took them behind the Memorial Hall in Laugharne for a few minutes of sex, lined up that queue of Irish labourers one morning off Victoria Street, danced through the streets without her underwear, and staged embarrassing confrontations with her lovers' wives in the town's bars. She was a woman in distress.

✻   ✻   ✻

During the remaining months of 1955 and the early part of 1956, Caitlin spent much of her time at The Boat House, still working on *Leftover Life to Kill* (which was eventually cut, shaped and crafted into a printable manuscript by her publisher, Roger Lubbock), and also beginning *Am I the Perfect Fool?* (which has not been published), in which she sought to defend herself and her marriage against Brinnin's closely argued charge that the Thomases were wanton, self-destructive, drunken and dissolute. Wyn Henderson kept her company most of the time, but occasionally Caitlin would visit London, usually staying with the Lockes, while Dolly Long looked after Colm, who was now attending Laugharne primary school.

Another thought was driving her on. Caitlin still wanted to learn as much as she could about Liz Reitell, whom she now looked upon as a rival even though Dylan was dead, and she was anxious to get away, far beyond the reach of the press, before *Dylan Thomas in America* was published in Britain.

Nearly two months ahead of its publication, the first articles started appearing in the tabloid newspapers, with *The Sunday Graphic* publishing interviews with Caitlin in its issues dated 19 and 26 February, and she knew well enough that Brinnin's book would be printed confirmation (or so it seemed) that Dylan killed himself with drink after years of debauchery. She confined herself to just one more public comment, agreeing to appear some time later on television with Daniel Farson. As the time for the live interview drew nearer, Caitlin refused to sit down in the studio and stood leering into the camera, her hand upon her hip. When Farson asked about Brinnin, she snarled, 'That bloody man was in love with my husband' – and Farson promptly ended the interview in little more than a minute, with the cameraman switching to the next item. Caitlin was not without friends. There were many who resented both Brinnin's disclosures and Farson's line of questioning, and that evening Constantine Fitzgibbon emptied a pint of beer over Farson's head.

By the time the book was published, Caitlin was gone, this time to the island of Procida, in the Bay of Naples, accompanied by Wyn Henderson. With Stuart Thomas supplying a monthly allowance, they rented an old house overlooking the sea with a garden of orange, lemon and apricot trees.

The children joined them there for the summer, and Caitlin soon found herself another lover, Mario, a dark-skinned Italian, her 'black boy' whom she described as 'perfectly ravishing . . . a complete black, hairy animal with no impeding brains whatsoever'.[6] But Liz Reitell was seldom far from her mind.

✷ ✷ ✷

Throughout their years together, Caitlin never ceased believing in the timeless quality of Dylan's poetry. That alone made everything else worth while, or at least sufferable, and she saw herself as part of the timelessness. Her father wrote poetry and so did she, but Caitlin rarely allowed anyone else to read her work. She was lacking in literary discipline, never submitting herself to the rigorous search for rhyme and metre, internal rhythms and developed argument that made Dylan's finer poems such major works, but Caitlin was good. 'She's a better poet than I am,' Dylan used to say, [7] and there was an element of truth in that. She would often suggest minor changes when he came down into The Boat House kitchen and showed her a few newly minted lines, and there could be little doubt in the mind of anyone who heard her talking naturally, freely and without inhibition that his technique of joining words in a bubbling sequence, employed most effectively in *Under Milk Wood*, came directly from her. It was how she spoke every day. For all Lubbock's careful editing, you can hear this voice in *Leftover Life* as well. And it was against this background of a shared literary experience that she acutely resented Brinnin hailing Reitell as the woman who sought to bring some shape and order into Dylan's life, providing not only comfort but day-to-day help with his schedule, health and wardrobe, and, worst of all, literary guidance.[8]

Before the book was published, Caitlin wrote a statement that appeared at its front, saying among much else:

> I am not quarrelling with Brinnin's presentation of Dylan. It is impossible to hit back at a man who does not know that he is hitting you, and who is far too cautious of the laws of libel to say plainly what can only be read between the lines.[9]

That was enough to trigger off the critics in both Britain and America; she was telling them they could lift stories from Brinnin's book about the state of her marriage and their lives of infidelity without fear of a writ. But she still did not say that what was bothering her most was his revelation that Reitell came briefly to fulfil the role in Dylan's life that she thought her very own.

✶ ✶ ✶

In fact, Brinnin told his readers little about Liz Reitell other than that she was his assistant at the Poetry Center, helped stage *Under Milk Wood* and made many of the arrangements for Dylan's third and fourth tours, accompanying him much of the time. We explained her background in chapter nine, but what kind of woman was she? Did Brinnin reflect her importance to Dylan correctly, or was this another of Brinnin's exaggerations? We are grateful to Arthur Miller, author of *Death of a Salesman* and *The Crucible*, for shedding some light on the matter.

After Dylan died, Reitell worked for some years as Miller's part-time secretary before moving to Missoula, Montana, to take up a job helping to produce publications for the Montana University's School of Forestry. She became active in various environmental groups, including the Montana Wilderness Association, the Great Bear Foundation and the Forever Wild Endowment, and also spent six years working for the Columbia River Inter-Tribal Fish Commission.

In an interview with a local newspaper, Reitell (by then known as Liz Smith and The Woman Who Loved Dylan Thomas) said, 'I had to fight for my own life after Dylan's death . . . I built on top of Dylan's death. Built on top – that is such a perfect phrase. "Oh well, you'll forget, time will pass, time will heal" – all those old saws. None of them are true, not when you have the absolute, elemental loss. I never forgot him.'[10]

Miller accepts that she was 'an intelligent, efficient, hearty woman' who may well have been helpful to Dylan 'as critic or as a sort of cultural guide; I think she knew a good deal about contemporary writing and had taste'.

However, early one evening Miller drove to the Chelsea Hotel and picked them both up in his car. He and Thomas were among a group of writers who had agreed to read from their work at a nearby high school:

> He was drinking rapidly, was fairly drunk but alert. I sensed an enormous sadness in him, a self-depreciation verging on open self-contempt. At the time I connected this with his selling his fame for the money that readings brought him. For he not only had to read but emote lyrically, in effect to pretend to feel on cue. When we went down and got into my car, a new Ford, he suddenly turned and asked, 'What are *you* doing this for?' Meaning that I was

not poor enough to have to do such readings, and that he never would be stooping to them if he hadn't had to.

I recall that he treated Liz offhandedly and with no great respect. She strove rather pathetically to ignore this and to assert her importance to him, or so it seemed to me. She laughed when nothing funny was said, striving to keep the atmosphere gay and light while he was visibly becoming more sodden and introspective. I figured she was probably useful to him in practical matters but I did not feel any deep attachment between them, at least not on his part. I might add that I never found her very attractive sexually, which may have warped my estimate of her importance to him as a lover.

Miller added that many years later, in the early '90s, Reitell visited him in the country,

and was quite changed. She showed us a tape of herself talking about Dylan and the passionate affair between them, again asserting her central role in his life, something I never witnessed and had to doubt. Of course, he may well have given her reason to believe in this role, and may for a time [have] believed it himself . . . She had a bald spot at the crown of her head and covered it with black shoe-polish, and she seemed to me to be totally self-absorbed and possibly delusionary with a fixed idea about her importance to the great poet.[11]

Caitlin had no such perceptions to guide her. No one put this contrary and to our mind convincing view that there was no great bond between Dylan and this other woman. Instead, Caitlin was left to believe that she had not only lost Dylan's bodily presence, but also that part of his mind that was hers. This all added to her instability and underlying sense of failure.

✻　✻　✻

While Caitlin was out in Procida, a journalist (Robert Pitman) tracked her down, describing her as a woman whose 'pretty green eyes were placid', with a figure (she was 39) 'as lithe as a teenage girl's'.[12]

Asking her 'the worst question first', Pitman sought a reaction to Brinnin's disclosures. 'It was a cruel book,' she said. 'I was just recovering from Dylan's death when someone handed me the typescript. It made me very ill.' But then she laughed. 'But Brinnin himself is a fascinating puzzle. How can you hit back at a man who does not know he is hitting you?'

Admitting she was 'better off as a poet's widow than as a poet's wife', Caitlin said she would never marry again. 'Apart from my feelings for Dylan, I believe that marriage is for a family. A woman may like the company of men, but she doesn't have to get married for that . . .'

✵   ✵   ✵

Caitlin moved on from Procida to Sicily, returned to Laugharne briefly over Christmas, finalised the text of *Leftover Life to Kill* and then, in February (1957), went off again. This time she stayed first in Rome and then in Anzio before moving on to Sardinia, where she would have bought a house if Stuart Thomas had sent the money. He did not, though, so on she travelled to Ischia (where her lover Mario was arrested for beating her up) and then back to Procida, where she made another half-hearted attempt to commit suicide. She dived from a rock, only to find herself floating contentedly in the water, with the waves gently washing her back to shore.

Her life was now shapeless and without meaning, despite international acclaim for *Leftover Life to Kill*. 'I doubt whether there is any personal record in the language so candid, unashamed and harrowing,' wrote John Lehmann in *The London Magazine*, while Elizabeth Bowen spoke in *The Tatler* of 'the savagery of total loss' and Cyril Connolly warned readers of *The Sunday Times* that 'Both deliberately and unconsciously, Mrs Thomas gives us a full-length picture of her character. She is egotistical, hysterical, jealous and quarrelsome, her own worst enemy, proud and violent. She kindles the woman-hatred in all woman-haters; to love her is a literal dedication. But what a reward! Generous, hearth-kindling, simple, truthful, trusting, like some large golden breathless dog: one is conscious of her real self before the world has warped it.' *The Sunday Express* said it was 'an extraordinary book about a happy marriage', while in London George Malcolm Thomson accurately observed in *The Evening Standard* that this was 'a final revolt against Dylan Thomas by the woman who never really accepted his fame and who resented his success'.

Lubbock sent her the different reviews, but Caitlin still kept moving on, partly to avoid Britain's crippling rate of taxes but also driven by restlessness and a need to find some peace of mind. In August, she returned to the home of the Macnamaras, to Ennistymon in Ireland's County Clare, with her mother, Brigid, Wyn Henderson and the children, but as soon as the school holidays were over, it was back to Italy again. This time it was to Rome, where Wyn Henderson found them an apartment on the Via Mogadiscio.

16

The Sicilian Walks into Her Life

Caitlin and Wyn Henderson travelled across Europe to Rome with another drinking friend, a writer and bit-part actor by the name of Cliff Gordon, who drove them in his car. They moved into a fourth- or fifth-floor apartment on the Via Mogadiscio, and soon began spending their evenings at the nearby Taverna Margutta on the Via Margutta, a favourite low-price, late-night hangout for writers, actors, musicians and people who vaguely worked 'in films', either as cameramen, technicians or production staff.

Gordon was not her lover (he was homosexual), just a drinker with vaguely Welsh connections who was happy to help them wash down plates of pasta with bottles of chianti, before Caitlin began turning to the hard stuff, as she did every night. They were an odd trio to look at. Gordon was short, portly and balding, Wyn was now extremely fat, and Caitlin was slim, fiery and aggressive, looking far younger than her years.

One evening a bronzed, thickly built Sicilian sitting at a nearby table looked across at them. Caitlin smiled, and without further ado he walked over, pulled up a chair and sat down at their table. 'Who she – Moby Dick?' he asked, stabbing a thumb towards Wyn Henderson. Without saying a word to the man who was to share the rest of her life, Caitlin immediately punched him on the nose. He smiled, barely flinching, and Wyn started apologising, realising they could converse in French.

His name was Giuseppe Fazio, he was 33 years old and he began chattering, flattering and bantering in a mixture of French, Spanish, German, Italian and pidgin English. He was smooth, but hardly sophisticated, and Caitlin could see immediately that this was a woman's man.

'We'll be having cocktails tomorrow night at seven – would you like to join us?' asked Henderson, and he was there at the Via Mogadiscio, right on the dot.

✳   ✳   ✳

Fazio was 11 years younger than Caitlin. He came from Catania, the main city in the east of Sicily that stands between Mount Etna and the sea. The family had once been rich, owning a large flour mill near the docks and several blocks of property in the city centre that were compulsorily purchased by the municipal authorities after the Second World War. His father died when Giuseppe and his brother Carmelo were very young, and their mother brought them up virtually on her own between managing the family businesses and running for civic office. At one time she was Mayor of Catania.

No one would call Giuseppe a literary man, but he walked with an air of authority. He and his brother were educated in Rome and Paris, and afterwards Giuseppe travelled the world, priding himself on his skills of seduction and knowledge of brothels, before returning to Sicily, joining the Italian Army during the Second World War and fighting against the British in North Africa. On one occasion when he was not wearing uniform, he was about to be shot by a German firing squad and saved himself by shouting passionately in German, 'Why are you doing this? Why are you trying to take the life of a young man like me?' The officer in charge immediately stopped the execution.

Another time, Giuseppe demonstrated his pugilistic skills by flooring seven men during a street fight in Catania. He found himself a hero when the case came before the city magistrates and was reported in the press.

With a constant fund of stories like that, and more than a touch of braggadocio, Caitlin found him immediately attractive.

✳   ✳   ✳

The next night, Fazio arrived at their apartment to find Caitlin and several other people drunk. They had started drinking wines, spirits and aperitifs with their midday meal.[1] The dining table was still littered with dirty plates, empty bottles and glasses of all kinds.

Being fairly abstemious, Fazio stood by the balcony window, sipping slowly, as Caitlin suddenly hurtled past him, trying to throw herself over the edge. He grabbed her by the feet and another guest, Geoffrey Copleston, helped pull her back. 'What the matter with you, crazy woman?' asked Fazio, holding her firmly until he was sure she would not try again. As soon as her trembling ceased and her body felt calmer, he let her go. She continued drinking heavily and started to dance alone. 'It was clear . . . Mrs Thomas was an alcoholic and that apart from Mrs Henderson, who was about to return to the United Kingdom, no one was doing anything to check her overindulgence,' said Copleston.[2]

The evening ended with more drama. As Cliff Gordon travelled down in the lift, he tried to give Fazio a kiss. That was a big mistake. Fazio punched him hard, and Gordon fell to the floor with a broken arm.

The next morning, Wyn Henderson went to see Fazio and told him, 'Caitlin likes you. She would like to see you again' – and he turned up in a brand new tiny red Fiat. 'I have come to take you out,' he said, without telling her he had gone down to a car showroom and put down a deposit of 10,000 lira, leaving her responsible for the monthly hire-purchase payments.[3]

✵ ✵ ✵

Within a day or two, Giuseppe moved into her apartment and began sharing her bed. Caitlin found this arrangement more than satisfactory, for he also prided himself on being able to reach a sexual climax six or seven times a night. 'That's one thing to be said for these Sicilians,' said Caitlin.[4] 'They don't give you much sleep – but they leave you alone during the day.'

Theirs became an intensely physical relationship, with Caitlin still fuelled by whisky – but she would never call it love. 'I only believe in one marriage, and, anyway, I wouldn't marry *him*,' she said,[5] not once but repeatedly, refusing to say 'I love you' in all the 37 years they were to spend together.[6]

'I can't stand the bloody man,' she would say savagely. 'He's a pure materialist. He worships money like they all do here . . . So far as I can see we have nothing in common . . . Just occasionally, when he's being simple and humble, which is practically never, he is alright. He has such enormous pretensions . . . but there are compensations.' Chief among these was that Fazio, for all his addiction to money, women and fast cars, was always attentive when she was ill, travelling far and wide to make sure Caitlin received nothing but the best medical advice. 'These Sicilians are like that. They look after you when you're sick, especially if you're a woman,' said Caitlin[7] and for one who had suffered so much, this was a strong factor in his favour.

✵ ✵ ✵

For the first time since Dylan's death, this became a household with just one man at the head of it. 'Caitlin was delightful sober, but terrible when she was drunk,' said Fazio,[8] who immediately began trying to persuade her to cut back her nightly intake of whisky, if not give it up altogether. He accompanied her to see doctors in Rome, and then down to Catania where she spent two and a half months at L'Ulivo Clinic under the care of a psychiatrist, Professor Enzo Arena, who treated her for 'mental confusion due to chronic alcoholism'.[9]

Fazio also became *in loco parentis*. Llewelyn was now in London, working as a copywriter for the J. Walter Thompson advertising agency and trying (unsuccessfully) to establish himself as a writer of science fiction, but Aeronwy lived at home and was proving a troublesome teenager, often defying her mother. Fazio began to lay down the law like a Sicilian father, telling her what time she had to be in at night, to dress modestly and to respect her mother. This only made matters worse. There were tears, shouting and occasional flashes of violent temper, and Aeronwy began to hate him. Colm, however, with his blond curls and mischievous charm, saw a gentler side of the Sicilian, who treated him as if he were his own son, sharing in childhood games, driving him up into the mountains and making sure he was given a place at the well-known San Giuseppe School, a classical institution that both Fazio brothers had attended.

'It was a pretty strict place with tough rules and religion, but it didn't do Colm any harm,' said Caitlin.[10]

The Trustees soon noticed a change in Caitlin's attitude. She became less of a pushover, and began questioning the way the Trust was run. Initially, this was not a problem. She continued to live over a thousand miles from Swansea, and provided her monthly allowance kept coming through, Stuart Thomas knew she was easily pacified with an extra cheque to cover some new, and sometimes necessary, item of expenditure. His life only began to get difficult when she found herself pregnant again, had a fourth child at the age of 49, and began searching for ways of breaking the Trust.

✳   ✳   ✳

Caitlin was now a relatively wealthy woman. Her share of the Trust's income from Dylan's works provided a reliable income. *Leftover Life to Kill* was a bestseller in both Britain and the United States, and was also translated into many languages. She followed this with *Not Quite Posthumous Letters to my Daughter* (1962), a dissatisfying work that brought in more money, basically advising Aeronwy to hang on to her virginity for grim life until she hooked a wealthy man. She then found herself unexpectedly earning substantial royalties from the stage play *Dylan*, written by Sidney Michaels and based partly on *Leftover Life to Kill*, partly on *Dylan Thomas in America*.

She received an advance of $2,800 from the producers, and when the play became a success on Broadway, with Sir Alec Guinness portraying Dylan, Caitlin shared 10 per cent of the weekly box-office takings.[11]

And yet, however much money came in, Caitlin never felt wealthy. She continued her whisky habit and never seemed able to bring her finances under personal control. Giuseppe, who gave up working soon after he met her, had expensive tastes in motor cars, importing the latest models from abroad – and outwardly this all lent credence to the belief that Dylan's widow was rolling in cash. Because she seemed to have no other financial needs, the Trustees of one of the funds established immediately after Dylan's death (led by Goronwy Rees) agreed to buy her and the children a plot of land on the shore of Lake Scanno in the Abruzzi mountains, south of Rome. There she and Giuseppe had a luxurious holiday home designed by an architect and built to their instructions, with ground-floor bedrooms, a room for their housemaid Sylvana (who travelled with them wherever they went), and a large first-floor lounge overlooking the lake.

✻   ✻   ✻

Her pregnancy was totally unexpected. Caitlin found herself putting on weight in the late autumn of 1962. Instead of going to a doctor, she began trying to slim, taking up swimming, riding horses for the first time since her teens and walking energetically through the Rome parks.

When she eventually did go to a doctor, Caitlin was astonished to learn she was expecting a baby. 'Having had so many abortions, I never thought I'd be able to have another child,' she told Tremlett.[12]

The baby was born in hospital in Rome on 29 March 1963, nearly three months prematurely and weighing only two pounds. For the first two months of his life, the baby – whom she named Francesco, after her father – was kept in an incubator, and at one point the fears for his life were such that Caitlin and Giuseppe stood by the cot while the child was given the Last Rites.

'I looked upon him as my own little miracle, and the hardest thing was not being allowed to touch him,' said Caitlin, who was not permitted to hold her baby in her arms or even kiss him during those first eight precarious weeks.

When it was thought Francesco might die, the doctor told her, 'I don't know whether he will live or die until I have seen the father.' Just one look at Giuseppe convinced him, 'The baby will live.'

✳   ✳   ✳

The first bout of open conflict between Caitlin and the Trustees came when her baby was just 15 months old. Money was still flowing in from the Broadway production of *Dylan*, and she continued to receive her allowance from the estate – but nearly all the funds that she and Giuseppe could raise between them were going towards the building of their new holiday home, which occupied much of his time while most of hers was devoted to motherhood, thoroughly enjoying 'something I never thought I'd experience again'. Because of the rising costs of the new house, they never seemed to have enough money – and then suddenly a bombshell arrived in the post from the Trustees.

The letter was signed by all three – Higham, Vaughan-Thomas and Stuart Thomas – but the drafting was clearly that of the Swansea solicitor, who disapproved of Caitlin's relationship with Giuseppe and considered it unseemly for a woman to have had a baby at the age of 49.

They told her she had received 'very heavy sums of money', leaving her with a total sum of monies within the Trust of 'no more than between £3,000 and £4,000', and while they were 'delighted to know that so much money is coming in from the play in New York', they thought this might not last much longer and she should be aware that:

> the American earnings have been paid over without deduction of tax, because certificates have been signed assuring the Americans that you are paying Italian tax. We don't know whether in fact you are and think it's very likely that you are not. But it is already known that the American authorities have been in touch with the Italian Revenue authorities on the question of tax in Italy . . . We are most anxious to impress this situation on you, because it could cause a virtual drying-up of funds available to you from any source, if the Italian authorities get as tough as we fear they may.[13]

And then came the two stings in the tale. The first was a strong suggestion that Giuseppe now controlled her finances – 'You yourself alone should operate your bank account and . . . you should allow no other person to operate it for you. It seems to us just possible that you are not aware of how much money has in fact been sent to Italy for you. If you invariably collect your own money from the bank, where it is sent regularly, you will then be in a position to dispose of it as you think fit.'

The second sting was in the next paragraph: 'The monthly monies from the trust fund have been suspended for the moment in order to try and accumulate some monies for you at a later date, when the play monies stop. It is not a question of trying to stop you getting your money, but merely saving it up for you for next year when you will undoubtedly require it after the play has finished.'

Caitlin was outraged by this letter, and so, too – predictably – was Giuseppe. Together they made a formidable team, taking on lawyers (and changing them frequently) with a fearless regard for costs or conventions. Stuart Thomas soon began to feel the lash of her tongue, and eventually could barely bring himself to utter her name. Caitlin was always 'the widow', Giuseppe 'the Sicilian' – and the small-town Welsh solicitor insisted on calling their son 'the bastard'. This did not provide the foundations for a happy relationship.

✳   ✳   ✳

What offended Caitlin most, apart from an unexpected interruption in her cash flow, was the thought that the Trustees, and Stuart Thomas in particular, seemed to believe they had a right to intervene in her private affairs. In her view, their function was limited to looking after the income of the Dylan Thomas Estate and distributing it in accordance with the Trust deed. 'It's none of their bloody business how I spend my money, who I choose to live with, what I earn elsewhere, or whether I pay taxes,' she insisted. [14]

Having learned to be cautious in her dealings with the Trustees, she avoided bringing matters to a head too soon since she was also engaged in a law suit that involved Stuart Thomas, but a deep distrust developed between them and she began looking for another solicitor.

The court case was one she brought herself, on Stuart Thomas's advice, against The Times Book Co. Ltd, seeking to regain possession of the original manuscript of *Under Milk Wood*. It will be remembered that shortly before he left for America for the last time, Dylan delivered the manuscript to Douglas Cleverdon at the BBC. Cleverdon arranged for his secretary to produce duplicate copies, returning the manuscript to Dylan, and agreed to let Dylan have three of the duplicated scripts to use in New York. These were handed over to him at the airline bar in Victoria, where Caitlin and the Lockes gathered to see him off.

'You have saved my life,' said Thomas, explaining that he had lost the original manuscript during a Soho pub crawl.[15]

'That seems an awful pity,' Cleverdon replied, recalling their discussion over the script for the past six or seven years, and saying he thought it one of the most interesting projects he had ever worked on.

'If you can find it, you can keep it,' said Thomas, giving Cleverdon the names of half a dozen pubs he had visited, adding, 'If I didn't leave it in any of them, I might have left it in a taxi.'

Cleverdon duly went to the Swiss Tavern, also known as the Helvetia, in Old Compton Street, where he asked a barmaid if anyone had found a script by Dylan Thomas. 'Here it is,' she said, reaching under the counter and producing Dylan's original, much-thumbed manuscript in its well-worn folder. It consisted of 23 foolscap pages in Dylan's own handwriting and 32 pages of the typescript he used in May 1953 for the New York readings, with numerous handwritten revisions.

Eventually, after having the manuscript specially bound, Cleverdon decided to sell it, hoping to raise money to enable him to buy a house in Islington. An old friend, the bookseller Jim Stevens Cox, agreed to act as his agent or intermediary, offering it for sale at the Antiquarian Booksellers' Fair in Albemarle Street, London, in May 1961, where it was bought for £2,000 by The Times Book Co. Ltd. The purchase was reported in *The Times* on 21 June, and Stuart Thomas, saying he was writing as Caitlin's solicitor, immediately wrote to the BBC asking how the manuscript had come on the market.

Cleverdon gave the BBC solicitor the version of events detailed in previous paragraphs, but Caitlin (persuaded by Stuart Thomas) challenged Cleverdon's veracity and eventually brought proceedings in the Chancery Court, claiming Dylan would never have given away such a valuable manuscript. The case took nearly five years to come to court, and turned into a *cause célèbre*, with Caitlin flying in from Rome to fight her battle personally, posing daily outside the court for press photographers and hosting expensive lunches for family and friends at the Wig and Pen Club.

Cox and Cleverdon employed counsel to defend their honour, and the case came before Mr Justice Plowman on 8 March 1966, lasting four days. Daniel Jones, Cordelia Locke and Ruthven Todd testified on Caitlin's behalf, but she lost, with the judge ordering her to pay not only her own costs but those of The Times Book Co. Ltd and Cleverdon and Cox. Plowman commented:

> I find myself forced to the conclusion that Mr Cleverdon was telling the truth
> and that I ought to accept this evidence.

Caitlin found herself many thousands of pounds out of pocket, but there was another long-lasting effect of the case. Jones made such a hash of his evidence that Plowman decided he was not talking sense, and Caitlin was mortified to learn as the proceedings ended that although the judge may have described her in his summing-up as 'the sole executrix' of Dylan's estate, she had actually lost all control of her inheritance.

✿   ✿   ✿

For the remaining 28 years of her life, Caitlin engaged in continual disputes with the Trustees, egged on by Giuseppe. She was not bothered about David Higham (and continued to use his agency to advise her on literary matters); nor did she concern herself much with Wynford Vaughan-Thomas, an amiable cove who knew better than to raise his head above the parapet unnecessarily, although both became enjoined whenever she wished to take legal action against Stuart Thomas in the courts. Just as he was continually abusive about her, so she referred to him as 'that lying Welsh bastard', and worse.

Her persistence sometimes paid off. Without her knowledge, Stuart Thomas frequently arranged for his friends to stay at The Boat House. Kingsley Amis lived there for a while and so did the journalist George Gale, who was a friend of Amis, but in 1967 Caitlin managed to get its ownership transferred to her and eventually sold it, stipulating that The Boat House could only be used as a museum in memory of Dylan Thomas.

To pursue her wider complaints against Stuart Thomas, she engaged a distinguished London solicitor, Anthony Rubinstein, giving him power of attorney. He began preparing a case against the Trustees that might have broken the Trust had it come to court. This hinged, in part, on an alleged mishandling of funds, but there were other issues that bothered Caitlin more than that.

What she wanted above all else, was to have the Trust deed varied so that Francesco would become an equal beneficiary with Llewelyn, Aeronwy and Colm, even though Dylan was not his father. Her argument was that the Trustees were handling her inheritance on her behalf (she was the 'settlor'), and therefore she had a right to seek a variation. Stuart Thomas resisted this firmly, with the support of Llewelyn and Aeronwy, arguing that under Italian law such a change would enable Giuseppe (as Francesco's father while the boy was a minor) to intervene in the Trust's affairs. Colm was more inclined to support his mother in the dispute.

An added complication was that Caitlin discovered, allegedly for the first time, that the 1953 Trust deed was amended in 1957, removing what little authority she had over the Trust's affairs and any right to be consulted over disposal of copyrights. Stuart Thomas claimed her signature was witnessed in London; Caitlin maintained she was in Rome at the time, and that Stuart Thomas flew out there and persuaded her to sign the deed on a night on which she was undoubtedly drunk, without telling her what she was signing. In an extra twist to the story, Caitlin managed to trace the woman who was said to have witnessed her signature in London – and the woman swore a handwritten affidavit that she did not. (We have copies of the 1953 and 1957 deeds and numerous documents relating thereto, but as the case never came to court we have confined ourselves to a neutral summary of the main issues.)

Just as the case seemed to be taking shape nicely from Caitlin's point of view, with Stuart Thomas's solicitors angling for an out-of-court settlement, she found herself thrown into gaol with unfortunate consequences.

✡   ✡   ✡

Late one October night in 1969, Caitlin and Aeronwy were travelling in a tiny Fiat in the centre of Rome. It was being driven by a friend from Catania, Maria Pettinato, and as they entered the Piazza S. Maria, she accidentally drove the wrong way down a one-way street into a square where cars were prohibited. They were stopped by a traffic policeman. It was 11.25 p.m.[16] Instead of politely saying 'Sorry' or 'Goodnight', they became abusive, and Aeronwy 'uttered words hardly current or orthodox', which included the epithet 'Nazi'.

While the policeman called in a colleague on his walkie-talkie, Caitlin climbed out of the car to confront him. Aeronwy and the driver disappeared. Caitlin called the policeman 'a brute', used various words that were left out of the statement when it was translated, hit him, bit him and boxed him around the ears.

With some difficulty, for she had been drinking wine, they bundled her into a police car and took her off to the women's gaol, where she was kept for five days, complaining bitterly that she had neither face creams, sleeping pills nor privacy and was even required to clean her own cell.

News of her imprisonment travelled fast. A short news story appeared in the London *Evening Standard*, and Llewelyn phoned his father-in-law, Stuart Thomas, suggesting they should fly straight out to Rome to see if there was anything they could do to help her. According to a subsequent statement by Stuart Thomas,[17] Caitlin met him on being released on bail 'and told me she bitterly regretted such action as she had taken against me in the past'.

Stuart Thomas clearly anticipated what might happen, for he arrived in Rome with a power of attorney for Caitlin to sign 'appointing her elder son, Llewelyn, to act as her attorney, to look after her financial affairs',[18] expressing the view that 'it would be as well if she kept control of her financial affairs in the hands of her own family'.[19]

Accordingly, Caitlin wrote to Rubinstein, saying, 'Please withdraw my case against Stuart Thomas. Stop it. Forget it,' adding that Llewelyn's intervention 'has convinced me it is the best thing to do'. Rubinstein duly handed over all the papers relating to the case that Caitlin intended to bring against Stuart Thomas, and that was the last she saw of them.[20]

This was the most crucial twist of all, for Caitlin was closer to breaking the Trust than perhaps she realised – but she had thrown away her hand, and the chance never came again.

✵ ✵ ✵

Temporarily, peace seemed to reign between the feuding Thomases. Friendly letters were exchanged again, and the Swansea solicitor travelled out to Rome on six occasions between October 1969 and May 1971, transferring a lump sum of £4,386 to Caitlin in October 1970 and arranging for her to receive an increased allowance of £350 a month. This amount soon went up to £375. The solicitor even agreed to find a way of making Francesco a joint beneficiary, confirming that in writing – but then failed to do so and the trouble started all over again.

Rubinstein was reappointed to represent Caitlin in her actions against the Trust, and she decided to sell most of Dylan's love letters (though not his last letters which she treasured most and kept in the leather wallet that was in his pocket when he collapsed at the Chelsea Hotel, and was returned to her after his death). She hoped the letters would raise enough at auction to finance a renewed assault upon the Trustees.[21]

This time she accompanied her efforts to break the Trust with a complaint against Stuart Thomas to the Lord Chancellor, head of the judiciary for England and Wales. Lord Widgery declined to intervene, but rather surprisingly suggested, 'It might be profitable for you to [consult] the Director of Public Prosecutions.'[22] Caitlin also formally requested the Law Society to investigate Stuart Thomas for professional misconduct.

The battle between Caitlin and the Trustees was now deadly serious, and was compounded by a totally new factor. She had conquered her alcoholism, having been told by Giuseppe that unless she did so he would leave her and take Francesco with him, warning that no Italian court would award custody of a child to a woman who was continually drunk and frequently violent.[23] Realising her arrest in Rome could be used as powerful evidence in any proceedings, Caitlin broke the whisky habit that had dominated her life for over 20 years. 'I didn't want to lose my child,' she told Tremlett,'[24] always referring to her son as Cico (pronounced 'Kee-ko'). 'My whole life now revolved around Cico, and I couldn't bear the thought of losing him.'

17

The Ground Is Laid for Him

Caitlin Thomas failed in all her attempts to break the Trust, and it may well be that her reputation damaged her chances. Lawyers have an ingrained tendency to look scornfully upon those who defy convention, particularly, perhaps, a widow who abused solicitors, engaged in unsuccessful litigation, was dilatory in paying legal bills, and constructed through her own writings and public behaviour an image of herself as a wild, violent, Irish drunk who engaged in years of flagrant promiscuity and refused to marry the father of her fourth child.

The odds were stacked against her and she knew it. Caitlin Thomas acquired a bad name, but reading through the papers relating to her complaint to the Law Society, a somewhat different picture emerges.

For the first time, she managed to manoeuvre Stuart Thomas into a position where he had to defend himself in writing, and his reply to her accusations makes curious reading.[1]

He denied knowing Caitlin was admitted to the River Crest sanatorium before Dylan died or that she tried to commit suicide on 24 November 1953, and also claimed that to the best of his knowledge she was still in New York at the time of Dylan's funeral. Thomas also maintained that he had known her many years before Dylan's death (which was untrue), and said he 'did not consider her to be an alcoholic'.

Stuart Thomas then gave a detailed account of how she applied for letters of administration 'on my advice', accompanied by himself and Daniel Jones, and avoided answering any questions that might have implied he knew about her mental state, saying instead, 'I have no evidence, nor was any produced to me, that Mrs Thomas was an alcoholic and suffering from melancholia. I am fully aware that occasionally she got very drunk and when she did she became very objectionable.'

Thomas also said he had 'no knowledge of the actual execution of the 1953 deed as I was away from the office when it was signed by Mrs Thomas', which is also curious, as we have a copy of the deed which shows that he signed it himself while his father witnessed Caitlin's signature.

Having said he thought Caitlin was in New York on the day of the funeral, Thomas totally contradicted this earlier statement by describing how she consulted Jones, Higham and himself that very day and 'requested me to prepare a suitable Trust, as she pointed out that she wishes, in view of her attitude towards money, to protect the interests of the children'.

Thomas insisted he either could not comment upon or could not recall various points she raised, denied any knowledge of her reasons for ending the chancery action against the Trustees in 1969 but admitted agreeing to seek a way of including Francesco among the beneficiaries. He said Llewelyn, Aeronwy and Colm decided not to agree to this after he advised them Francesco's inclusion 'would give considerable powers to his father, Señor Fazio'.

The letter was masterly in the way he managed to avoid answering questions or admitting that he should have known Caitlin was unfit to take key decisions, while emphasising how difficult she could be, particularly when drunk. It had the right effect. The Law Society duly informed her they were satisfied her main motivation was to seek a variation in the Trust, advising, 'If you wish to pursue your claim, you should do so by means of an application to the court.'[2] Its Senior Assistant Secretary said the council 'were satisfied that Mr Stuart Thomas had not acted in any way unprofessionally'. Curiously, the letter ended with an encouraging comment: 'I sincerely trust that your application to the court will be successful.'

✢ ✢ ✢

Just why Stuart Thomas was so determined to maintain personal control of the Trust is hard to explain. David Higham died on 30 March 1978. No one was appointed to replace him for eight years. With Wynford Vaughan-Thomas 'happy to leave everything to Stuart',[3] this left the Swansea solicitor very much in control. His fees were frequently excessive[4] and his battles with Caitlin provided a fund of personal anecdotes with which he would amuse his friends, but there had to be more to it than that.

Ironically, for all his faults, Stuart Thomas probably did more than anyone to establish the value of Dylan Thomas's copyrights and their coherence as a body of work. Had Caitlin been left in personal control of her inheritance, she would probably have sold it off for drinking money in the years immediately following Dylan's death, when she was by her own admission in no fit state to make decisions.

As it was, with the Swansea solicitor treating the estate as his personal responsibility, *Under Milk Wood* was translated into and published in 50 languages; the recorded and film versions became hugely popular throughout the world; the *Collected Poems* (Dylan Thomas's other major copyright) remain in print on a global basis; cinema films were made, based on two of his other works, *The Doctor and the Devils* and *Rebecca's Daughters*; television films were produced, based on six of Thomas's short stories; and the Trustees oversaw an authorised biography, *The Life of Dylan Thomas* by Constantine Fitzgibbon (1965), with a companion volume *The Selected Letters of Dylan Thomas*, which Fitzgibbon edited (1966). They also co-operated in the publication of *Dylan Thomas: Letters to Vernon Watkins* (1957), and helped Paul Ferris when he was writing his biography *Dylan Thomas* (1977) and editing *Dylan Thomas: The Collected Letters* (1985).

Stuart Thomas also co-operated to a degree in over 30 other books, mostly works of literary criticism that required his consent to quote from copyrighted material, and helped to ensure that even lesser copyrights like *Quite Early One Morning, Collected Stories, Adventures in the Skin Trade, Portrait of the Artist as a Young Dog* and *A Prospect of the Sea* remained in print in one form or another in different languages.

However, Caitlin's opinions were never sought, biographies appeared without any input from her, she continued to live in Rome with Giuseppe and their son, and Stuart Thomas carried on administering the Trust virtually singlehandedly until Tremlett suggested to her in 1978, when she was visiting London with Francesco, that the time had come when she ought to consider putting her side of the story in a book written with him. They lunched with a London publisher who agreed to publish the book, but then Caitlin changed her mind and said she would prefer to write it herself. The manuscript turned out badly and when Tremlett declined to act as her editor, she flew off to Ireland where Constantine Fitzgibbon's widow, Theodora, worked on the manuscript instead, slashing it to ribbons. This collaboration came to a sticky end when Theodora passed some remark implying she had been closer to Dylan during the war than Caitlin realised, and Tremlett was again invited to pick up the pieces. He again said no, arguing that it would be better to start afresh. Eventually, after seven years' talk and correspondence and another delay caused when Caitlin and Giuseppe decided to leave Rome to settle in Catania, they agreed to begin working on a manuscript together in October 1985.

✳ ✳ ✳

Some degree of calm had now been restored to her relationship with Stuart Thomas. After managing to get the better of her in the various disputes between 1966 and 1978, Thomas learned to keep his distance. He rarely expressed an opinion on her relationship with Giuseppe, never gave interviews to the press, and provided she kept silent too, the monthly allowance would arrive on time at her bank in Italy. If ever she complained about anything, the cheques would stop – and Thomas knew this was all it took to bring her into line, having once taught her a sharp lesson by leaving her without money over Christmas. This was a strange way for a solicitor to behave, and it was always an uneasy kind of calm needing only the slightest hint of umbrage to set the dispute alight again.

✳ ✳ ✳

When Caitlin and Tremlett agreed to work on a book together, there were signs of alarm. He was advised that Stuart Thomas disapproved, that Caitlin was senile, that her memory had gone and that, perhaps, she was suffering from Alzheimer's disease. Tremlett refused to believe this, for her letters from Sicily were warm, witty and very much to the point. When he persisted, travelling out to Catania in October 1985 to conduct 50 hours of tape-recorded interviews and returning there again in March 1986 for Caitlin to approve the manuscript line by line, Stuart Thomas began consolidating his position. Having been challenged so many times before, he may have sensed Caitlin was going to use whatever she earned from this collaboration to mount another attack. If he did, he was right; this was precisely what was on her mind.

The Trust was now virtually a shell. No one had replaced David Higham. Wynford Vaughan-Thomas was in his late seventies and dying of cancer,[5] and Stuart Thomas himself was in his early seventies and becoming frail . . . but still he hung on like a limpet, bringing in two personal friends, Kingsley Amis and Michael Edward John Rush, as new Trustees, without consulting Caitlin or informing her afterwards. She did not hear about the new Trustees for nearly a year, and was appalled at the choice of Amis.[6]

Battle-lines were being drawn. If she did decide to renew her campaign against him, Stuart Thomas would be able to say, truthfully, that the Trust had now been strengthened, since Kingsley Amis was an author of considerable renown and Rush a professional man of good reputation. Thomas was ready for her to make the next move, but it was not the one he expected.

* * *

Caitlin earned substantial monies from her collaboration with Tremlett. Their book *Caitlin* was published in Britain in hardback and paperback and was serialised by *The Sunday Times* and *The Western Mail*. It was also serialised by *The Toronto Globe* in Canada and *The Australian Women's Weekly*, published in two hardback editions and also in paperback in the United States and translated into Swedish and German.

Stuart Thomas may have been expecting an immediate onslaught of the kind he had experienced several times before, but it did not happen like that. Caitlin returned to Laugharne in October 1986 for the first time in 30 years to promote the book, attracted long queues for her signing sessions in Laugharne, Swansea and Cardiff, and gave daily press, radio and TV interviews for over a fortnight. She was clearly frail, white-haired and sometimes unsteady on her feet because of spinal degeneration caused, so she was advised by doctors in Catania and Munich, by her years of alcoholism prior to 1970, but there was no doubting the sharpness of her wit or her mental agility. She also demonstrated surprising physical stamina. While having morning coffee in Carmarthen with Aeronwy, Tremlett and his wife, she developed an alarming muscular spasm. Refusing to go to a doctor, she insisted on walking five miles 'to get this damn thing out of my system'. That night, she leapt out of a chair to kick a passing cat at Tremlett's house.

With his usual attention to all matters medical, Giuseppe discovered there was a clinic in Munich specialising in the kind of spinal operation that Caitlin needed, reinforcing the upper vertebrae with metal rods so that she would not have to wear a neck brace. It would, at the same time, ameliorate a problem she was having with incontinence, which Caitlin found defeminising. (She was still the most meticulous of women in her mid-seventies, spending between two and three hours every morning on ballet exercises and facial and body treatments.) The operation was delicate, but doctors advised her that if it was successful her life would be happier. She would have less trouble with her sense of balance and become more mobile – and she was willing to take the risk.

While in South Wales, Caitlin lunched with Stuart Thomas at a Chinese restaurant in Swansea. He was affable enough, but sought to discourage her from spending so much money on medical treatment at the private clinic in Munich. This left her disgruntled. 'I am sure that bloody man is waiting for me to die,' she told Tremlett that evening.

✲ ✲ ✲

By now Tremlett had a close relationship with Caitlin. They kept in touch for seven years before he arrived in Catania to spend three weeks interviewing her daily at her home. This was originally a small, lava-built, one-storey building on the lower slopes of Mount Etna that Giuseppe had inherited from his mother. (Lava, the molten rock thrown up by volcanic eruptions, sets into a hard stone when it cools. In Sicily, this is cut into building blocks and paving slabs.) Since returning to Catania from Rome two years earlier, Giuseppe had overseen the design and construction of a new house built with the old one as its foundation.

This was now the family home, and Caitlin also had the original building, with its massive walls and ancient-looking vaulted ceilings, as a private study where she wrote every day. Unfortunately, the site lay next to what was now the municipal rubbish tip. Flies were a constant problem, and at night a pack of wild dogs could be heard howling and fighting as they scrambled for food among Catania's garbage.

'I hate this house,' said Caitlin. 'Nearly all the money I get goes into it because of Giuseppe's building mania, and I don't like the place at all . . . I don't want to spend my old age here, or die here. I'd rather be back in Rome, where Cico is at university, because I miss him so much. Cico has always been attentive to me . . . I couldn't go back to England and end up like Granny Thomas, who used to put aside half a crown a week so she'd be buried tidy. I don't like being a granny, anyway. I'm not the type. I've always enjoyed Aeronwy's company, but she hates Giuseppe – and if I went over to her, I'd become babyminder-in-chief. And I wouldn't like that, either.'

When Caitlin and Tremlett were talking together, while Giuseppe drove down into Catania for his demi-tasse at the trattoria, she continued to talk waspishly about the various failings of her family, saying, 'I'm a pretty sad person. I think I have always been sad. Some people are born jolly, but I was not . . . I was much busier with Dylan . . . The last 30 years have been a blank, not a complete blank because I was pleased to be able to achieve sobriety . . . I haven't really come to life again since Dylan died, and I can't talk about this with Giuseppe or Cico because it all happened so long ago.

'I did tell Giuseppe how I felt one night, it must have been nearly 20 years ago, and I cried a lot, but we've never talked like that again . . . Whenever anything comes up now about Dylan, I'm careful to discuss it lightly . . . Giuseppe isn't a bad man. He has stood by me when a lot of men wouldn't, poor bugger, but Stuart was always able to say that Giuseppe was living off me because he wouldn't go out and get a job. It was never as simple as that.'

This conversation led into a discussion about religion, with Caitlin talking about the Irish Protestant tradition in the Macnamara family (her father's side) and the Quaker beliefs of the Majoliers (her mother's). When Tremlett asked which she preferred, or whether she had a personal faith of her own, Caitlin smiled, hesitated and then said, 'I've never had any time for that stuff.'

A few evenings later Giuseppe drove them into Catania, after Tremlett said he would like to look around the massive cathedral, with its Norman chapels, monument to the composer Bellini, who is buried there, and relics of St Agatha, who was martyred in Catania in AD 252. As he and Caitlin walked through the crowded cathedral, they became temporarily separated and he turned to see her on her knees below a statue of the Virgin Mary and the infant, making the sign of the cross in Catholic fashion, across her breast and from her forehead, downwards. Their eyes met, she smiled, tucked her arm in his, and not a word was said until they were alone again the following day.

'You told me you didn't believe in religion,' said Tremlett.

'I've never lost my faith in the baby Jesus,' Caitlin replied. 'I identify with the imagery of the innocent child. That has always meant a lot to me.'

✳   ✳   ✳

For many years, Caitlin believed Stuart Thomas deducted too much money from her allowance to cover income tax and she wondered whether or not it all reached the Inland Revenue. To help her resolve this point, and also make sure her income from *Caitlin* was handled correctly, Tremlett recommended an accountant to her, who in turn found her a solicitor when Stuart Thomas refused point blank to recognise the accountant's authority.[7]

The solicitor was also a circuit judge and a respected member of the Law Society, and when a warning to Thomas would not budge him, a writ was issued in the Cardiff District Registry of the High Court, Queen's Bench Division (No. 1988/T/540), on 23 March 1988. It required Thomas, Rush and Amis to produce the Trust's accounts for the year ended 5 April 1987, to provide a breakdown of Stuart Thomas's expenses over that and other years.

This did the trick. Within a fortnight, Caitlin learned that there was a balance due to her in the Trust's accounts of over £40,000. Over the next 16 months, she received in total £75,000, less her own legal expenses. For the first time in 35 years, she managed to humble Stuart Thomas – and followed it by going ahead with her operation in Munich, putting away her surgical collar, and buying herself an exercise bike.

✳   ✳   ✳

Midway through this last legal challenge, Caitlin returned to Laugharne. By then she knew that Stuart Thomas had been holding back the £40,000, but none of this had yet come through and she had been told the operation in Munich would cost £20,000. By that time, Tremlett was working on the first draft of his biography *Dylan Thomas: In the Mercy of his Means*, and she agreed to help him if he flew out to Catania. He phoned to confirm the travelling arrangements, and she phoned back to say she and Giuseppe would prefer to come over to Laugharne.

In a telephone conversation some weeks earlier, Tremlett had said that if she was a British citizen who had been paying British taxes, deducted at source, for the past 35 years, why not explore the possibility of having the operation done in Britain as a National Health Service patient rather than pay £20,000 to the clinic in Munich? Now, Caitlin said she wanted to see if she could do just that, and would also bring over various papers that would help Tremlett in his research.[8]

She and Giuseppe arrived in Laugharne on 21 May, staying in a cottage on the main street, and that evening, after Caitlin had gone to bed early, Giuseppe arrived on Tremlett's doorstep, saying, 'This fucking country drives me mad.' He clearly did not like seeing Dylan's portrait in shop windows and hanging on an inn sign outside Brown's Hotel, or The Boat House being run as a shrine in the poet's memory. 'Fucking Dylan – he was no fucking man,' said Giuseppe, who frequently threatened over the next few days to fly back to Catania without Caitlin. She stood her ground and said, 'I'm not leaving without the fucking money.' She bombarded her solicitor several times a day, on one occasion saying, 'You have disappointed me . . . I trusted you and I had faith in you and you have let me down . . . Don't you want to represent me? Why is this going on so long? Why haven't I had the money?'

Tremlett could hear the solicitor spluttering apologies at the other end of the phone, and as Caitlin ended the conversation she turned, smiled mischievously and said, 'I never know how to deal with these fuckers . . .'

Her mind was as sharp as ever, but her body was weakening. At supper one night she spilt some wine. 'You've dropped your glass, Caitlin,' said Giuseppe. Immediately, she replied, 'That wasn't me, it was my hand.' She also affected deafness, but this seemed to come on mainly when Giuseppe was being argumentative. When Tremlett commented on this, she grinned and said, 'I know, I do put it on a bit.'

One morning Caitlin persuaded Giuseppe to drive over to Newcastle Emlyn where her accountant opened an account for her with Midland Bank. She wanted him to collect some money. As soon as he had gone, she told Tremlett, 'Now we can talk . . .' and began to seek his advice on what arrangements she needed to make regarding the disposal of her body after she died.

'That's a bit difficult for me to answer,' said Tremlett, suggesting this was something she ought to discuss with her children or Giuseppe.

'Don't be a coward,' she said. 'I'm asking you! I don't want to talk to *them* about it,' she added, explaining that Llewelyn and Aeronwy did not know she was in Laugharne and she found it difficult to talk to them because they always sided with Stuart Thomas, and Colm was in Australia. 'I couldn't talk to Cico about it; he gets too emotional, and if I try to raise the subject he tells me I'll live for ever . . .'

'Well, what do you want?' asked Tremlett. 'Do you want to be buried or cremated?'

'I don't want to be burnt like the Jews,' she said, in a chilling reference to the Holocaust.

'So you want to be buried?'

'I suppose so . . .'

'With Dylan or in Catania?'

'Do I have the choice?'

'Of course you do,' said Tremlett. 'No matter what goes on in a family, they usually respect your wishes over a matter like this.'

'Would they let me be buried here?'

'It's up to you. The decision is yours. You have a total right,' said Tremlett. 'You probably own the grave. When someone dies, the family buys the grave and there's usually room for three or four more coffins. That's why they dig them so deep.'

'I can't remember what I did when Dylan died,' she said.

'That's easy enough to sort out,' said Tremlett, explaining that all churches kept a plan of their graveyards, showing who was buried in each plot. He then arranged for her to meet the vicar privately.

'How are you going to explain this to Giuseppe?' Tremlett asked.

'That's no problem. I know how to handle him,' she said. 'He'll do whatever

I ask if it's a matter of honour . . .' Caitlin then asked Tremlett to take her for a drink, something she had not done in Laugharne in well over 30 years. They walked across the street to Brown's Hotel. 'Is it all right if I have a lager?' she asked. 'You can have whatever you like,' said Tremlett. As they sat down, the landlord Tommy Watts joined them. Other customers walked over to shake her hand, saying 'Welcome home, Mrs Thomas', without realising for a moment what this meant.

Turning to Tremlett she said, 'You have taken a weight off my mind.' And that was the last that was said.

✵   ✵   ✵

Although she regained mobility after her operation in Munich, Caitlin became more frail as she approached her 80th birthday. She rarely left Catania. Tremlett last saw her in April 1990. He was working on a book in North Africa, and travelled home via Sicily. Giuseppe made him welcome and Caitlin greeted him warmly, handing him a letter. 'I've been trying to write to you for weeks,' she said, 'but I've been having trouble with my hand. It starts to shake some days and I can't write properly. I don't want people reading letters like that, because that's how they'll remember me. So this is probably the last letter you'll ever get from me . . .'

Early in 1994, Caitlin fell off a stool in a pizzeria in Catania, fracturing her hip. This made her bed-bound and gangrene set in. She suffered considerably for the next seven months, and Francesco gave up his job to nurse her and sit by her bedside. He was now an accomplished dancer, and she enjoyed watching him dance in the last weeks of her life, accompanied by his dancing partner.

Caitlin Thomas died on 1 August 1994 and her body was flown back to Laugharne for burial with Dylan, just as she had requested. Tremlett was invited to write an obituary for *The Guardian,* in which he referred to the moment in Catania Cathedral when he noticed her on her knees before the statue of the Virgin Mary and the infant Jesus.

'That was very nice, George, but I don't think Mummy was religious,' said Francesco, who accompanied her coffin from Sicily to West Wales. 'We were together every day, and she never talked like that.' Francesco added that neither he nor Giuseppe had ever gone to church with her in Catania. Colm was equally dismissive on the day of the funeral. 'You were being sentimental,' he said.

✵   ✵   ✵

The funeral was held at St Martin's Church on Wednesday 10 August. The order of service wrongly stated that she died on 31 July, but this was a minor point, for Caitlin died late at night and far away. The funeral was conducted by the Revd D.B.G. Davies, who had discussed her funeral with her six years earlier. It was the usual, simple Laugharne ceremony, with Psalm 23 ('The Lord is my Shepherd') and the hymns 'Immortal Invisible' and 'King of Glory, King of Peace'.

Reporters, photographers and TV camera teams scrambled across the churchyard with hundreds of strangers, many of them tourists wearing beach clothes, to join Caitlin's children, Brigid and Stuart Thomas, who was himself dying of pancreatic cancer. The funeral had a strangely eerie air, for as the coffin was being carried out of the church there was an awesome crash of thunder. All eyes looked skywards. 'Caitlin's arrived,' said Tommy Watts, who was leading the bearers.

Brigid died a day after returning home to Hampshire, and Francesco delayed going back to Sicily to attend her funeral too. Three weeks later, Tremlett received a call from Giuseppe, who was recovering from the burst stomach ulcer that prevented him from attending the funeral. Father and son had been going through Caitlin's papers, and to their astonishment discovered a diary, various manuscripts and other documents she had never mentioned.

'I think you ought to come over here and see them,' said Giuseppe, and Tremlett did. He flew to Catania on 6 October and was shown two boxes of papers that began to explain how Caitlin Thomas acquired the courage and inner strength to survive not only the traumatic events of October and November 1953 – the collapse of her marriage, Dylan's death at the hands of Milton Feltenstein and her own humiliation by the same man – but also her suicide attempts, 20 years of alcoholism, the betrayal of trust by John Malcolm Brinnin, a life with Giuseppe that was less than bliss, her feud with Stuart Thomas and her unfortunate relationship with Llewelyn and Aeronwy: she found God.

Now this is not so strange as members of her family might suppose. Dylan was a more religious man than is generally believed, but this was overshadowed by the falsehoods that surrounded his death. Many of his poems draw strongly on biblical imagery. As Vernon Watkins wrote in his obituary for *The Times*, 'There was nothing God ever made that Dylan Thomas, the revolutionary, wanted to alter.' Or, as Thomas put it himself in the preface of his *Collected Poems*:

I read somewhere of a shepherd who, when asked why he made, from within fairy rings, ritual observances to the moon to protect his flocks, replied: 'I'd be a damn' fool if I didn't!' These poems, with all their crudities, doubts and confusions, are written for the love of Man and in praise of God, and I'd be a damn' fool if they weren't.

Dylan insisted his children should be christened in church, retained a detailed knowledge of the Bible from his Sunday School days and, in the opinion of Aneirin Talfan-Davies, came close to embracing Catholicism in his latter days. But this was something he never talked about; it was another dimension of the inner man.

Something similar happened to Caitlin, or perhaps they always shared it, for these boxes of private papers included poems and aphorisms, statements of faith and her *Pearls of Wisdom on the Way to the Grave*.

On 21 October 1977, engaged in her bitter dispute with Stuart Thomas, she wrote, 'I can't risk waiting for God to come to me . . . God has got to be prepared for, the ground has got to be laid for Him. I have to be available for Him. I have to make space all around me, and time stretches ahead, and silence, for Him to approach me.'

On 24 November 1977 she wrote, 'God is the Divine Life. Life is Divine if we make it so. If we do not make it so, life is merely organic. When we die, life dies with us. The Divine Life goes on.'

Two days later, on 26 November 1977, she wrote, 'Nobody has made so many mistakes in their life as I have. My whole life has been one fat mistake and, now that it is too late, I am beginning to find out a few things . . . Life is Divine in itself; any kind of life, and it can be made more and more Divine. There is no end to Divinity.'

On 9 March 1978 she wrote, 'Am I undergoing a sign of imminent death? Is it the calm before the death rattle? It may well be. It is my just time, but no such luck. With Dylan's dying I could feel something precious and irretrievable dying inside of me forever.'

There were innumerable other thoughts like these committed to paper, either in diary or literary form, totalling in all, so the Fazios estimated, at least 8,000 pages, and among them lay one tiny sheet of torn notepaper that appeared to be tear-stained and had evidently been folded and refolded so many times that it was in danger of falling apart. This was:

MY EPITAPH

Nothing is imperceptible
Nothing is unintentional
All is inescapable

Postscript

The death of Dylan Thomas had extraordinary ramifications. Medical errors and malpractice, attempts to conceal the truth, fear of civil charges, women rivalling for the role of widow, betrayal of trust, Caitlin running amok, abortions, litigation and, hanging over it all like a cloud, the smell of the whisky bottle . . . none of it would have happened had a poet not been struck down in his prime by a doctor who should have known better.

Failure to save a patient's life always lies heavily on a doctor's conscience. He may spend every working day trying to help people with life-threatening conditions, often realising death is inevitable, but the memory of someone dying when he could have been saved will always trouble him most.

This is why the surviving hospital staff in this case recall what happened so clearly. For 40 years they have lived with the knowledge that Dylan Thomas died unnecessarily and probably would have lived another 30 or 40 years had he been given the right medical treatment.

Blame for what happened is fairly evenly spread, with Dylan Thomas putting himself at risk by ignoring his doctor's advice for over 20 years and failing to seek medical attention when he clearly needed it. He was a fool not to disclose full details of his medical history when he first met Feltenstein.

If Brinnin's conscience was not sorely troubled, it should have been, for he left a sick man to travel the length and breadth of the United States without looking after him properly. One can see now that his account of those travels, *Dylan Thomas in America*, was inaccurate and one-sided. Brinnin should have had more sense than to rely so heavily on the word of Liz Reitell, who clearly panicked when Thomas was ill and, whether knowingly or unwittingly, gave wrong information to Feltenstein and subsequently withheld the whole truth. She knew what she had done and was fearful of the consequences. Among Brinnin's papers at the University of Delaware, we found a letter from Reitell to Brinnin, undated but written in 1954, in which she says, 'No lawyers after me yet.'

Guilt weighed even more heavily on the conscience of Dr Milton Darwin Feltenstein, as well it should have done. His first grievous errors were made in May 1953 and are curiously missing from Brinnin's account. Feltenstein should never have prescribed drugs like morphine, cortisone or benzedrine without first establishing what was wrong with the patient. Blood and urine samples should have been taken that first day. Had they been, Thomas's diabetes would have been discovered and his life saved.

Even worse was Feltenstein's failure to examine his patient with due care when he continued pumping these dangerous drugs into Dylan Thomas's body during October and early November 1953. The poet's life could have been saved right up until the night of Wednesday 4 November, when Feltenstein administered the final fatal overdose of morphine that plunged Thomas into a coma.

There are many questions that will remain unanswered so long after the event. Why did it take Feltenstein at least an hour to get Thomas into a nearby hospital? Why did he claim authority over the patient when he had none? Had he previously tried to find Thomas a bed in the Beth Israel Hospital and failed? Could that have caused the delay? Why did he continue to claim Thomas was suffering from alcoholism even after diabetes had been confirmed? Why did Reitell not tell the hospital doctors of Thomas's previous ill health in New York? And why did she and Brinnin not challenge the way the admission diagnosis at St Vincent's was changed from diabetic shock to alcohol poisoning?

One can understand Mahoney's anxiety to protect the good name of St Vincent's. He was not responsible for Dylan Thomas's death, neither were his staff, so why should they incur opprobrium? By not mentioning that diabetes was known to be the primary cause of Dylan Thomas's collapse, Mahoney managed to head off any question of a formal enquiry or claim for damages. And there were several people, especially Brinnin, Reitell and Feltenstein, who were saved embarrassment – or worse.

✳   ✳   ✳

Because of Brinnin's devastating portrayal of Dylan Thomas as a drunken adulterer who lost control of his skills, no one challenged his account of Thomas's death for ten years. In 1965, Constantine Fitzgibbon, who had a far more serious drink problem than Dylan Thomas ever did, wrote the first authorised biography. He obtained a copy of the autopsy and referred to Feltenstein's use of morphine, but dealt perfunctorily with Dylan's final days in New York, missing the truth of what happened at the Chelsea Hotel and St Vincent's.

The first serious research into the facts of Dylan's death was conducted by Dr B.W. Murphy, a psychoanalyst from Maryland, who published a lengthy article, 'Creation and Destruction: Notes on Dylan Thomas' in *The British Journal of Medical Psychology* (Vol 41, 1968). Murphy interviewed Mahoney and reviewed Dylan's medical treatment at St Vincent's as part of his research, but accepted Brinnin's version of what happened and did not challenge the suggestion of delirium tremens. Unfortunately, Dr Murphy was not a practising physician and was willing to rely on the legend of alcoholism, as this was the foundation for his psychoanalytic theory that Dylan Thomas died from neurosis. Had Murphy known that Thomas had suffered from diabetes, his theory would have been in serious jeopardy.

Overall, Paul Ferris also relied largely on Brinnin and a correspondence with Reitell for his 1977 biography, although he did establish that Feltenstein injected the final half-grain dose of morphine, albeit without realising the implications.

✳   ✳   ✳

There is another interesting side issue that we have decided to deal with separately from the body of the book, and that is the curious parallel between the death of Dylan Thomas and that of the Irish playwright and storyteller Brendan Behan. Both men became renowned as geniuses who drank themselves to death — and they were both diabetic.

Thomas and Behan came from humble backgrounds. Neither completed any formal education, but they grew up in households with books and relatives who taught them the classics from an early age. While Thomas was listening to Shakespeare on his father's knee, Behan was reading by the age of three and published his first article at 12. Both built their early reputations on poetry and then showed enormous talent as actors, performers, playwrights and prose writers. Both started out as thin youths until drink and untreated diabetes caused significant weight gains that left them obese. Both married tough, good-looking, intelligent women who provided a stable atmosphere for their creative work, but neither wife was able to keep enough order in her husband's life to prevent his disintegration. Thomas knew he had diabetes by the time he was 19, but continually kept this and many other aspects of his life secret from his wife; Behan knew he was diabetic at the age of 31, but kept it secret from no one.

Success in America came to them both. Just like Thomas, when Behan was away from his wife, Beatrice, he had affairs with women who became his nursemaids. As each broke his ties with wife and home, he spiralled into chronic ill health and blackouts and, in Behan's case, alcoholic seizures. Thomas and Behan hated and feared doctors, and found themselves unable to adhere to a regime of stable diet, weight loss and regular sleep and work habits. Behan died from an alcohol-induced coma while Thomas really died from a morphine overdose and steroid injections which pushed him into diabetic shock.

Their deaths had very different effects on their wives. Beatrice Behan knew of Brendan's diabetes eight years before he died and was able to prepare herself. Caitlin, on the other hand, was given no warning, and she never really recovered from the shock she received in New York, when she was carried away in a strait-jacket from the place where her husband lay dying. The hardest kind of grief to cope with in sudden death is one where there is no explanation; Caitlin died 40 years later without knowing what happened, and she suffered terribly.

✻ ✻ ✻

Feltenstein died in 1974 with the case still on his conscience. He refused to discuss it with biographers or journalists, and his secrets would have died with him had he not felt compelled to share his distress with his friend and colleague Dr Joseph Lehrman.

Remarkably, McVeigh never discussed the case with his wife and family. Had it not been for his willingness to challenge Feltenstein's diagnosis with Turnball, the truth would never have come out. McVeigh died in 1984. Turnball has been ill with cancer for some time.

Mahoney retired in 1967 and went to live in Groningen, Germany, hoping to write a biography of one of his teachers, Dr Otfrid Foerster. Due to failing eyesight, Mahoney was unable to finish the book and died in 1990. Pappas visited Mahoney almost yearly in his retirement, and even organised a fund for him when he fell on hard times in later life. Pappas and Mahoney shared the secret of Dylan Thomas's death for over 30 years. By habit and training, doctors never discuss a patient's medical secrets with laymen, but this case was different; Dylan Thomas died unnecessarily, and this troubled them all.

✻ ✻ ✻

In our preface, we posed the question of whether or not it really matters how Dylan Thomas died. Having told the story, we still believe it does. As a direct result of medical failure and his own unwillingness to face the truth, his death cost him the respect that was his due, devastated his widow and left a trail of mayhem in its wake. Our researches prove that none of this should have happened.

James Nashold
George Tremlett

May 1997

Appendices

Notes

CHAPTER ONE

1 *Collected Letters*, edited Paul Ferris, p.903
2 *Caitlin*, Caitlin Thomas and George Tremlett, p.176
3 Barbara Holdridge interview, New York, September 1996
4 *Conversations with Stravinsky*, Robert Craft
5 *President Kennedy, Profile of Power*, Richard Reeves, p.243
6 Dr Joseph Lehrman interview, New York, 1996. Dr Lehrman, a pseudonym, was a neurologist and psychiatrist at Beth Israel Hospital, New York, and a colleague of Dr Feltenstein who discussed Dylan Thomas's case with him in the spring of 1954. Dr Lehrman was a graduate of the College of Physicians and Surgeons of Columbia University and did his training at Queen's General Hospital and Cornell University. After his training, he was an Adjunct Professor at Beth Israel Hospital. He also served in the US Army from 1942 to 1945.
7 *Collected Letters*, Ferris, p.891
8 Reitell letter to Brinnin, dated 4 June 1953, Brinnin Collection, Special Collections, University of Delaware
9 *Caitlin*, Caitlin Thomas and Tremlett, p.177
10 *The Life of Dylan Thomas*, Constantine Fitzgibbon, p.343

CHAPTER TWO

1 *Dylan Thomas*, edited E.W. Tedlock, p.77
2 *Dylan Thomas*, Paul Ferris, p.55
3 *The Life of Dylan Thomas*, Fitzgibbon, p.45

CHAPTER THREE

1 *The Life of Dylan Thomas*, Fitzgibbon, p.36
2 Anecdote told by Wynford Vaughan-Thomas to Tremlett
3 *Collected Letters*, Ferris, p.50
4 *The Life of Dylan Thomas*, Fitzgibbon, p.81
5 *Lippincott's Quick Reference Book for Medicine and Surgery*, George E. Rehberger, 'Diabetes Mellitus'
6 *Collected Letters*, Ferris, p.39

CHAPTER FOUR

1 Anecdote told by Mervyn Levy to Tremlett
2 *Collected Letters*, Ferris, p.101
3 *Collected Letters*, Ferris, p.129
4 *Collected Letters*, Ferris, p.140
5 *Manual of Medical Therapeutics*, edited by M.J. Orland and R.J. Saltman, p.405
6 *The Life of Dylan Thomas*, Fitzgibbon, p.159
7 *The Life of Dylan Thomas*, Fitzgibbon, p.162
8 *Collected Letters*, Ferris, p.187
9 *The Life of Dylan Thomas*, Fitzgibbon, p.146
10 *Dylan Thomas*, Ferris, p.129
11 *Collected Letters*, Ferris, p.201
12 *Portrait of the Artist as a Young Dog*, Dylan Thomas, pp.195–96
13 *Important to Me*, Pamela Hansford Johnson, p.142
14 *Collected Letters*, Ferris, p.222
15 *Dylan Thomas*, Ferris, p.143

CHAPTER FIVE

1 *Caitlin*, Caitlin Thomas and Tremlett, p.161
2 *Collected Letters*, Ferris, p.410
3 *Collected Letters*, Ferris, p.511
4 *Dylan Thomas*, Ferris, p.188
5 This account is based on a report of the subsequent court case which appeared in *The Welsh Gazette* on 12 April 1945. Killick was committed for trial at the Cardiganshire Assizes in June, when he was acquitted. According to Caitlin in 1985, she and Dylan and their house guest Mary Keene all agreed to tone down their evidence against him because Vera Killick was a family friend.

CHAPTER SIX

1 Discussed by A.J.P. Taylor in *A Personal History*
2 *A Personal History*, Taylor, pp.149–50
3 *Caitlin*, Caitlin Thomas and Tremlett, p.99
4 *Living in Wales*, broadcast talk, 23 June 1949
5 It is often forgotten, not least by Thomas's biographers, that the British film industry briefly boomed just after the war. Thomas worked on two scripts for British National Pictures, *Three Weird Sisters* (1948) and *No Room at the Inn* (1948), and several other projects for J. Arthur Rank's Gainsborough Pictures, including *The Shadowless Man*. His other film scripts included *Betty London*, *Me and My Bike*, *The Beaches of Falesa* (based on a short story by Robert Louis Stevenson) and also *Rebecca's Daughters* and *The Doctor and the Devils*, which were both filmed many years after his death. Karl Francis directed *Rebecca's Daughters* (1992), starring Peter O'Toole, and Freddie Francis directed *The Doctor and the Devils* (1985), starring Jonathan Pryce and Twiggy, with the script adapted by Ronald Harwood.
6 *A Personal History*, Taylor, p.107

CHAPTER SEVEN

1 *Collected Letters*, Ferris, p.747
2 Brinnin may not have realised when he wrote *Dylan Thomas in America* that Thomas himself wrote long, detailed letters describing his travels, sent to Caitlin and his parents. They can be found in Ferris's *Collected Letters*.
3 *Dylan Thomas in America*, Brinnin, p.25
4 *The Party's Over Now*, John Gruen, p.26
5 Peter and Florence Grippe interview, Orient Point, New York, August 1996
6 *Caitlin*, Caitlin Thomas and Tremlett, p.124
7 *The Days of Dylan Thomas*, Bill Read
8 *Dylan Thomas in America*, Brinnin, p.48
9 These details of Thomas's stay in Iowa come from *Dylan Thomas in Iowa* by Ray B. West Jnr, an article in the magazine *The San Francisco Fault*, October 1972.
10 *Best of Times, Worst of Times*, Shelley Winters, pp.31–40
11 *Dylan Thomas in America*, Brinnin, p.75
12 *Dylan Thomas in America*, Brinnin, pp.76–77
13 *A Walker in the City*, Alfred Kazin, p.12

CHAPTER EIGHT

1 *Caitlin*, Caitlin Thomas and Tremlett, p.140
2 *Collected Letters*, Ferris, p.732
3 *Caitlin*, Caitlin Thomas and Tremlett, p.143
4 *Dylan Thomas in America*, Brinnin, p.35
5 *Caitlin*, Caitlin Thomas and Tremlett, p.145
6 *A Goldfish Bowl* by Elisabeth Lutyens, quoted in A *Pilgrim Soul: The Life and Work of Elisabeth Lutyens*, Meirion and Susie Harries, p.143
7 *Dylan Thomas in America*, Brinnin, p.152
8 Letter to James Nashold, September 1995
9 *The Life of Dylan Thomas*, Fitzgibbon, p.310
10 Letter to Nashold, October 1995
11 Letter to Nashold, October 1995

CHAPTER NINE

1 *Caitlin*, Caitlin Thomas and Tremlett, p.125
2 *Dylan Thomas*, Ferris, p.287
3 *Collected Letters*, Ferris, p.879
4 *Dylan Thomas in America*, Brinnin, p.177
5 *Dylan Thomas in America*, Brinnin, p.188
6 *Dylan Thomas*, Ferris, p.289
7 *Portrait of Dylan*, Rollie McKenna, p.68
8 *Conversations with Stravinsky*, Craft
9 *Dylan Thomas in America*, Brinnin, p.221

CHAPTER TEN

1 Barbara Holdridge interview, New York, September 1996
2 *Collected Letters*, Ferris, p.889
3 *Collected Letters*, Ferris, p.900
4 *Caitlin*, Caitlin Thomas and Tremlett, p.176
5 *Portrait of a Friend*, Gwen Watkins, p.145
6 *Time* magazine, 6 April 1953
7 *Time* made its opinion of Dylan Thomas even clearer after his death, describing him as 'a slob, a liar, a moocher, a thief, a two-fisted booze-fighter, a puffy Priapus who regularly assaulted the wives of his best friends, an icy little hedonist who indifferently lived it up while his children went hungry . . . Though he looked like a choirboy, he argued like a Bolshevik, dressed like a bum, drank like a culvert, smoked like an ad for cancer, bragged that he was addicted to onanism and had committed an indecency

with a Member of Parliament.'

8 *Collected Letters*, Ferris, p.127

9 *Portrait of a Friend*, Watkins, p.145

10 *Portrait of a Friend*, Watkins, p.145

11 *John O'London's Weekly*, 7 August 1953

12 Portrait of a Friend, Watkins, p.139

13 Notes by Aneirin Talfan-Davies on the International Eisteddfod, included in *Quite Early One Morning*, p.175

14 *Collected Letters*, Ferris, p.892

15 *Collected Letters*, Ferris, p.910

16 The word 'tear' has two meanings. When pronounced to rhyme with bare it means to pull apart, rend or lacerate. When read like beer, it is the saline moisture in one's eye. Caitlin thought she knew which one was right; Dylan thought differently, because he was quoting a phrase from *Over Sir John's hill*:

fishing in the tear of the Towy

17 *Portrait of a Friend*, Watkins, p.139

CHAPTER ELEVEN

1 *Dylan Thomas in America*, Brinnin, p.252

2 *Dylan Thomas in America*, Brinnin, p.255

3 *Dylan Thomas in America*, Brinnin, p.258

4 *Dylan Thomas in America*, Brinnin, p.259

5 This last letter from Caitlin is now among the Brinnin papers at Delaware.

6 Letter from Arthur Miller to Nashold

7 *Dylan Thomas in America*, Brinnin, p.268

8 Letter from CuRoi, sent to Tremlett by the New York lawyer Eric Corbett Williams and quoted in *Dylan Thomas: In the Mercy of his Means*

9 *Dylan Thomas in America*, Brinnin, p.272

10 *Dylan Thomas in America*, Brinnin, p.274

11 *Merritt's Textbook of Neurology*, edited Lewis P. Rowland, p.270

CHAPTER TWELVE

1 This section of the chapter is based on an interview with Dr Jerry Turnball (a pseudonym), New York, September 1966. Turnball was a graduate of New York University School of Medicine and completed his residency at New York University and St Vincent's Hospital. He was an officer in the United States Navy from 1942 to 1945. He returned to private practice

on Long Island, New York, until his retirement.

2 *Dylan Thomas in America*, Brinnin, p.279

Other parts of the chapter were based on interviews with Dr Joseph G. Chusid and Dr George Pappas. Chusid was a graduate of the University of Pennsylvania School of Medicine where he also underwent residency training in neurology and psychiatry. He was a Fellow of the Illinois Neuropsychiatric Institute before becoming an Attending Physician in Neurology and Chief of Electroencephalography at St Vincent's.

Dr Pappas was a graduate of New York State University Medical College and completed his surgical and neurosurgical training at NYU and St Vincent's Hospital. He was an Attending Physician and briefly succeeded Dr Mahoney as Chief of Neurosurgery at St Vincent's before pursuing a private practice in New York.

3 This odd spelling is correct. Sir William's family name was spelt MacEwen, but while he was a medical student at Glasgow University he changed the spelling of his own name, apparently believing 'Macewen' more distinguished.

CHAPTER THIRTEEN

1 Interview with John Malcolm Brinnin, Key West, Florida, July 1996
2 *Caitlin*, Caitlin Thomas and Tremlett, pp.182–83
3 *Leftover Life to Kill*, Caitlin Thomas, p.61
4 *Portrait of Dylan*, McKenna, p.83
5 Zeckel charged a fee of $80 for this advice, but was never paid. Phillip Wittenberg, attorney to the Dylan Thomas Memorial Fund, thought the fee was inappropriate as Caitlin was committed to River Crest against her will.
6 *Leftover Life to Kill*, Caitlin Thomas, p.79
7 Chusid interview, New York, September 1996
8 Interviews with Chusid and Pappas
9 *The Last Days of Dylan Thomas*, Rob Gittins, p.191
10 *Portrait of a Friend*, Watkins, p.152

CHAPTER FOURTEEN

1 *My Friend Dylan Thomas*, Daniel Jones, p.6
2 *My Friend Dylan Thomas*, Jones, p.7
3 *My Friend Dylan Thomas*, Jones, p.106
4 *The Times*, 10 November 1953
5 *The Daily Mirror*, 18 December 1953

6 *The Spectator,* 13 November 1953

7 It was reported on the front page of *The Daily Telegraph* and also on p.8 of *The Times* that Dylan Thomas left an estate worth only £100 (24 December 1953).

8 Admittance papers, Holloway Sanatorium

9 Admittance papers, Holloway Sanatorium

10 See note 7

11 *My Friend Dylan Thomas,* Jones, p.83

12 Jones would say privately that he thought she was clinically mad, but was always willing to support Stuart Thomas when the latter argued that she was in a fit state to sign the legal documents.

13 At a dinner organised by the Dylan Thomas Society in October 1986, Tremlett found himself sitting between Mrs Jones and Caitlin, who leaned across and said in an audible stage whisper, 'The last time I met that bloody woman I tried to strangle her.'

14 This incident was observed by two young men working on the early shift at Laugharne Bakery. They could barely believe their eyes.

CHAPTER FIFTEEN

1 These figures were in a schedule attached to the disputed Deed of Variation that was signed in 1957.

2 *Leftover Life to Kill,* Caitlin Thomas, p.88

3 *Leftover Life to Kill,* Caitlin Thomas, p.88

4 *Leftover Life to Kill,* Caitlin Thomas, p.89

5 *Leftover Life to Kill,* Caitlin Thomas, p.90

6 *Caitlin,* Paul Ferris, p.179

7 This was something Thomas used to say frequently, but it is also recorded by Brinnin, *Dylan Thomas in America,* p.35.

8 On publication of *Dylan Thomas in America,* Brinnin was widely abused for breaching the Thomases' confidence in a vulgar manner for monetary gain. He clearly resented Caitlin's tirades against him. When the book was republished in 1988, he added a preface claiming she once admitted never having read it. This was not true. The book was sent to her before publication in manuscript form and she wrote to David Lougee saying it was an 'astonishing tour de force' and had 'spoilt the summer for me with the dirty taste in my mouth' (*Caitlin,* Ferris, p.170). And was she right about Brinnin being homosexually attracted to Dylan? Nashold put that question to Brinnin directly, and he replied, 'I loved Dylan, Jim, but we were never lovers, if that's what you mean.'

9 This statement is published at the beginning of *Dylan Thomas in America*, and cleared the way for the book to appear without Caitlin issuing a libel writ.

10 *The Missoulian*, 19 September 1986

11 Letter from Arthur Miller to Nashold

12 *The Sunday Express*, 8 July 1956

CHAPTER SIXTEEN

1 These details come from a sworn statement by Copleston dated 16 March 1972. He agreed to give evidence for Caitlin in her case against Stuart Thomas.

2 See note 1

3 Tape-recorded interview with Caitlin Thomas

4 Caitlin Thomas to Tremlett

5 *The Sunday Express*, interview with Graham Lord, 5 February 1967. She said this repeatedly during the years Tremlett knew her.

6 Giuseppe and Francesco both confirmed that she never once said 'I love you' to Giuseppe (when they visited Laugharne in 1995). However, Caitlin taught herself Italian and one night over supper said to Giuseppe in front of his son, 'I am very fond of you, Papa.' Francesco said, 'This was a big moment in our life as a family.'

7 Caitlin Thomas to Tremlett

8 Giuseppe Fazio to Tremlett, 1995

9 Caitlin was also admitted to clinics in Rome in 1966 and again in Catania in 1967, and eventually managed to conquer her alcoholism completely by 1971. Thereafter she had ten years of 'total sobriety'. In the last ten or 12 years of her life, she would have a glass of red wine with her supper, diluting it with Seven-Up. She achieved her sobriety by attending Alcoholics Anonymous three times a week for ten years in Rome.

10 Caitlin Thomas to Tremlett

11 In his archives, Tremlett has a complete record of the box-office takings, together with contracts, letters and original typescript of the play *Dylan*. He bought the file from a book dealer in 1996.

12 This is a point of some significance, for Tremlett has documentary evidence that two of Caitlin's abortions were paid for by the Trustees, i.e. after Dylan died. During his lifetime, she admitted four other abortions and also said she had 'tried everything from bottles of gin to throwing myself downstairs'. Two of the abortions were arranged in Swansea, and Tremlett thinks Caitlin probably had seven abortions in all, which makes this very late pregnancy all the more remarkable.

13 Letter from the Trustees to Caitlin, dated 27 July 1964

14 Caitlin's comments to Tremlett after she gave him a copy of the letter

15 These details come from verbatim quotations of the judge's summing-up and evidence given by witnesses.

16 These details come from a translation of Caitlin's statement to the Rome police.

17 From a statement by Stuart Thomas dated 4 January 1972

18 See note 17

19 See note 17

20 Stuart Thomas confirmed in his statement that the papers were handed over, but Caitlin said he always refused to let her have them back.

21 The letters were offered for sale through Sotheby's in 1975 with a reserve of £8,000. They were withdrawn at £2,100 and subsequently sold privately to an American collector.

22 Letter from Lord Widgery dated 24 May 1976

23 Caitlin told Tremlett this in Giuseppe's presence in May 1988, and he confirmed that this was true.

24 Caitlin to Tremlett, May 1988

CHAPTER SEVENTEEN

1 Letter from Stuart Thomas to the Law Society, dated 13 June 1977

2 Letter from the Senior Assistant, Secretary of the Law Society, to Caitlin Thomas, 23 June 1978

3 Wynford Vaughan-Thomas to Tremlett

4 We have examined copies of the accounts which show that by the late 1980s, Stuart Thomas was charging fees of over £20,000 each year plus other expenses to the Trust. On one earlier occasion, Caitlin challenged his habit of charging air flights to Rome against her personal account, regardless of whether or not she invited him over. This came before the Taxing Master who reduced Stuart Thomas's bill from £3,675.85 to £1,600, saying he was 'extremely out of sympathy' with the claim.

5 Wynford Vaughan-Thomas died at his home in Fishguard on 4 February 1987, aged 78. The cancer spread from his colon to other parts of the body, yet he lived much longer than expected. He remained cheerful and no one, least of all Caitlin, bore him any ill will for his largely passive role in the Trust's affairs. It will be remembered that Amis and Stuart Thomas had been friends since the early '50s. Rush, a solicitor with a distinguished career in local government in South Wales, was a friend of them both.

6 In a letter to Tremlett, Caitlin said she was appalled at the choice of Amis,

whom she considered 'a vulgarian' who had always been jealous of Dylan's talents. Although a successful novelist, Amis never managed to master the art of writing poetry.

7 This was in a letter dated 27 January 1987 in which Stuart Thomas stated unequivocally, 'I have had conduct of this Trust since the death of Dylan Thomas in 1953' and 'For many years Mrs Thomas has been living with a Sicilian known as Giuseppe Fazio . . . In the past Giuseppe Fazio has exercised strong and improper influence over Mrs Thomas to her financial detriment. For this and other reasons, not least Mrs Thomas's vulnerability, her situation is one that calls for extreme caution on the part of all concerned.' He ensured this letter was countersigned by Llewelyn and Aeronwy.

8 This was in May 1988.

Acknowledgements

The authors wish to acknowledge the many people, places and resources which contributed to the research for this book. A delicate balance must be struck in any new book about Dylan Thomas because his life and work created such powerful emotions among his friends and audiences, who each remembered the poet in often distinctly different ways. Even after 40 years, memories of events were as clear and strong as if they had just happened – and this was no more true than among the doctors and nurses who attended Dylan at his death.

Special appreciation must be extended to the many present and former staff of St Vincent's Hospital in New York who agreed to be interviewed so that the record of Dylan's death could be set straight. Dr Richard Rovit and Dr Raj Murali opened many doors, including one which led to Dr George Pappas who, despite his poor health, acted as a constant source of sound advice and wisdom.

We would also like our thanks to go to Jerome Agel, Patricia Albright, Julia Bowers, John Malcolm Brinnin, Andreas Brown, Dr Ron Burke, T.O. Cannon, D. Castleman, Joan Champie, Dr Joseph Chusid, Dr John Comer, Patrick Cropper, Thomas Rain Crowe, Louis Dudek, Dr Garofalo, John Giorno, Lois Gridley, Peter and Florence Grippe, John Gruen, Dr Charles Hirsch, Barbara Holdridge, Fred Janes, Alfred Kazin, Carl Kirchway, Dr and Mrs Edward Laws, Dr Joseph Lehrman, Mervyn Levy, Judy Mayo, Rollie McKenna, Susan McGuire, John McPartland, the family of Dr William McVeigh, Rebecca Melvin, Arthur Miller, Florence Miller, Madeleine Mullin, Sister Katherine Muldoon, Dr Tim Murray, Jack Nelson, Gabriel Neruda, Anke Nolting, Noel

Osment, Dr William Panke, Robert E. Parks, Gail Pietrzk, Will and Rosemary Rees, Dr Franklin Robinson, Joanne Seltzer, Steven Siegel, Dave Slivka, Rose Slivka, Dr Eugene Stead, Hannah Stein, Peter Swales, Dr Jerry Turnball, Theodore Watts, Tommy Watts, Anita Wellner, Martha Wells, Eric Corbett Williams, Douglas Williams and Jane Wilson.

A number of institutions generously assisted our search for documents and photographs or provided us with information about former staff members, including the Departments of Neurosurgery and Neurology, St Vincent's Hospital; Beth Israel Hospital; Columbia University, College of Physicians and Surgeons; the Special Collections, New York Public Library; Pierpont Morgan Library; Young Men's and Young Women's Hebrew Association; Office of the Chief Medical Examiner, City of New York; Gotham Book Mart; *The New York Times Book Review*; the Chelsea Hotel; Duke University Medical Center Library, Perkins Library, Duke University; Special Collections, University of Delaware Library; Baily/Howe Library, University of Vermont; Rare Books and Special Collections, The Francis A. Countway Library of Medicine, Harvard Medical School; the University Archives, University of Pennsylvania; Yale University School of Medicine.

Perhaps no other poet than Dylan Thomas has had so much written about him, and we found many important anecdotes about his health among the many books and articles written about his career and particularly his four tours of America. To these authors we owe a debt and acknowledge their work. One of the most important books about the last years of Dylan's life will remain John Malcolm Brinnin's *Dylan Thomas in America* (Little Brown, 1955), and we have also referred to *Dylan Thomas* by Paul Ferris (Hodder and Stoughton, 1977); *Dylan Thomas: The Collected Letters*, edited by Paul Ferris (Dent, 1985); *The Life of Dylan Thomas* by Constantine Fitzgibbon (Dent, 1965); *Dylan Thomas: A Bibliography* by J. Alexander Rolph (Dent, 1956); *Dylan Thomas: His Life and Work* by John Ackerman (Oxford University Press, 1964); *Welsh Dylan* by John Ackerman (John Jones Ltd, 1979); *Dylan Thomas: Early Prose Writings*, edited by Walford Davies (Dent, 1971); *Leftover Life to Kill* by Caitlin Thomas (Putnam, 1957); *The Days of Dylan Thomas* by Bill Read (Weidenfeld and Nicolson, 1964); *Poet in the Making: The Notebooks of Dylan Thomas*, edited by Ralph Maud (Dent, 1968); *My Friend Dylan Thomas* by Daniel Jones (Dent, 1977); *Important to Me* by Pamela Hansford Johnson (Macmillan, 1974); *The Last Days of Dylan Thomas* by Rob Gittins (Macdonald, 1986); *Dylan Thomas: No Man More Magical* by Andrew Sinclair (Holt, Rhinehart and Winston, 1975); *Conversations with Stravinsky* by Robert Craft (Faber and Faber, 1959); *Dylan Thomas: The Poet and His Critics* by R.B. Kershner (American Library Association, 1976); *Remembering Poets* by

Donald Hall (Harper and Row, 1978); *President Kennedy, Profile of Power* by Richard Reeves (Simon and Schuster, 1993); *On the Air with Dylan Thomas*, edited by Ralph Maud (New Directions, 1992); *Dylan Thomas: Letters to Vernon Watkins* (Dent and Faber and Faber, 1957); *The Nine Lives of Dylan Thomas* by Jonathan Fryer (Kyle Cathie, 1993); *Dylan Thomas: The Legend and the Poet*, edited by E.W. Tedlock (Heinemann, 1960); *Caitlin* by Caitlin Thomas and George Tremlett (Secker and Warburg, 1986); *Dylan Thomas: In the Mercy of his Means* by George Tremlett (Constable, 1991); *A Personal History* by A.J.P. Taylor (Hamish Hamilton, 1983); *Best of Times, Worst of Times* by Shelley Winters (Muller, 1990); *A Pilgrim Soul: The Life and Work of Elisabeth Lutyens* by Meirion and Susie Harries (Michael Joseph Lutyens, 1989); *Portrait of Dylan* by Rollie McKenna (J.M. Dent and Sons Ltd, 1982); *Portrait of a Friend* by Gwen Watkins (Gomer Press, 1983); *Quite Early One Morning*, edited by Aneirin Talfan-Davies (J.M. Dent and Sons Ltd, 1954); *Caitlin: The Life of Caitlin Thomas* by Paul Ferris (Hutchinson, 1993); *Contemporaries* by Alfred Kazin (Little Brown, 1962); *Brendan Behan* by Ulick O'Connor (Hamish Hamilton, 1970); *A Walker in the City* by Alfred Kazin (Harcourt Brace, 1951); *The Discovery of Insulin* by Michael Bliss (University of Chicago, 1982); *The Chemistry and Chemotherapy of Diabetes Mellitus* by Alexander Marble (Charles C. Thomas, 1962); *The Medical Casebook of Adolf Hitler* by Leonard and Renate Heston (Stein and Day, 1980); *The Pharmacological Basis of Therapeutics* by Alfred Gilman and Louis Goodman (Macmillan, 1985); *Neurology in Clinical Practice* by Walter Bradley (Butterworth-Heinemann, 1991); *Merritt's Textbook of Neurology*, edited by Lewis P. Rowland (Williams and Wilkins, 1995); *With a Great Heart* by Sister Marie de Lourdes Walsh (St Vincent's Hospital, 1964); *The Party's Over Now, Reminiscences of the Fifties* by John Gruen (Viking Press, 1967); *Wise Men Fish Here* by Frances Steloff (Booksellers House, 1994); *Quick Reference Book for Medicine and Surgery* by George E. Rehberger (Lippincott, 1920); *Manual of Medical Therapeutics*, edited by M.J. Orland and R.J. Saltman (Little Brown, 1986); *Spyclopedia* by Richard Deacon (Macdonald, 1987) and *Elizabeth Bishop, Life and Memory of It* by Brett Miller (University of California Press, 1993).

The following articles were also helpful in providing further background material on Dylan's life and health: *Creation and Destruction: Notes on Dylan Thomas* by B.W. Murphy, *Dylan Thomas in Iowa* by R.B. West Jnr, *Alcohol and Poetry: John Berryman and the Booze Talking* by Lewis Hyde, *An Evening with Salvador Dali and Dylan Thomas* by Gabriel Neruda, *Is Medical Rivalry Threatening Yeltsin's Chances for Recovery?* by Lawrence Altman and *A Thin, Curly Little Person* by Howard Moss.

INDEX